Building the
Virtual State

Building the Virtual State

Information Technology and Institutional Change

Jane E. Fountain

BROOKINGS INSTITUTION PRESS
Washington, D.C.

Copyright © 2001
THE BROOKINGS INSTITUTION
1775 Massachusetts Avenue, N.W., Washington, D.C. 20036
www.brookings.edu
All rights reserved

Library of Congress Cataloging-in-Publication data
Fountain, Jane E.
  Building the virtual state : information technology and institutional change / Jane E. Fountain.
    p.   cm.
Includes bibliographical references and index.
  ISBN 0-8157-0078-4 (cloth : alk. paper)—ISBN 0-8157-0077-6 (pbk. : alk. paper)
  1. State governments—Data processing. 2. Electronic government information. 3. Internet. I.Title.
  JK2445.A8 F68 2001   2001001614
  352.13´0285—dc21   CIP

9 8 7 6 5 4 3 2 1

The paper used in this publication meets minimum requirements of the American National Standard for Information Sciences—Permanence of Paper for Printed Library Materials: ANSI Z39.48-1992.

Typeset in Sabon

Composition by Cynthia Stock
Silver Spring, Maryland

Printed by R. R. Donnelley and Sons
Harrisonburg, Virginia

For Michael, Elena, and Emily
And for Mom and Dad

Contents

Preface

THE INQUIRY THAT resulted in this book began as an attempt to understand how information technologies affect decisionmaking in complex organizations. At the outset, I wanted to understand how public managers were using information technology. Over time, it became equally important to better conceptualize the role of information technology (IT) within the institutional perspective. Institutional theories and their central concern, choice within constraints, span political science, sociology, and economics. Yet I could not find in any of these disciplines an adequate treatment of the relationship between IT and organization. The analytical framework developed in this book, technology enactment, is meant to extend institutional perspectives to account explicitly for the importance of information technology in organizational life.

As a field researcher whose terrain is complex organizations in government, I initially chose a quintessential Weberian bureaucracy, the army, in which to explore my research questions. My field research on the army, which I began in 1989 before the Internet became publicly accessible, convinced me that the causal arrow between IT and organization needed to point in both directions. I found that organizational structures and processes as well as institutionalized norms, beliefs, and values exerted a strong influence on information technology by shaping the perceptions of individuals, their understanding of an information system and its potential, and the ways in which they would try to implement and use new information technologies and applications. The enactment framework was sketched in its barest outlines. It took nearly a decade to fill in enough conceptual detail so that a more secure scaffolding could be erected.

The intellectual and physical journey that included the writing of this book took me from the northern desert in Washington State, where the army holds war games at the Yakima Firing Range, to the shadow of the United States Capitol and the elegant perimeter of the mall in Washington, D.C., where federal office buildings hum with digital and human activity, to the gritty port of entry at Otay Mesa, California, where seamless global trade meets the reality of lines of trucks that extend for miles and hold hundreds of goods awaiting inspection at the border between the United States and Mexico. When the Internet and World Wide Web burst upon the American scene early in the 1990s, this new form of digital telecommunication forced me to rethink the relationship of information technologies to organizations. For a brief time, I assumed that the Internet had made connectivity a public good by reducing connection costs dramatically. I anticipated that its effects would overwhelm organizational forms and individual resistance and that its simplicity of connection would lead to rapid organizational change. If this were so, I reasoned, surely researchers should try to capture dramatic structural changes in organizations, economic sectors, and government. During most of the 1990s, I assiduously sought out and tracked some of the most important uses of the Internet in the federal government, gaining extraordinary access to the projects and thinking of innovative, deeply committed appointees, senior executives, public managers, and operators. I was surprised to find eerily similar social, organizational, and political effects on their perceptions, design, and use of information systems in the networked world of the Internet.

The in-depth field studies whose results are reported in this book were not chosen at random. They represent innovative uses of networked computing in settings where the initial prospects for success were high given the intrinsic value and feasibility of the project, the caliber of leadership and management, political support, and adequacy of resources. The field study results are based upon hundreds of interviews (many of them taped and transcribed for analysis), mostly with the public servants who are building the virtual state. I promised them anonymity, even when they did not request it. Because the studies are an effort to understand information technology as its users view it, I let government actors speak using their own language to show how they are making sense of and negotiating fundamentally new forms of coordination, control, and communication.

In addition to these richly textured field studies, this inquiry is informed by a detailed classification and analysis of nearly fifty semifinalists and finalists in the Innovations Program in American Government, a Ford Foundation and Kennedy School of Government program that honors and celebrates cutting-edge government projects. This analysis supported observations based upon field research that even the most innovative uses of IT typically work at the surface of operations and boundary-spanning processes and are accepted because they leave the deep structure of political relationships intact.

It is impossible to adequately thank all those who made this study possible. My first debt goes to the public servants who generously shared their time, experience, and insights. In particular, I am grateful to the three outstanding leaders whose projects are detailed in this book. Robert Ehinger directed the International Trade Data System project office with enormous energy and commitment to public service and provided access to project staff, field sites, and materials. James Van Wert, the champion of the U.S. Business Advisor, was the first government official to tell me about the potential of multiagency websites at the beginning of the Internet "revolution." Lt. General Paul E. Funk (ret.), as assistant division commander, generously provided access to the Ninth Infantry Division (Motorized) and insight into the changing nature of military organization. In addition, the ideas and concepts in this study were developed in discussions with hundreds of public servants in Washington, D.C., across the United States, and in graduate and executive programs at the Kennedy School of Government at Harvard. I am particularly grateful to more than 500 participants in Harvard's Senior Managers in Government Program, with whom I discussed and tested concepts and their practical applications.

Among the colleagues who were of particular help in the development of the ideas presented in this book or in extending other types of support are Alan Altshuler, Maria Eugenia Arias, Chris Avery, Eugene Bardach, Michael Barzelay, Lewis Branscomb, Garry Brewer, Jean Camp, Paula Caproni, John DiIulio, Paul DiMaggio, Steven Kelman, Don Kettl, Todd R. La Porte, Charles Lindblom, Jerry Mechling, Charles Perrow, Roger Porter, Robert Putnam, Gene Rochlin, David Eddy Spicer, and Robert C. Wood. I owe a strong debt of gratitude to colleagues and public managers who read, reread, and commented on several chapters of the manuscript. These include Carol Chetkovitch, Cary Coglianese, Pepper Culpepper, Chris

Demchak, Sheila Jasanoff, David Lazer, Jane Mansbridge, Viktor Mayer-Schoenberger, Laurence O'Toole, Zachary Tumin, and two anonymous reviewers.

Many of the ideas presented in this volume were worked out in seminars and lectures. I benefited from presentations and discussions with colleagues at the Kennedy School of Government at Harvard through the Faculty Research Seminar, the Politics Research Group, and the Visions of Governance in the 21st Century Project. In addition, some chapters began as papers delivered at the annual meetings of the American Political Science Association, the Association for Public Policy and Management, the Public Management Research Conference, and the Academy of Management.

I am particularly grateful to Dean Joseph Nye and Academic Dean Frederick Schauer for their interest, encouragement, and deep appreciation of the implications of the Internet for governance. The project would not have been possible without sustained support from the Visions of Governance in the 21st Century Project, the Dean's Research Fund, and a sabbatical that provided the opportunity for uninterrupted reflection and writing. I also received support from the Innovations in American Government Program, the Strategic Computing and Telecommunications Program in the Public Sector, and the Harvard Information Infrastructure Project. I am grateful to the Kennedy School Case Office for permission to draw from case materials. The financial support that launched the study of the army came from a Yale University Fellowship and a Mellon Foundation Fellowship in the Social Sciences, which provided a year in residence to pursue interdisciplinary research at the Yale Institution for Social and Policy Studies. I am deeply grateful to Garry Brewer and Paul DiMaggio, who played critical roles in the early stages of this project. The final revisions were completed while I was a fellow of the Radcliffe Institute for Advanced Study at Harvard University in 2000–01.

Camiliakumari Wankaner was unflagging in her assistance, administrative support, and pursuit of elusive references. Barbara Slater earlier provided superb administrative and secretarial support. Laurel Blatchford provided able research assistance. Janet Mowery edited the manuscript with care. Christopher Kelaher and Janet Walker of the Brookings Institution Press shepherded the manuscript to completion with alacrity and offered valuable editorial advice. Carlotta Ribar proofread the pages, and Robert Elwood provided an index.

The unique contributions of one's family are impossible to recount or repay. My gratitude to Michael Serio and to our daughters, Elena and Emily, lies in a realm beyond words.

PART ONE

Theory

CHAPTER ONE

Introduction

THIS BOOK DEALS equally with the Internet and with institutions, the latter a dominant concern of political and social thought since antiquity. In governments around the globe, from Indianapolis to India, from San Francisco to Singapore, from Chile to China, policymakers view the Internet either as a force to increase the responsiveness of government to its citizens or as a means to further empower the state. In developing nations, new wireless information and communication technologies signal an unprecedented opportunity to hasten the pace of development and connection to the developed world. A marked increase in the growth of transnational financial, legal, and regulatory systems—made feasible by the Internet—has raised serious debate about the future, the location, and the structures of governance. In authoritarian regimes, the Internet threatens domination by the state over information and communication but at the same time, paradoxically, serves as an instrument of consummate state surveillance and control over society. The choices we face in the present regarding the use of digital tools and the institutional arrangements in which they are embedded will influence the way governments work around the globe during the next century and beyond.

The analytical framework I advance extends and refines institutional theory to encompass recent fundamental developments in information technologies. This intellectual territory lies virtually uncharted by institutional theorists in political science, sociology, and economics or in the related practical fields within public policy and management and organizational behavior. As the use of the Internet unfolds, questions central to institutional thought persist with increasing force. How are bureaucratic policymakers using networked computing? Are they negotiating new institutional arrangements as a consequence? To what extent and in what ways are they constrained by current institutional arrangements? What extensions of institutional theory are necessary to take account of fundamental change in organizational communication, coordination, and control? My purpose is to advance theory to inform answers to these questions. By clarifying and extending concepts and relationships, central tasks of theory-building, this book also contributes to practice.

Enter the Virtual State

A key phase of the Internet's impressive growth began in 1993, coinciding with the initial period of a major government reform effort, the National Performance Review, led by Vice President Al Gore. Having focused initially on developing regulatory and legal regimes conducive to e-commerce, the government then turned to the task of building digital government, in part through the strategy of creating virtual agencies. The virtual agency, following the web portal model used in the economy, is organized by client—for example, students, seniors, small-business owners, or veterans; each site is designed to provide all of the government's services and information from any agency as well as links to relevant organizations outside government. Web portals, extending to government the business concept of 7 x 24 x 365 (being available seven days a week, twenty-four hours a day, 365 days a year), would restructure the relationship between state and citizen to be simpler, more interactive, and more efficient. A virtual state (my term) is a government that is organized increasingly in terms of virtual agencies, cross-agency and public-private networks whose structure and capacity depend on the Internet and web.

Cost savings, although sizable in many instances, have not been emphasized during these early efforts. Yet they are potentially enormous.[1] The U.S. Department of Commerce estimates that the cost to the government of processing a payment would be reduced between $1.65 to $2.70 for traditional administrative processing and from $0.60 to $1.00 for web-based processing.[2] Public agencies process hundreds of millions of paper-based transactions annually in the form of bill payments and document submissions and could achieve similar efficiencies across a range of transactions. The Department of Education services approximately 20 million student loan accounts. It pays a contract fee of twelve dollars per toll-free telephone call for access to student account information in the department's central processing system, which stores the database of Title IV student aid, student loan origination, and aid disbursement to schools. Web-based queries to this database cost only a few cents.[3]

Movement from paper-based to web-based processing of documents and payments typically generates administrative cost savings of roughly 50 percent—more for highly complex transactions. This figure ignores additional savings of money, time, travel, and effort to citizens and intermediate institutions. The sum of the following transactions with government—birth registrations; elementary, secondary, and college enrollment; motor vehicle registration and inspection; voter registration; construction permits for new housing; and patent and trademark applications—was nearly $443 million per year in 1999, according to the U.S. Census Bureau.[4] The sheer volume of government transactions suggests the enormous savings electronic transaction processing alone could provide.

Forrester Research, a private research firm, predicts that by 2006 governments at the local, state, and federal levels will receive 15 percent of their total collections, or $602 billion, over the web.[5] This figure is significant not only for its impressive size, but also because private vendors and e-government providers typically charge a percentage fee for each transaction. Thus digitizing government can create a particularly lucrative new market. If no other pressure for electronic government existed, the market potential for businesses alone would move digitization forward. By the summer of 2000, nearly every federal agency and most state and larger local governments provided information and some services on the web. The median number of web-based state government services was four. Forms may be downloaded and taxes filed electronically, professional licenses obtained or renewed digitally, and state employment databases, sex offender registries, and government contracts searched online.[6]

The web's potential to support more efficient procurement means government benefits financially and administratively. In fiscal year 1999, U.S. government expenditures at all levels for procurement equaled $584 billion, of which $177 billion was federal defense spending.[7] Many large firms using web-based procurement to put supply chains on the web gain transparency and improve markets. Some have reported savings of 20 percent annually from use of the web for business-to-business exchange, although more recent estimates are smaller.[8] Similar government savings are estimated to yield nearly $117 billion per year.[9]

In addition to the development of web-based government-to-citizen (G2C) services and government-to-business (G2B) digital procurement processes, development of government-to-government (G2G) connectivity promises to yield significant benefits. Agency autonomy, competition, and lack of interoperability ("stovepipes") have long hampered coordination, slowed communication, and diminished opportunities for joint policy problem-solving in government. Open standards and protocols on the Internet allow all computers to be connected, resulting in the remarkable connectivity, size, range, and richness of the web. Yet the technical infrastructure for linking the computers of the government is no substitute for the institutional infrastructure required to support coordinated practices, procedures, cultures, incentives, and a range of organizational, social, and political rule systems that guide behavior and structure agencies.

The major challenge for government is not the development of web-based G2C transactions but reorganizing and restructuring the institutional arrangements in which those transactions are embedded. Policymakers have barely contemplated integration or reorganization behind the web, in the bricks and mortar of government. Moreover, it is clear that the current information infrastructure in most government agencies could not support e-government at any appreciable level, meaning that the Internet alone cannot interconnect agencies and the public. The initial euphoria that greeted e-commerce has been replaced with a growing awareness of the painstaking and painful organizational and industry restructuring that will be necessary to further exploit the coordination, control, and communication potential of the Internet. Government is following a similar trajectory. Unlike private firms, however, government reorganization is far more difficult and highly political because of the embeddedness of agencies in long-standing institutions. The reorganization of government as a consequence of the Internet signals an institutional transformation of the American state.

These reform challenges demand scholarly inquiry. This book seeks to break new ground by incorporating networked computing into institutional perspectives on governance and organizations. The intellectual precursors of this study are firmly situated in three broad streams of theory and research rooted primarily in political science, organizational and economic sociology, and studies of technology and organization.

The first stream, the study of governance, has been inextricably linked to institutions since antiquity. Robert Dahl observed: "That the character of a regime and the qualities of its people are somehow related has been a commonplace of political philosophy since the Greeks."[10] Aristotle argued that effective democratic institutions are intimately connected to the social and economic development of the demos. Plato, in the *Republic*, noted that similar institutions of governance vary depending upon the cultural characteristics of the citizenry. In the mid-nineteenth century, as constitution building in the nation-states gained impetus, John Stuart Mill sought to devise the institutional structures and processes of representative government that would protect individual rights and interests.[11]

More recently, interest in institutions has encompassed a range of overlapping and, at times, competing research programs.[12] Robert Putnam has furthered our understanding of the relationship among democratic institutions, politics, and social capital.[13] James March and Johan Olsen have contributed to institutional thought by delineating both rational choice and boundedly rational organizational bases of politics.[14] Robert Keohane and Joseph Nye have argued that realism in international relations fails to account for the effects of complex interdependence, international institutions, and the importance of "soft power."[15] International relations scholars have long examined the underpinnings of international regimes that govern in the absence of overarching authority.[16] Historical and comparative studies of government institutions, particularly those that examine the autonomy, capacity, and development of the state, have emphasized the political conflict and negotiation underlying institutional change and development as well as the strong effects on development of history, culture, and structural inertia.[17]

Other political scientists and sociologists have used an institutional lens to examine individual and organizational relationships and behavior in the policymaking process.[18] Researchers in this stream tend to focus on policymaking as it is actually carried out by individual and organizational actors rather than on more formal models of legislative or interest group behavior.[19] As Hugh Heclo observed, political sociologists have attended to the social relationships and social conditions that lead to public policies and the effects those policies have on social structure. Political scientists cast their analytical gaze on the political relationships, political forces, and political effects of policy. Yet public managers and other government actors are both social and political.[20] The analytic distinctions are imposed on the phenomena. The organizational, and more structural, variant of this mode of inquiry is perhaps best exemplified by Edward Laumann and David Knoke in *The Organizational State*, which views policymaking from the perspective of constellations, or networks, of public, private, and nonprofit organizations.

The second broad stream from which this book draws is the new institutionalism in organizational theory and sociology.[21] At the turn of the twentieth century, Émile Durkheim, the founder of sociology, defined it as "the science of institutions, of their genesis and of their functioning."[22] John Meyer, Richard Scott, and Brian Rowan have explained the roles of symbols and rituals in institutions and their relationship to legitimacy.[23] Paul DiMaggio and Walter Powell accounted for similarities in organizational forms and practices within organizational fields not as the result of rational choice but more often as the product of institutional isomorphism, processes by which organizations in a given field conform to normative influences, mimic others, or are coerced by powerful actors in their environments to adopt practices.[24] Other sociologists incorporate self-interest and incentives into institutional analysis to construct a choice-within-constraints framework that overlaps substantially with the new institutional economics.[25]

Mark Granovetter, in a seminal article published in 1985, argued that economic action is embedded in ongoing social structures and social relations.[26] His clear conceptual account of embeddedness in institutional and economic life reinvigorated a long-standing but dormant line of research in economic sociology. Embeddedness, according to Granovetter, affects both individual action and institutions. His approach sought a "third way" between "an atomized, undersocialized conception of human action [developed] . . . in the utilitarian tradition" and an oversocialized conception of the individual as one who has internalized norms and obligations to such an extent that terms such as "interests" and "choice" lose meaning.[27] Subsequent research has further developed the antecedents, characteristics, and outcomes of embedded network relationships, explored the mechanisms by which networks and embeddedness influence economic behavior, and explored the links between institutions and networks.[28]

The third major stream of research informing this book considers the relationship between information technologies and organizations. Max Weber recognized clearly the rapid development of bureaucracy in the nineteenth century as a response to the industrial revolution. Bureaucracy was needed to control decentralized, complex operations and to coordinate rail transport. He explained bureaucracy as a technology of control through its structuring of information into cases and channels, its strict reliance on impersonal relations, and inevitable tendency toward rationalization.[29] More recently, Alfred Chandler, the business historian, traced the evolution of the modern corporate form and its practices.[30] James Beniger has placed the "information revolution" in more than a century of efforts to gain speed and control over material processing. He argued that developments in computing typically respond to crises of control.[31] JoAnne Yates traces the dominant modes of managerial communication in complex organizations to their roots between 1850 and 1920 as written, formal communication subsumed earlier, less formal means.[32] Stephen Barley has explored the relationship between information technology (IT) and the organization of work.[33] Other researchers also have focused on the social and structural mechanisms by which individuals and organizations use new information technologies and on the effects of information technology on organizations and the design of work.[34]

This book seeks to integrate and to refine and extend research in these three broad streams. With few exceptions, little detailed inquiry on embeddedness and the role of networks has been conducted on government organizations and institutions. Laurence O'Toole has observed that public management "increasingly takes place in settings of networked actors. . . . Yet the standard writings to which most administrators turn for advice to improve performance devote relatively little attention to acting effectively in such situations."[35] Networked arrangements in government are prominent and likely to increase. The federal budget appropriates only a small proportion of the total to single-agency programs; nearly all major federal policies require a constellation of public, private, and nonprofit organizations.[36] Researchers have used the term "the hollow state" to denote that government increasingly takes place in the private and nonprofit sectors.[37] This book seeks to extend research on embeddedness and networks to better align research with current phenomena.

Studies of technology and organization have remained persistently ignored by social and policy scientists except those with an explicit interest in technology. Information technology has yet to be theorized in the institutional perspective or in other central paradigms of political science and sociology with the exception of communications studies. Although theories of technology adoption and innovation have a long history, particularly in economics, the ways in which information technologies interact with behavior, ongoing social relations, and organizational structure and process have yet to be adequately conceptualized and remain the province of research programs relatively isolated from the mainstream. As Heclo wrote in a different context, "One of the things most astonishing to posterity about our own times will be not how much we understood but how much we took for granted."[38] A century from now, social and policy scientists will look back with amusement and no small amount of condescension at the glacial pace with which social scientists moved to consider fundamental changes in information processing and their implications.

Enacting Technology

Institutional theories provide accounts of the constraints that institutions impose on action. These theories explain stability and coherence in collective and individual action but tend to leave essential and pressing questions unaddressed. How do institutions change? If institutions constrain action, how and why do only some actors and some organizations conform? How does technology enter institutional theory as a variable? By what mechanisms are institutions affected by fundamental changes in information processing and communication? In what ways do enactments of information technology strengthen or weaken constraints posed by institutions?

The analytical framework I advance is introduced here in simplified form in figure 1-1. Its elaboration and support form the substance of this book. This framework contributes to institutional theories by treating information technologies endogenously. Information technologies are transformed in the process of being designed and used. I distinguish *objective technology* from what I call *enacted technology*. Objective technology includes the Internet, other digital telecommunications, hardware, and software; enacted technology consists of the perceptions of users as well as designs and uses in particular settings. The Internet is merely a telecommunications spinal cord that computers connect with throughout the globe. It is a breathtaking achievement, but its force as an agent of change lies in the fact that it reduces some communication and coordination costs to nearly zero and affords an enormous array of new uses.

Information technologies differ from production or manufacturing technologies, the referent for "technology" in most institutional and organization theories. Information technologies are much more decomposable, flexible, and open to myriad designs and uses. Industrial technologies are brawn. Information technologies are brain and nervous system. Industrial technologies replace arms, hands, and muscle. Information technologies

FIGURE 1-1. Technology Enactment: A Basic Framework

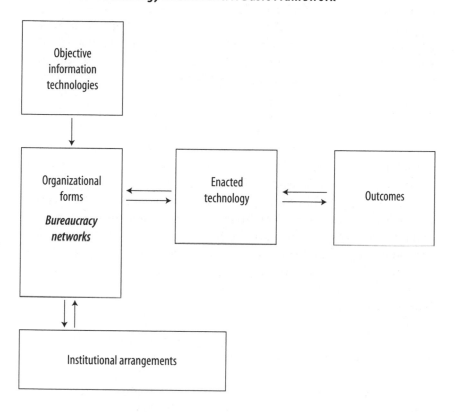

replace communication, thinking, and calculation. They are far more complex in their application, use, influence, and effect. Institutional theory has not yet accounted for information technologies and their role.

Institutional and organizational arrangements mediate technology enactment. In this framework, organizational arrangements refer to bureaucracy and interorganizational networks, both of which are dissected in later chapters.

Political scientists often use the term *institution* as a rough synonym for government. Many social scientists, however, distinguish between organizations and institutions, although the analytical distinction is blurred. Organizations are technical instruments in which products or services are produced and exchanged in a market and in which rewards are given for "effective and efficient control of the work process."[39] In contrast, institutions generate rules and requirements to which actors and organizations must conform if they are to receive support and be deemed legitimate in their authorizing environment. Organizational environments reward effectiveness, efficiency, and control over production. Institutional environments reward normative requirements for appropriateness and legitimacy and, in some cases, conformity to procedure, presentation, symbols, and rhetoric. Government agencies possess both organizational and institutional elements and must function in both environments. They are expected to be efficient and effective in their core activities but operate in a legislative, oversight, and political environment that requires conformity to a range of requirements that have little or nothing to do with economic output. Institutional arrangements range from micro-level elements in organizations to macro structures in the state and society.

Information technologies and organizational/institutional arrangements are connected reciprocally. Both function in this framework as dependent and independent variables. Each one has causal effects on the other. Institutions and organizations shape the enactment of information technology. Technology, in turn, may reshape organizations and institutions to better conform to its logic. New information technologies are enacted—made sense of, designed, and used (when they are used)—through the mediation of existing organizational and institutional arrangements with their own internal logics or tendencies. These multiple logics are embedded in operating routines, performance programs, bureaucratic politics, norms, cultural beliefs, and social networks.

Therefore, outcomes are unpredictable and variable in their rational, political, and social features. The effects of the Internet on government will be played out in unexpected ways, profoundly influenced by organizational, political, and institutional logics. In many instances the Internet does not lead to institutional transformation but is enacted to strengthen the status quo. Consider the use of information systems that speed up the processing of information, monitor employees more closely, and produce detailed monthly reports of activities. Little has changed structurally in this scenario. The same processes simply run faster and employees operate under tighter controls. In other instances technology is used explicitly to create change. Information technologies are not so much adopted or implemented as they are enacted by decisionmakers.

Reciprocal effects between technology and institutions are not sequential and direct but complex and highly interdependent, forming a new kind of virtual politics. When different logics intersect or conflict, the results are unpredictable. A high level of uncertainty, stemming in part from the pace of technological change, contributes to the production of unanticipated consequences and externalities in positive and negative variants. The negotiations, conflicts, and struggles among bureaucratic policymakers constitute the building of the virtual state. The outcomes of these struggles will shape its contours.

In most accounts of information technology and its influence, the causal mechanism that connects technology and institution is direct:

information technology → predictable institutional change

In these accounts, networked computing leads to a set of predictable changes, including flattened hierarchies, greater use of cross-functional teams, and more collaborative cultures; and more permeable organizational boundaries lead to greater use of interorganizational networks.[40] However, at least two decades of research on technology and organization demonstrate conclusively that these predictions, while possessing a certain technological logic, are not borne out in general.[41] To cite one example, Harold Leavitt and Thomas Whisler predicted in the 1950s that information technology would lead to the disappearance of middle-management layers.[42] It was clear even fifty years ago that automation could easily accomplish many of the routine tasks performed by middle managers. Yet the inarguable logic of IT did not lead to this change until the mid-1980s, when organizations began deep restructuring efforts in the face of an economic downturn, increased global competition, and a political culture that allowed massive downsizing in the economy. As Fernand Braudel observed about the industrial revolution, the technologies for such a revolution were in place for many years and in several countries. They sparked a "revolution" in Great Britain when economic necessity and institutional arrangements interacted synergistically with technology.[43]

An institutional perspective alerts us to the fact that government is likely to use the Internet differently than firms in the economy use it. The development of the virtual state is not likely to resemble the growth of electronic commerce. Government reform is qualitatively different from restructuring in firms and industries. Ironically, the substantial efficiency gains driving the development of e-commerce and industry change are disincentives for bureaucrats to use the Internet in government. Whereas dramatic efficiency gains and cost savings in the economy are rewarded through profits, promotions, stock price increases, and market share, similar gains in government are rewarded with budget cuts, staff reductions, loss of resources, and consolidation of programs. In this instance, incentives and rewards in the institutions of government are the obverse of those in the market. During the current first wave of digital government euphoria, when information and services are beginning to migrate to the web, efficiency gains and their political implications are not apparent. But during the next wave, when government-to-government channels develop further, bureaucratic decisionmakers will rapidly experience the perversity of incentives for institutional transformation.

Over the next decade, government decisionmakers will make important choices about the development of electronic government. Deliberate and informed decisions regarding alternative designs and uses of technology and institutional arrangements will require clarifications of the challenges and implications. Management and digital government consultants, eager to exploit the huge government market for digital tools, have already predicted that Congress will have to force the restructuring of agencies in order for government to take advantage of the benefits of the Internet and avoid bureaucratic gridlock.[44] These predictions suggest the pressure that governments might face to keep pace with changes in the economy. Without a conceptual framework to guide analysis and practice, researchers might simply document internecine bureaucratic struggles alternately with cases of dramatic innovation rather than helping decisionmakers to structure decisions and their consequences.

The Structure of the Book

The analytical framework summarized here is an outline for the chapters that follow. The study is grounded in the experience of the federal government, yet its lessons apply to state and local governments as well as to other democratic institutions around the globe. Part I of the book, which focuses on theory, dissects and analyzes organizational and institutional structures. Chapter 2 provides the historical and political context of national government reform in the United States during the National Performance Review (later called the National Partnership for Reinventing Government). Chapter 3 analyzes the chief properties of networked computing and its current uses in American government. Chapter 4 takes up bureaucracy, whose demise has been greatly exaggerated, and asks whether Max Weber would recognize the structures now called postbureaucratic. The network form and its characteristics are the subject of Chapter 5. Many experts have argued that networked governance replaces and supersedes bureaucracy. Whether or not this is true, the network form is growing in use and importance. Chapter 6, the central theoretical chapter, addresses institutions and presents a detailed discussion of the technology enactment framework and some of the initial propositions derived from it.

Part II focuses on practice. Three detailed case studies examine the ways in which bureaucratic policymakers—senior civil servants and appointees— are enacting technology for public purposes. Government actors in the bureaucracy, more than any other group, will construct or reconstruct the American state in an information age. When institutional arrangements and technology affect one another, they do so as a consequence of the actions and decisions of political actors. Their engagement with the structure of government and the policymaking system—and their role in making sense of and integrating new technologies into the nervous system of government—dwarfs that of any other group.

At the beginning of the Clinton administration, government reform efforts emphasized technology as a catalyst for modernization and the importance of bottom-up change as a way to revitalize the bureaucracy. Chapters 7 and 8 examine the development of the International Trade Data System, a governmentwide G2G and G2B system for processing international trade. The case scrutinizes the relationship between state and economy as international supply chain integration increases the volume and pace of the movement of goods and services across international borders. The International Trade Data System represents the kind of restructuring likely for G2G channels to be developed. If the state is to adequately regulate a global economy in which agricultural products, pharmaceuticals, assembled goods, and inputs cross international borders with impressive frequency, it has little choice but to develop information systems that integrate and facilitate the work of the nearly sixty-three separate agencies with partial jurisdiction over trade.

Far less ambitious than a governmentwide information system, a G2C web portal integrates the information and services of "bricks and mortar" agencies in cyberspace. Presented in Chapter 9, the development of the U.S. Business Advisor, the nation's first federal government web portal, brought together for the first time information and services from several agencies that serve or regulate business. Small-business owners could search one website for all regulations, laws, and information enforced or available through the government. The Business Advisor provides online approval for small-business loans up to $150,000, online tutorials, and indexes of export opportunities and regulations from around the globe. This case study explores the institutional and political challenges of building such virtual agencies.

Well before the Internet was publicly accessible, large organizations used intranets, including shared databases, e-mail, and other digital tools. No part of government pursued this path more vigorously than the army, in its efforts to modernize after the Vietnam War. In Chapter 10, I examine the user-as-developer approach followed in the Ninth Infantry Division, once the high-technology testbed for the tactical army, to develop automated battlefield management systems. The unanticipated consequences of technology enactment in the army provide surprisingly relevant and timely lessons for civilian government.

These cases were not selected at random and are not intended to be representative of all government technology efforts. They were chosen as examples of the intricate interdependence between individual action, institutional structure and practice, and networked computing. They allowed me to observe firsthand the processes by which government actors learn to use new technologies with transformative potential. The dramatic surge of activity following the release of the Internet for public use provided an unparalleled opportunity to observe a natural experiment in institutional transformation. I "test" propositions against empirical evidence to generate theory rather than to evaluate predictive theory. These cases represent cutting-edge experiments that were expected to achieve dramatically important results. In all instances, senior-level support was strong. The size of the effort and the political backdrop varies with each case, as does the level and type of interorganizational integration. The cases illustrate the sorts of challenges that will become more pressing and frequent as governments around the globe move beyond simply putting information and services on the web to the more complex challenges of institutional transformation.

Why is this inquiry important? In the face of momentous social transformation, a curious silence echoes through much of the academy. A review of the first-tier journals in organization theory and political science yields an almost imperceptible nod to the Internet. It is as if an information revolution were not taking place among experts on organizations and institutions. A troubling gap is growing between the importance of the Internet and its effects on government and society and the attention of social scientists to this empirical phenomenon. Social scientists, with few exceptions, have barely taken account of fundamental changes in communication, information processing, coordination, and control enabled by networked computing. It may be that the din of popular attention to the

Internet produces an understandable antipathy toward the topic among social scientists. Social science should avoid the trendy in order to focus on questions of deep and enduring concern to society. Yet the information revolution represents a fundamental, deep, and disjunctive shift in society, economy, and government. It is a revolution in its effect, not in its speed. This book fills a gap rather than standing in opposition to well-developed approaches to the topic. There are no well-developed approaches.

Evolutionary theories tell us that individuals will find the most efficient and best-suited forms of the Internet and its use in government through a competitive process that will separate the good ideas from the bad. If this is so, policymakers have only to continue muddling through until the separation process occurs. Such wishful thinking, though appealing, is highly problematic. Rational-actor models tell us that individuals will find the most efficient uses of the Internet in government, and that better performance and utility will result. If efficiency were the only, or even the chief, criterion of institutional performance in government, this might be a plausible account. Technological determinism tells us that the power and ubiquity of the Internet and the pace of technological change have overwhelmed human capacities to plan, design, or consider alternatives. In such a view, technology itself leads inexorably to new institutions that were planned and anticipated by no individual. These theories provide partial insights. This book is for those who believe that institutions matter.

If organizations, institutions, and technologies carry different and conflicting features, and if the emergence of interagency networks forces a confrontation among these different elements, what, exactly, can be said about the details of this new politics? Under what conditions are costs and disappointments likely to be high? What steps can actors take to improve governance? If we are to exercise control over our future we must understand our core institutions, their constituent elements, and the mechanisms by which they change with far greater clarity than we now do. If we are to control information technology rather than relinquishing control to fate, evolution, competition, determinism, cyberutopianism, a technocratic elite, or "the Internet," it will be more important to understand the interplay of technology and institution through human action than to develop dramatic predictions of a future over which we are powerless.

CHAPTER TWO

Leveraging Cyberspace to Reinvent Government

THIS CHAPTER PLACES the institutional development and the information technologies that are the subject of our inquiry in their concrete setting. In 1993 the Clinton administration under the directorship of Vice President Al Gore undertook a major government reform effort. First called the National Performance Review (NPR), in 1998 the initiative was renamed the National Partnership for Reinventing Government. The mission and objectives of this reform effort are, of course, important, but for our purposes the rhetoric, symbols, stories, and subculture of the reform are equally significant. A raft of criticism has been directed at the NPR, some of it justified. In spite of its flaws, the focus of reformers on leveraging cyberspace, using the Internet to create a new infrastructure and "logic" for organizing in the federal bureaucracy, has rapidly moved the American state toward the digital age.

In addition to laying out the central features of government reform under the NPR, in this chapter I dissect the logics of objective information technology that affect organizations and institutions and survey a variety of technology-based innovations in government to illustrate how bureaucratic policymakers have enacted technology during the 1990s. Although technology use has led to the alteration of some structures, most agency enactment of information technology has been what I call "plug-and-play."

That is, whenever possible, decisionmakers have used information technology in ways, however innovative, that leave deeper structures and processes—such as authority relations, political relations, and oversight processes—undisturbed. Organizations tend to patch information systems onto existing structures in ways that may enhance efficiency and capacity but that otherwise maintain the status quo.

A Partnership for Reinventing Government

The National Performance Review was launched on March 3, 1993, to "create a government that works better and costs less."[1] The momentum of the reform effort was created, in part, by the worldwide phenomenon of the New Public Management, a loose collection of policy and management initiatives designed to increase efficiency, accountability, and performance in bureaucratic states largely through greater use of markets and market-based management systems.[2] The NPR explicitly sought grassroots activists within the federal government who would use their detailed familiarity with government to identify and suggest hundreds of process improvements to streamline the federal bureaucracy. The NPR differed from most earlier American government reform efforts in resisting the temptation to restructure agencies. It emphasized redesigning process flows, increasing customer service to citizens, and leveraging the potential of information technology (IT) to enhance the capacity of government. The NPR headquarters staff, located in the White House, invited civil servants from agencies throughout the government to form reinvention teams. Two hundred and fifty civil servants scrutinized agency procedures and governmentwide systems in a search for improvements. Within five months NPR published its first report, *The Gore Report on Reinventing Government.* According to one history of the NPR by a staff member:

> The Vice President presented the report to President Clinton on September 7, 1993. The President and Vice President made a tour of the country to promote the report. The President issued directives to implement a number of the recommendations, including cutting the work force by 252,000 positions, cutting internal regulations in half, and requiring agencies to set customer service standards. In addition, the Congress adopted a law developed during the study phase of our task force—the Government Performance and Results Act— that required agencies to develop strategic and performance plans,

along with measures of performance, and publicly report progress annually. . . . In general, we focused on how the government works, not on what it should be doing. We chose to target the overhead costs, not the organizational structure, of agencies.[3]

The Senior Executive Service, the highest ranking civil servants in the government, intentionally were not given leadership roles in the reinvention process. Indeed, they were perceived as part of the problem rather than part of the solution. The Government Performance and Results Act mandated that agencies develop measures of success and work toward those measures in demonstrable ways. An intensive effort to cut red tape by streamlining performance programs, standard operating procedures, and business processes was undertaken. Under executive order, agencies were required to identify their "customers," develop customer service strategies, design standards for serving clients, and work out monitoring efforts to measure compliance with those standards.[4] Performance-based management became the norm in the federal government during the NPR, a move away from a bureaucratic focus on process and procedure to one on outputs, outcomes, and results. Similarly, regulatory reform shifted attention from identification of procedural violations to building partnerships with industry to jointly solve regulatory problems.

The use of information technology to revitalize, improve, reform, and modernize government lay at the center of the NPR. In September 1993, NPR staff produced "Reengineering through Information Technology," a report that included thirteen recommendations for using IT to reform government (see table 2-1).[5] Recommendations ranged from addressing a vacuum in technology leadership in the federal bureaucracy to the more mundane need to establish electronic mail throughout the government, the lack of which was a source of embarrassment and a reflection of agency autonomy and isolation. Several national and governmentwide information systems fell under the sponsorship of the NPR. Those information systems targeted by the NPR included the International Trade Data System (the subject of Chapters 7 and 8 of this book), a national law enforcement network, intergovernmental electronic tax filing capability, and a national environmental database index. Many of these initiatives began well before the NPR yet found renewed impetus following the explosion of the Internet and with visible White House support.

By the time the National Performance Review changed its name to the more active National Partnership for Reinventing Government, it claimed

TABLE 2-1. Reengineering through Information Technology (an NPR Document)

Category	Recommendations
Leadership	Strengthen leadership in information technology (IT).
Electronic government	Implement nationwide, integrated electronic benefits transfer. Develop integrated electronic access to government information and services. Establish a national law enforcement/public safety network. Provide intergovernmental tax filing, reporting, and payments processing. Establish an international trade data system. Create a national environmental data index. Plan, demonstrate, and provide governmentwide electronic mail.
Support mechanisms for electronic government	Improve government's information infrastructure. Ensure privacy and safety. Improve methods of IT acquisition. Provide incentives for innovation. Provide training and technical assistance in IT to federal employees.

Source: Office of the Vice President, "Reengineering through Information Technology," NPR Accompanying Report, September 1993 (www.npr.gov/library/reports/it.html [March 13, 2001]).

to have reduced the size of the federal work force by 351,000 and to have saved $137 billion in government spending. A later phase of reform concentrated on building interagency initiatives, virtual agencies, and the government version of electronic commerce, electronic or e-government.

The Internet as an Enabler of Virtuality

From the 1960s to the mid-1980s the technology of computing was radically transformed from one that used free-standing devices for calculation to a communication system unrivaled in extent and memory in human history.[6] During the 1960s the idea of using computers for communication was unusual. Although modems had been invented in the 1950s, connecting computers for information transfer through the telephone system was difficult and fraught with error. The Internet was first developed in the late 1960s as a small experiment funded by the Defense Advanced Research Projects Agency (DARPA) to allow scientists to run programs on remote computers. Early in the 1990s, with the development of the first web browser, Mosaic, the Internet rapidly took form as a global system connecting millions of computers.[7] For users of the Internet it has become commonplace to communicate instantly and globally.

The Internet and a growing array of information and communications technologies fundamentally modify possibilities for organizing communication, work, business, and government. These technologies influence society and economy in ways reminiscent of the printing press, and, more recently, the steam engine, railroad, and electricity. As a revolutionary technology, the Internet—by which I mean the Internet and a host of related information technologies—provides the technological potential to influence the structure of the state as well as the relationship between state and citizen.

During the 1990s alone, process redesign efforts and innovations provided evidence that IT in conjunction with government reform efforts is likely to result, over the long run, in substantial modification of the form and capacity of the administrative state. Technology has been used to help change agency structures and has led, in some cases, to vertical and horizontal compression: a reduction in the layers of command and functional division of labor in bureaucracies. Information technology in conjunction with the redesign of organizational process flows has diminished the amount of red tape and accelerated the delivery of government services for some members of the public. Government information and an increasing number of services are available via the Internet and the World Wide Web to those with access.

Commenting on the policy implications of the Internet, Thomas Kalil, former senior director of the National Economic Council, observed:

> People with shared interests are using the Internet to solve problems, accomplish tasks, and create resources that would be well beyond the reach of any one person or organization. The Internet is being used to created virtual libraries, . . . organize massive volunteer efforts, and filter information in collaborative fashion. The ability to leverage the efforts of large numbers of networked users has important economic, social, and political consequences. This phenomenon is important to policy makers because it can potentially be used to leverage scarce taxpayers dollars and promote applications of the information infrastructure.[8]

According to Kalil, the political potential of the Internet derives from its function as a "distributed, massively parallel supercomputer that is connecting not only microprocessors but people, information repositories, sensors, intelligent agents, and mobile code." Steven Whitehead has used the term "cyberspace leveraging" to mean the use of "computer networks to harness the power of a large population of networked users," that is, to leverage the "small efforts of the many" rather than the "big efforts of the few."[9] As part of the democratic process, ease of access is central to influence, but to date the use of the Internet for political participation remains biased in favor of the educationally and economically advantaged.

As a medium that currently supports extremely low cost communication among millions, the Internet, and the access it provides to the web, differs markedly from other communications media. Its ability to enable many-to-many communication, or communication within and among groups of individuals, separates it from one-to-many (broadcast) media, including newspapers and magazines, television, and radio. Moreover, digital information is remarkably malleable, meaning it can be easily retrieved, stored, indexed, transmitted, and revised. In their current pioneering state, the Internet and the web together possess a cost structure radically different from that of any other mass media technologies. Their potential is available to nearly any interest group with access to the Web. It is not clear how the cost structure will change as the Internet is combined with other media and as its commercial potential is further exploited.

The Internet and World Wide Web enable government agencies to restructure their interactions with citizens. Some agencies—or interagency groups—have developed client-based systems to provide government information and services. Others have developed electronic commerce by constructing web-based bidding arenas for government contracts. The government has also developed information-based networks. In January 1999 the Internal Revenue Service (IRS) accepted its first credit card payment over the Internet. Previously the IRS allowed taxpayers to file returns online. But since 30 percent of those who filed their taxes online owed money, they still had to mail in a check or money order. Before accepting credit card payments, the IRS had to determine how to reconcile tax returns with payments and how to credit taxpayer accounts accurately. Once it did that, in 1999, 20,000 citizens used credit cards to pay their taxes.[10]

When the first national atlas of the United States was produced in 1970 it weighed twelve pounds, and the production run was limited to 15,000 copies. In 1997 the United States Geological Service (USGS) coordinated the production of the second national atlas on the web. Internet users may now create their own maps at www-atlas.usgs.gov using data from the USGS, the Census Bureau, the Environmental Protection Agency, and other agencies. Jay Donnelly, the atlas's managing editor, observed, "With the World Wide Web as the publishing medium we no longer have to restrict content. We can make the digital representations of maps available to the public regardless of theme."[11]

Users who design their own maps may combine demographic, environmental, geographic, geologic, and other types of data from various agencies:

> Users can create a map that displays the nation's streams and watersheds overlaid with data on toxic releases or Superfund sites. USGS has produced hard-copy maps for the project, but the days of the 12-pounder are gone. These are separate maps on specific subjects such as the nation's principal aquifers/groundwater resources, watershed boundaries and the distribution of federal and American Indian–owned land. Most recently the USGS released a shaded relief map of North America. It will issue a map on the nation's wetlands next. All printed maps have Web-based counterparts.[12]

Similarly, the Environmental Protection Agency (EPA) provides environmental and regulator data to the public over the web. EnviroMapper (www.epa.gov/enviro/html/em/index.html) includes data on water quality, toxic releases, hazardous waste, and Superfund sites. In order to monitor the environment, the EPA spends $400 million annually to collect data. The EPA realized that by posting its vast repository of geographic information systems and regulatory data on the web, all users, including environmental activists, corporations, and concerned citizens, would have the ability to create customized maps without staff assistance from EPA. Thus the disintermediation of public information possible through the web at the same time reduces agency workload and costs. By placing its data on the web, the agency estimates it will save $5 million annually.

The term "virtual," as I use it in reference to the state, refers to capacity that appears seamless but that exists through the rapid transfer and sharing of the capacity of several discrete units and agencies as their partners. For example, by rapidly transferring memory across several disks to optimize free disk space, a computer may have a virtual memory that is much larger than its actual memory. A virtual circuit may function as an actual circuit when in fact it is a packet-switched network.[13] Similarly, clients interact with a virtual government agency as if they are interacting with a coherent physical organization when in fact they are interacting with several agencies that may be integrated only through digital networks. As the state becomes increasingly networked through information systems, interagency arrangements, public-private partnerships, intergovernmental agreements that join federal, state, local, nonprofit, and private actors, and web-based services that link the websites of hundreds of organizations, we may speak of a virtual state. Virtuality is a function of the apparently seamless integration of disparate, jurisdictionally separate, often geographically dispersed parts.

The Internet and the web, although by no means the only information technologies to influence bureaucratic reform, have enabled disjunctive changes. Although interorganizational arrangements and the embeddedness of economic activity in social networks were topics of practical and scholarly interest well before the widespread use of the Internet and the web, the effect of these technologies on the rate and scale of network formation has been extraordinary yet poorly understood.[14]

A transformation of communication as fundamental as that brought by the Internet and the web should not be underestimated. Lucian Pye, one of the central scholars of communication and politics writing pre-Internet, observed: "Communications is the web of human society. The structure of a communication system with its more or less well-defined channels is, in a sense, the skeleton of the social body which envelops it. The content of communications is of course the very substance of human intercourse. The flow of communications determines the direction and the pace of dynamic social development."[15]

Functional differentiation and the clear division of labor as means of organizing information and information processing in complex organizations are giving way to the structuring of information using computer-based information systems. By removing the artificial boundaries between subunits and people, more of the burden for organizational structure can be assumed by information systems. Hierarchy diminishes in importance as a means of control as teams have come to manage more work and make decisions. As a consequence, roles and job descriptions have become more fluid in order to accommodate cross-functional and network configurations. Entire units and jobs in bureaucracy were once devoted to the management of paper files. Not only clerical work, but also report writing and an array of middle-management tasks were devoted to accumulating and sorting information. Although it is now clear that many mid-level managers perform critical tasks that cannot be automated, much of the routinized information processing that was performed in the middle strata of complex organizations is now handled by computers. In addition, the digital file allows information to be made available "anywhere, anytime" around the globe if the information system is so designed.

Virtual Agencies

Agencies have a growing ability to integrate information, decisionmaking processes, and flows across organizational boundaries. As integration efforts continue, notions of jurisdiction are likely to change. Integrated information processing not only greatly speeds the flow of information and services across organizations but also modifies some rationales for jurisdiction by significantly lowering transaction costs. Internal contracting within the federal bureaucracy, public-private partnerships, and networks among federal, state, and local agencies, nonprofits, and firms are proliferating. These network arrangements are more complex than simple outsourcing contracts. The ability to organize, coordinate, and control complex policy domains is changing and will continue to modify the structure of government, the relationship between competition and collaboration among government actors, and government-business relationships.

The federal government has adopted the idea that clients of government (individuals and firms) should have a single point of entry for government information and services. This movement extends the notion of "one-stop shopping" and makes the information providers responsible for minimizing search costs.[16]

Shared databases within agencies made it possible for personnel responsible for providing public services to offer a wide range of information as well as to retrieve and modify citizens' documents, often in real time. The customer contact units of the Social Security Administration, the IRS, and the Immigration and Naturalization Service, among others, rely on shared databases to provide current services to the public. Shared databases across agencies, without regard to jurisdiction, allowed an even wider range of information and services to be integrated at the point of contact between the public and the state. More recently, the Internet has increased the possibilities and pressure to integrate across an even wider variety of traditional boundaries in order to reduce search costs for the public and to solve policy problems that cannot be adequately addressed without such integration. Integration of information in websites and databases may not—and in most cases does not—imply any actual integration of programs or services. Thus agencies can achieve virtual integration—

producing virtual agencies—often without changing their structure, jurisdiction, or budgetary autonomy.

Networks of government actors have always been an important feature of the federal government. It is the growth in their use that is startling. That growth invites the reformulation of concepts such as jurisdiction, accountability, and command-and-control hierarchies. Among the questions raised by the growth of interagency networks are: What are the long-term effects of socializing individual and corporate actors to view, for example, "trade administration" or "services for senior citizens" as a single entity rather than as a number of agencies, cultures, and jurisdictions? Is there a dynamic force within the virtual integration of programs that may lead to other forms of agency integration? When should actual, rather than virtual, restructuring occur? What are the criteria that should guide decisions about degrees and types of integration?

One of the precursors of structural change in the nation-state appears to be data standardization across agencies. Shared databases are not possible without standardized data, and, once developed, they create a platform for further integration efforts. Thus data standardization, catalyzed by the Internet, represents a significant rationalization of agency and interagency processes. First, standardization renders redundancies across agencies transparent. Second, standardization weakens the rationale for having different agencies collect and store highly similar or identical data elements. Third, data standardization suggests new forms of analysis that may lead to changes in the structure and organization of agencies. Fourth, structural changes in the federal bureaucracy are inevitable as redundant data collection, storage, and analysis by different agencies is eliminated. The political battles revolve around which agencies will win and which will lose ownership of data.

The Information Network for Public Health Officials (INPHO) is housed at the Centers for Disease Control and Protection of the U.S. Public Health Service. It "is an initiative to build an information infrastructure serving community, state and federal public health practitioners" and gives "public health agencies new access to formerly centralized information" in an effort to unite the public health and medical care communities.[17]

Virtual integration in international networks has also proliferated, often with coordination by the U.S. government. For example, in 1996 the Office of Arms Control and Nonproliferation in the Export Control Division of the Department of Energy (DOE) developed and put at the service of the international nonproliferation community an automated system to coordinate efforts against the spread of nuclear weapons. According to program documents:

> The Nuclear Suppliers Group Information Sharing System (NISS), is a high-speed, highly-reliable, low-cost system whose transmissions are secure against eavesdroppers. . . . Each NISS user feeds information into NISS on its own local computer terminal and has synchronous access to the entire NISS computerized database through geographically-distributed architecture. The information from NSG members flows to a central location at DOE's Los Alamos National Laboratory, where the data is updated automatically every 24 hours. . . . The system enables the 32 member countries of the Nuclear Suppliers Group (NSG) to keep informed on what each member is doing to deny proliferation-sensitive materials, equipment, and technology to would-be proliferant countries. Awareness of an NSG member's denial action puts the other NSG members on guard against proliferant efforts to find an alternative supplier and eliminates the possibility of suppliers economically undercutting each other. DOE notifies member states of denials as well as other information on nuclear-related exports simultaneously.[18]

Not surprisingly, the concept of a virtual agency captured the imagination of the NPR staff. The central idea was to create networked constellations of individuals, programs, services, information, and agencies on the web to "virtually" reorganize agency information and services in ways that would better serve all constituents.

At a 1996 conference on virtual agencies sponsored by the Defense Technical Information Center (DTIC) for the federal government, the topics addressed included: creation of a one-stop guide to federal statistical information using a robot program to collect key HTML pages and documents from over 4,000 URLs and to create a comprehensive set of indexes; FedWorld's proposal to support all of an agency's online needs; and virtual social work, which envisioned "a converging, synergistic world of the digital economy, electronic commerce, digital democracy, electronic government, virtual communities of place and interest, virtual agencies and organizations."[19]

Through virtual diplomacy the communication and coordination attributes of the web allow potential changes in policymaking structure and practice even across sovereign state boundaries. The role of the State Department as an intermediary between U.S. agencies and their international counterparts is changed as a result. Similarly, direct international communications and coordinating alter the role of international organizations.

Federal interagency websites, or virtual agencies, would enable service integration not possible outside cyberspace. The number of federal interagency websites indicates the magnitude of this effort (see box). By November 2000 the number of interagency websites had grown to twenty-six, covering nearly all policy domains. For example, Access America for Seniors, a government web portal for seniors, compiles information and services from nineteen agencies. Afterschool.gov is a virtual agency that connects citizens to the resources of fifteen federal agencies "that support children and youth during out-of-school time." The U.S. Business Advisor, the first of the NPR-sponsored virtual agencies, co-locates all information and services from the government used by small-business owners.

Vision versus Reality

The visionary initiatives highlighted here contrast with other more challenging technology issues struggled with by the NPR. In October 1993 President Clinton signed Executive Order 13011, which established the Government Information and Technology Services (GITS) Working Group

---

Federal Interagency Websites

Access America for Exporters	FedStats (statistics)
Access America for Seniors	Financenet
Access America for Students	Healthfinder
Afterschool	Inspector General Network
BudgetNet	PAVNET (Partnership Against
CodeTalk (Native American)	Violence Network)
Commonly Requested Federal	Recreational Opportunities
Services	Web Pages For Kids
Consumer Protection	U.S. Business Advisor
disAbility	U.S. NonProfit Gateway
Federal Business Opportunities	U.S. State and Local Government
Federal Consumer Information	Gateway
Center	Veterans
Federal Information Center	Youth Info
Federal Resources for Education	Workers[20]
Excellence (FREE)	

to implement the recommendations of the initial NPR report in part by promoting the development of innovative technologies and government practices, seeking the views of government and outside experts, and recommending opportunities for cross-agency cooperation and the sharing of infrastructure services.[21]

A status report on the original IT initiatives of the NPR also noted that the federal government was lagging behind the private sector for several reasons—regulatory, legislative, and cultural—and that it lacked access to current technologies and services.[22] The NPR staff felt that the government lacked a coherent overall plan for using the potential of technology in government and that it lacked leadership in this area. They wanted to provide a government counterpart to Clinton's commitment to make technology the "engine of economic growth" in the economy. But most of the rhetoric focused on government-to-citizen, or first-wave, use of the Internet, such as online student loan applications and approvals, electronic fingerprinting of criminals to create a national crime database, and one-time entry of information for seniors to cover Medicare and pension programs throughout the government.

The rhetoric of the NPR reflected the hyperbole and lack of analysis that dominates popular management writing on cyberissues. Political rhetoric understandably serves purposes other than neutral analysis.[23] But political rhetoric cannot substitute for reasoned, empirically based analysis and analytical frameworks required to guide government officials undertaking major structural reform while absorbing significant personnel cuts and near static appropriations to agencies. Internal government documents—notably from the General Accounting Office, the Office of Management and Budget, and the federal information resources management community—tend to ignore institutional change, focusing instead on information resource management issues such as the life cycles of computer systems, their cost and capacity, and proper methods of systems planning and procurement. What has been missing is sustained examination of the implications of networked information and organizations for policymaking, the capacity of the state, and governance.

CHAPTER THREE

Networked Computing

I N CHAPTER 2 we examined virtual agencies in the context of the National Partnership for Reinventing Government. This chapter completes our examination of the attributes of networked computing and its uses in American government. The level of
hyperbole and mythology regarding information technologies calls for a
careful appraisal of attributes and technology enactment before proceeding further in our inquiry. Information technology differs from other technologies in its capacity to manipulate symbols used in all types of work. It

Examples of IT innovation in this chapter from the Ford Foundation–Harvard
University Innovations in American Government Awards Program were selected as
part of a systematic analysis of IT-based innovation in government. I am grateful to
Alan Altshuler, director of the Innovations in American Government Program at the
John F. Kennedy School of Government, for access to all finalist and semifinalist applications to the awards program. I examined more than fifty detailed applications,
submitted from 1993 to 1999, that advanced to the finalist and semifinalist ranks of
an annual competition of innovations in government held at Harvard University. The
study found that most technology innovations, although highly useful and creative,
did not involve structural changes in an agency or program. Typically, these innovations were better characterized as "plug and play"; that is, they could be tacked on to
existing structures with little modification.

has the potential to affect coordination as well as production and decisionmaking processes within and across institutions and organizations. In theory, particularly in theories of machinelike bureaucracy, information technology should make feasible a wide range of efficiencies through its effects on coordination and information. One of the chief potential effects of advances in information technology on bureaucratic organization has been the ability to structure information processing and flows using networked computing rather than through the strict delineation of roles, organizational relationships, and operating procedures. In practice, however, gains in efficiency and effectiveness depend critically on organizational structure and design rather than on technological infrastructure.

To the extent that information is power, the ability to design communication and information flows unavailable in the Weberian bureaucracy and to locate information anywhere that individuals have access to networked computers signals the potential for significant shifts in power. Current communication and search costs for web-based information located anywhere on the globe are virtually zero. The implications of this political economy of information for the structure and capacity of the state are enormous.

Information technology makes some structural features and operations relatively inexpensive and easy to implement. Think, for example, of the ease of website creation and making government information accessible to anyone with a computer, a connection, and an Internet service provider. Networked computing can make other decisions more difficult, however. For example, once an agency has established an active Internet presence, it may be more difficult to justify providing face-to-face service, even though many citizens still lack Internet access. Thus technology, by changing the costs and benefits of design choices, influences design, structure, and politics. Moreover, large technical systems, such as the legacy information systems and software used in the federal government, carry sunk costs—in the form of the dollars spent on putting the expertise, contracts, and physical infrastructure in place to begin with. Thus decisions made during the initial phases of system design strongly constrain subsequent choices. Because of such "path dependence," then, choices regarding some technologies may be said to be determinist. In sum, technologies themselves influence choice, but the relationship is indirect, sometimes subtle, and exercised in combination with other economic, cultural, political, and social influences.[1]

Information technology is enacted by governments to support dominant societal values. In the United States prevailing uses of IT support economic competitiveness and efficiency and provide some attention to democratic values of equality and liberty. In contrast, the central government of the People's Republic of China (PRC) enacts networked computing as an instrument of social control and surveillance. Technologies used for jamming, blocking, and filtering information dominate. In the royal Islamic government of Saudi Arabia, the state exercises more selective societal control, using some of the most sophisticated filtering technologies in the world. Similar information technologies may be used in dramatically different ways, as these examples demonstrate. However, the current open-source standards and protocols of the Internet and World Wide Web mean that authoritarian states must employ strong measures to maintain societal control in a networked world.

Effects on Distance, Time, and Memory

Information technologies affect information flows, coordination, and the work of the bureaucracy by altering the relationship between information and the physical factors of distance, time, and memory. When information is digitized and shared, geographic distance becomes less relevant—and in most cases irrelevant—to information flow, making possible geographically distributed partnerships, collaborative problem-solving, and highly coherent organization.[2] Time also may be said to become more fluid as a bureaucracy uses asynchronous communication. Store-and-forward systems and shared databases have reduced time delays in production and decisionmaking that were the consequence of multistep, linear information flows. The Social Security Administration can shift incoming calls from one time zone to another in order to expand its telephone-based service to the public beyond the typical federal workday. Thus, for example, calls dialed at 5:10 P.M. eastern standard time may be forwarded west to a center still in the middle of its business day.

Organizational memory (storage, organization, and retrieval), which exists in part in the form of shared databases, collects data from and provides it to all authorized points in agencies. This digital memory also maintains information in easily retrievable and malleable form over time. As part of a shared database, that part of organizational memory that was traditionally stored on paper in files and managed by clerical staff can be accessed systematically, analyzed for patterns, and used to benefit administration and future decisionmaking. But unlike paper files, digital information may be structured to reveal patterns and exceptions, thus creating much more than the simple memory that is stored in a file cabinet. These three properties of information flow and coordination—time, distance, and memory—allow agencies to more easily establish and build intra- and interorganizational networks among members who share production processes but are located in geographically separate settings.

Telecommunications networks allow decisionmakers to place nearly any digitized information anywhere to be available any time and in nearly any format. With this telecommunications infrastructure comes the ability to virtually network employees and work both within agencies and, increasingly, across agencies and entities. Information (the "files") located in shared databases or intranets, and now more frequently available on the web, can appear in any location and at any time a computer is available. Thus government information and services can be available at kiosks in malls, through personal computers in homes, at town libraries, in small rural settings and large urban centers, from Washington headquarters, and at remote field locations in the wilderness, desert, or U.S. territories.[3] For example, the General Services Administration designed "Government Services Express," service centers located where citizens tend to carry out their daily errands: in shopping malls. Service centers opened in 1999 near San Francisco at the Milpitas Great Mall and north of Boston at the Liberty Tree Mall in Danvers, Massachusetts. Constructed and administered in partnership with state and federal agencies, the kiosks allow anyone to read and print a variety of government information and forms as well as to carry out some transactions, including filing federal income tax forms. Video teleconferencing is available at centers for citizens who require advice that is not available in text form.[4]

In 1993 the U.S. Department of Education began to build a network of teachers to improve policymaking. Its "Goals 2000 Teacher Forum" invites teachers to voice their policy ideas in person and, beginning in 1995, via satellite teleconferencing. The department also maintains a computer network of outstanding teachers who provide feedback and input to policymakers. Forum participants and other award-winning teachers are included in a database of experts in education as potential mentors for other teachers. The department in this case serves as a central node for the network as well as a facilitator of dialogue. The rich, ongoing social connections enabled by the Internet and network approaches to policymaking blur the boundary between teachers and federal officials in the policymaking process.[5]

Simultaneous Centralization and Decentralization

Coordination and control have been central to theory and research on organizations, management, public policy, and administration. Traditionally, the tension between organizational centralization and decentralization was caused by the complex tradeoffs involved in determining the best location of the decisionmaking authority. Local field offices make policy and operational decisions based on region-specific information and experience. In contrast, federal headquarters, where agencywide policy is made, must maintain equitable operations across regions. But excessive central control impedes local responsiveness and adaptation and imposes reporting requirements that can be onerous. When headquarters must have all the relevant information in hand before local decisions can be made, delays are inevitable.

But data collected at remote field locations, once digitized, can be as easily available at headquarters as in its field locations and may be easily transferred without going through several layers of hierarchy. The creation of telecommunications networks can greatly reduce the space (files), staff, and tasks needed to manage data. Similarly, information generated at headquarters can be easily transferred to and enhance the activities of field locations. Telecommunications networks, increasingly linked to the Internet and web, allow bureaucracies to centralize some tasks and decentralize others. The design challenge is to structure field units to maximize the benefits of local knowledge while using centralized systems to maintain control and prevent redundancy. The results of local activity in digital form are transferable to central databases almost immediately. Simultaneous centralization and decentralization are possible, but as a practical matter agency officials have the ability to make structural adjustments without all of the constraints imposed by the traditional tradeoff between centralization and decentralization.

During one month in 1989, Hurricane Hugo devastated the southeastern United States and the Loma Prieta earthquake damaged parts of northern California. These disasters triggered relief efforts of the Federal Emergency Management Agency (FEMA) for 450,000 people that were the equivalent of those needed in three typical years. The enormity of these crises led the agency in 1995 to begin developing, as part of a larger modernization program, an integrated computer system for disaster relief. One new feature of the system is Automated Construction Estimating (ACE), which streamlines the delivery of aid to disaster victims: to save time, FEMA field inspectors transmit the results of home damage inspections (which serve as the basis for disaster awards) via handheld computers directly to the Disaster Field Office for data entry and transmission to headquarters. Similarly, disaster victims' information is transmitted electronically to the central processing facility at headquarters, resulting in greater data accuracy and more completed inspections each day.[6]

The ability to enter data into a digital system only once, combined with the capability to rapidly transfer data from field units to headquarters and to use software to calculate the amount of damage compensation, has resulted in significant capacity gains. Greater operating capacity at the field level and more rapid response were achieved in combination with—rather than at the expense of—greater center control.

Data can be available at headquarters and field locations in forms useful to decisionmakers at several levels. Critical management tasks include deciding which data are needed at which organizational locations, how current those data should be, and in what formats they would be most useful to the decisionmakers who will use them. Multiple sources and easy availability of centralized data collected from branch offices help avoid the problems created by outdated information and information that has been filtered through several hierarchical layers. Information systems allow for objective data reduction and near real-time transmission. When field personnel lack the information to make effective operational decisions because it is located only at headquarters, then agencies may benefit from the decentralization of those data. Many managers perform suboptimally because they are not fully aware of agency goals, lack the informational resources to make informed decisions, or lack motivation because incentives do not align with objectives.[7] When performance incentives are linked to control systems through shared information, the effect on performance is powerful and meaningful.

Redesigning Production Processes

Classical management theories assume a positive correlation between task complexity and a person's position in the hierarchy. In the quest for efficiency, functional specialization in many jobs has been carried to an extreme in order to simplify, and often to deskill, tasks.[8] In the federal bureaucracy, systems of job classification and seniority initiated during the late nineteenth century and increasingly elaborated until the 1980s fueled excessive functional specialization. Diseconomies produced by the coordination required to join increasingly numerous small and specialized jobs soon overshadowed the efficiencies of functional specialization.[9] As complexity increases so does specialization, with consequent increases in interdependence and coordination.[10] Traditionally, coordination has been achieved in large measure through direct supervision. Between 1993 and 1996, when 350,000 jobs were eliminated in the federal bureaucracy, supervisory positions were eliminated at twice the rate of nonsupervisory managerial positions. Approximately one-third of the work-force reductions targeted first-line supervisors, those at the lowest supervisory rungs.[11] Although in many cases this severe downsizing preceded the coordination gains that were expected from the use of information systems, it is not surprising that the supervisory ranks were attenuated. Theorists as early as the 1950s predicted the demise of middle management as a direct result of computer use in complex organizations.[12]

A first-line supervisor at an automated government facility of the Immigration and Naturalization Service reported to me that he spent a whole afternoon once a week hand-tallying numerical information supplied by his staff of approximately twenty-five immigration information operators, including the types and number of phone calls handled by the operators during the week. This occurred in a facility considered "state of the art," in which each operator and the supervisor already used desktop personal computers and advanced call-center technologies. That task alone accounted for 10 percent of the supervisor's time annually.[13]

Computerization has made it possible to combine many excessively specialized positions into "enlarged" jobs for individuals or teams. For example, during the late 1980s the Social Security Administration, which serves nearly 50 million citizens by disbursing welfare, disability, and survivors' and retirement benefits, customarily transferred requests for claims from administration telephone operators who received them from a separate claims processing unit. Citizens typically waited several weeks for a return call from a clerk in the claims processing unit, who would then collect information to initiate a process. By retraining operators and reprogramming computers at the telephone centers, the agency combined the initial steps of the claims process with the existing tasks of telephone operators.[14] Such compression of the horizontal and vertical flows of information and decisionmaking at SSA and across governments has significantly reduced coordination needs.

The aggregation of tasks, in which operators are given more responsibilities (including some that may have been classified at a higher pay grade) using computer-based information processing and "decision support tools," is often described as "empowerment" or "job enlargement." "Decision support systems," including access to databases and modeling software, give clerks low in the hierarchy the ability to make more decisions because the rules (or standards) they are to follow are embedded in software rather than in the decisionmaker. But the range of potential choices the "empowered" operator can make is often limited by the software, thus embedding control formerly exercised by supervisors. Moreover, an operator's decisions are visible to those in charge, and the system may automatically report deviations from standard procedures. (An important debate about the nature and motivation behind the "empowerment" of operators is discussed in Chapter 10.)[15] It should be obvious that any new discretionary authority granted to government employees is balanced, perhaps overshadowed, by the immense ability of IT to monitor, capture, and display employee activities.

Rationalization and the automation of information flows have been central features of restructuring efforts in the federal bureaucracy. Clerical tasks, the work that permeates government, are heavily affected by information technology. These tasks, often classified as "information work," include accounts processing, claims processing, social security administration, tax administration, welfare disbursements, student loan processing, and a large number of other linear, multistep processes.

The Postal Rate Commission, for example, must conduct hearings on all rule-making cases such as proposals for rate increases and post office closings. Rule-making is conducted as a legal proceeding and includes the phases of discovery, cross-examination, hearings, the submission of briefs, and finally a recommendation to the Postal Board of Governors. A proposed rate increase, for example, typically entails ten months of proceedings. Citizen and business response, or pleadings, during hearings may amount to 35,000 pages of documents, which must then be reproduced as many as 150 times, resulting in 5.2 million printed pages.

To handle this volume, the commission has developed a document management system, called Operating Online, which scans information into digital form. All digital files are publicly available on the Postal Rate Commission website at www.prc.gov. Although the $370,000 system will save only $150,000 a year in costs, the availability online of all documentation related to hearings reduces the costs of rule-making.[16] Most agencies with regulatory mandates have developed similar document management systems.

During the rule-making process, the information agencies must manage comes in the form of public comment, petitions, extensions, and adjudications. A docket, the voluminous file containing all information related to a proposed rule, must be managed by clerical staff. In 1993 the Department of Transportation—whose rule-making authority ranges from the regulation of air bags to the transport of hazardous materials—managed nine "docket rooms" and relevant staff. If materials were lost, there was no ability to track them, and researching a docket was an arduous task. Then the docket management process was moved to the web and opened to the public at the Docket Management System (DMS) website, www.dms.dot.gov. Now, the system lists the most requested dockets. In the fall of 1999, when one of the most requested dockets was a Maritime Administration attempt to reregister eight ships, designed to carry liquefied natural gas, under a foreign flag, the site received more than 12,000 requests for information (or hits) from the petitioning firms and from crew members of the ships that would be affected by the reregistration.[17]

Decision support systems also modify the design of decisionmaking processes, or "knowledge work." The knowledge worker adds value to information by virtue of training, education, and experience. Among the knowledge workers in government are specialists who develop loans and other financial instruments, provide counseling, write contracts and regulations, and design legislation, as well as budget analysts, logisticians, and lawyers. All are potential users of decision support tools. The following examples illustrate the complexity of analysis conducted in the federal bureaucracy, which when conducted well is largely invisible to the polity.

From 1978 to 1997, ten airline accidents were attributed to ice formation on aircraft. In response to these tragedies, the Federal Aviation Agency strengthened the rules for de-icing aircraft before takeoff and implemented a decision support system to help in the decisionmaking process. The process for deciding when to de-ice is dynamic and complex. Three different de-icing fluids may be used, each with different costs and chemical properties. The Environmental Protection Agency requires de-icing fluid to be recovered following its use. Climatic variations, including humidity and temperature, as well as flight delays all must be considered. The new decision support system, named Weather Support to De-Icing Decision-Making (WSDDM), uses data from Doppler radar, surface weather instruments, and snow gauges to help air traffic controllers and pilots reach the most efficient de-icing decisions.[18]

Similarly, the development of the $540 million Advanced Weather Interactive Processing System (AWIPS) by the National Weather Service allows forecasters to monitor and detect precursors of severe weather and issue earlier warnings. Supercomputers used for atmospheric modeling combined with an information system that integrates several data sets allow extremely rapid data analysis. In May 1999, seventy tornadoes in Kansas and Oklahoma resulted in fifty fatalities and more than $1 billion in property damage. Weather experts report that the number of casualties would have been much higher without the degree of advance warning made possible by the system.[19]

Performance Measurement as Control

Control processes allow agencies to measure performance and to gather timely, clear, and accurate feedback on the degree to which standards have been met. Decisionmakers must then interpret those results and make strategic and operating decisions based on their interpretations. Control systems traditionally serve three functions in management. First, they help decisionmakers use resources more effectively by providing feedback on the production process. Second, they provide coherence to disparate performance units and divisions to bring them into greater conformity with agency goals. Third, they supply data for strategic decisionmaking.[20] Information systems not only provide the potential for efficiency gains but also have led to the development of powerful new tools for control.

A simple but important illustration is provided by the Office of Thrift Supervision (OTS), the Treasury agency that regulates savings and loan associations. OTS implemented the Savings Institution Risk Management Program to minimize losses in savings and loan investments as a consequence of a rise in interest rates. A computer-based model permits OTS to identify institutions with the greatest risk of investment loss and also allows individual institutions to monitor their own interest rate risk and adjust their exposure to avoid losses or increase their capital cushion without costly government intervention. The model uses a stress test to predict each savings and loan institution's potential loss under different interest rate scenarios. The interest-rate risk model is an off-site monitoring tool that permits the regulator and the institution to analyze fundamental industry financial elements in a more timely way and with greater accuracy than is possible by traditional on-site examination. The Treasury analysts who developed and now manage the system report: "The implementation of our system has greatly reduced the possibility that we will ever experience another thrift crisis that is interest rate risk related. We believe the system has fundamentally changed risk management practices in the industry for the better."[21]

A second example illustrates the importance of control systems in health care. The Indian Health Service administers hospitals and health care centers throughout the United States for American Indians and Alaska Natives. It also monitors health risks specific to those populations. The Indian Health Performance Evaluation System (IHPES) was developed in response to new hospital accreditation standards by the Joint Commission on Accreditation of Healthcare Organizations. A system designed with measures of risk specific to Native American populations was thought to be more effective than the national risk management systems developed throughout the health care industry. For example, because diabetes is epidemic among Native Americans, the system monitors hospitals and health care facilities to be sure that blood sugar is regularly checked, that eye and dental exams are given, and that nutritional education is made available. By monitoring precursors of diabetes as well as the use of diagnostic procedures and preventive care and counseling, the system is used proactively rather than simply as a retrospective measurement tool.[22]

Community Connections is an initiative pioneered by the United States Department of Housing and Urban Development (HUD) in early 1994. Before the program's implementation, HUD mandated twelve separate housing and community development programs from every state and locality. Because these programs were uncoordinated, they hindered community development, prevented citizens and communities from sharing information, and frustrated evaluators' attempts to measure agency progress. Community Connections replaced the programs' separate applications with one consolidated plan that uses performance measurements to trigger funding for over $10 billion in HUD programs. Performance data are analyzed using a computer program that replicates community features using mapping software, demographics, and HUD information. All of these maps are available on the web.[23]

Information technology cannot determine the appropriate performance measures or standards for agencies. But once those are established, software analysts can embed routines, rules, and standards in programs and procedures to make data collection easier, data collation automatic, and the generation of reports simple. Information technologies rationalize and standardize elements more powerfully than standard operating procedures and supervisors. Embedded rules in software applications subtly but clearly identify the aspects of tasks that are discretionary. Information-based organizations thus codify knowledge and inculcate habits in a somewhat different but much more powerful manner than traditional bureaucracies. In many but not all ways, the control problem in government has never been easier to manage. During the twentieth century, the bureaucratic state moved from direct supervisory control to bureaucratic control and now, in information-based organizations, is moving to embedded control.

Enabling or Deskilling?

Information technology formalizes the knowledge and know-how of skilled workers and thereby makes it relatively independent of those actors. The routines, procedures, knowledge, expertise, and problem-solving maps used by workers at all levels can, in part, be "objectified" (or formalized) by being designed into equipment and machinery, including, of course, software, hardware, and telecommunications. This formalization is similar in many respects to the formalization of work in organizations through the development of routines, standard operating procedures, and performance programs.[24]

Through the formalization of work and decisionmaking, IT may be used either to deskill work or to complement and enhance the abilities and skills of those using it.[25] A debate that persisted throughout much of the twentieth century and continues into the present argues whether technology increases discretion, creativity, and skill in bureaucracy or alienates and deskills workers. One more recent stream of this debate has focused on the discretion of decisionmakers over the design of technology as a mechanism of coercive control and deskilling or as a tool to enable greater discretion, to leverage expertise, to promote joint problem-solving, and in general, to complement and leverage human capacity.[26] Designers do influence how information systems are used and the ways in which they shape organizational arrangements. As Paul Adler and Bryan Borys put it:

> According to one rationale, the user is a source of problems to be eliminated; according to the other, the user is a source of skill and intelligence to be supported. In one, labor is a source of error, and the goal of design is to get the operator out of the control loop; in the other, equipment is seen as inherently limited, and the goal of design is to ensure the operator can intervene effectively to rectify problems.[27]

In the army, a concept known as the "user as developer" was adopted to explicitly put users into the design phase of new information systems. Through its traditional approach to development, the army had had significant experience developing and building information systems that were both out of date and inappropriate for users by the time they were ready to be used. By adopting an evolutionary approach in which designers were asked to "build a little, test a little," the army was able to reduce costs, shorten development cycles, and produce information systems that were closer to the needs of its personnel (see Chapter 10 for more detail).

In this chapter and the last we have seen that the Internet has the potential to fundamentally affect organizational coordination, control, and communication. Bureaucratic policymakers are using information technologies to reshape service delivery, enforcement and control, relationships between headquarters and field units, and the boundary between state and society. Complex rule-making takes place increasingly on the web. Risk management programs embedded in networked computing influence decisionmaking throughout the government. Performance measurement, again embedded in decision support systems, shapes behavior and decisionmaking and provides clear data patterns for analysis and policy refinement.

The growth of virtual agencies and networks of several variants suggests that bureaucracy may be changing and that government networks are increasing. But what are the structural elements of the bureaucratic state? And what are the implications for the use of information technology and the structure of the American state? To answer these questions, and to probe more deeply the organizational and institutional arrangements that I argue shape the enactment of technology, the next two chapters analyze two predominant organizational forms, bureaucracy and the network.

CHAPTER FOUR

Bureaucracy

> The reduction of modern office management to rules is deeply embedded in its very nature.
>
> *Max Weber*, Economy and Society

S INCE THE INDUSTRIALIZATION of the United States in the late nineteenth century, government has required a complex administrative and policymaking machinery in order to manage its day-to-day operations and implement legislation. The rhetoric of "post-bureaucracy" notwithstanding, this administrative machinery, and the career public servants within it, continues to be an essential intermediary between elected officials and society. It transforms the often vague and ambiguous decisions and judgments of the executive, the legislature, and the judiciary into operational and organizational rules and programs. Its attributes and vitality are more than ever of crucial concern to government and, ultimately, to citizens. In an industrialized society and economy, the state is central to contemporary political life.[1]

This chapter develops ideas first published in "The Virtual State: Toward a Theory of Federal Bureaucracy in the Twenty-First Century," in Elaine Ciulla Kamarck and Joseph S. Nye Jr., eds., *democracy.com? Governance in a Networked World* (Hollis, N.H.: Hollis, 1999). I am grateful to the Visions of Governance in the Twenty-First Century Project at the Kennedy School of Government, Harvard University, for financial support and to the faculty associated with that project for early comments on many of the points discussed in this chapter.

It is commonplace to claim that information technology changes the structure of organizations. Attention to network organizations signals one significant move away from bureaucracy. The reduction of red tape and flattening of hierarchies in government over the past decade have signaled further change. Yet few researchers interested in technology have addressed the bureaucratic "structure," or the modern state, in much detail. Here and in the next chapter on interorganizational networks I attempt to do just that as a means of examining the dynamics of virtual agencies and the growth of digital government. The result will be a better understanding of the ways information technology is actually used and how current uses interact with agency structure and practice. This inquiry will also help formulate a response to the question: Is there a transformation of the bureaucratic state taking place that can be at least partially attributed to the information revolution? If so, what are some of the political and policy implications of these structural modifications? Of course, any discussion of bureaucratic structure must begin with Max Weber, and so our excursion into the bureaucratic form begins.

Weberian Bureaucracy

Although Weber depicted bureaucracy as an ideal type, he also argued early in the twentieth century that bureaucracy is the only form of organization able to cope with the complexity of modern enterprise.[2] In fact, wherever complex coordination of activities has taken place since ancient times, bureaucracy has of necessity sprung up.[3] During the twentieth century we became a society of organizations.[4] Weber's depiction of this organizational form proved central to twentieth-century public administration, to the Progressive agenda from approximately 1920 when the English translation of his work first appeared, and to the normative construction of the role of the bureaucrat.[5] Weber outlined the key elements of bureaucracy in the economy and the state as follows:

Characteristics of Modern Bureaucracy

Modern officialdom functions in the following manner:

I. There is the principle of *official jurisdictional areas*, which are generally ordered by rules, that is, by laws or administrative regulations. This means:

(1) The regular activities required for the purposes of the bureaucratically governed structure are assigned as official duties.

(2) The authority to give the commands required for the discharge of these duties is distributed in a stable way and is strictly delimited by rules. . . .

(3) . . . Only persons who qualify under general rules are employed.

In the sphere of the state these three elements constitute a bureaucratic *agency*, in the sphere of the private economy they constitute a bureaucratic *enterprise*. Bureaucracy, thus understood, is fully developed in political . . . communities only in the modern state, and in the private economy only in the most advanced institutions of capitalism.

II. The principles of *office hierarchy* and of channels of appeal[6] . . . stipulate a clearly established system of super- and subordination in which there is a supervision of the lower offices by the higher ones. . . .

III. The management of the modern office is based upon written documents (the "files"), which are preserved in their original or draft form, and upon a staff of subaltern officials and scribes of all sorts. The body of officials working in an agency along with the respective apparatus of material implements and the files, make up a *bureau*. . . .

IV. Office management, at least all specialized office management— and such management is distinctly modern—usually presupposes thorough training in a field of specialization. . . .

V. When the office is fully developed, official activity demands the *full working capacity* of the official. . . . Formerly the normal state of affairs was the reverse: Official business was discharged as a secondary activity.

VI. The management of the office follows *general rules*, which are more or less stable, more or less exhaustive, and which can be learned. Knowledge of these rules represents a special technical expertise which the officials possess. It involves jurisprudence, administrative or business management.

The reduction of modern office management to rules is deeply embedded in its very nature.[7]

Weber's rational-legal ideal type was meant to indicate how bureaucracy could replace personalistic, patrimonial, patriarchal governance in society and economy.

James March and Herbert Simon argued the impossibility of developing principles that would guide the structuring of organizations.[8] Such principles were a mainstay of classical management theory and had guided the development of the American state during the first half of the twentieth century.[9] Richard Cyert and James March, analyzing firm behavior, laid out the elements of bureaucratic politics by showing how individual actors pursue their interests and goals apart from compliance with an overarching organizational goal or mission.[10] Graham Allison developed these ideas from organization theory to explain the role of organizational processes and bureaucratic politics, or the seemingly uninterrupted bargaining among government officials, that typifies government decision-making.[11] James Q. Wilson, also drawing upon these theoretical streams, notes what every student of government and organizational behavior knows, that some agencies adhere to rules, but many do not.[12] The balance of powers articulated in the Federalist Papers by James Madison constrains agency behavior to a greater extent than conformance to rules. That Weber's ideal-type bureaucracy masks a startling variety of bureaucratic forms and practices, in their details, is an important one. One of the most important limitations of the Weberian framework is the absence of flesh and blood—that is, a view of government decisionmakers and their activities even in highly bureaucratized organizations.

The modern American state is a bureaucratic state. Researchers cannot theorize the role of information technology in the bureaucratic state without paying considerable attention to its structural elements. Fundamental concepts of governance follow logically from Weber's conceptualization, including jurisdiction, hierarchy, merit, documentation, and professional training in administration. If bureaucracy is outmoded or deficient, which of these elements has changed? As James Beniger observes in his masterly analysis of control systems:

> Few turn-of-the century observers understood even isolated aspects of the societal transformation . . . then gathering momentum in the United States, England, France, and Germany. Notable among those who did was Max Weber (1864–1920), the German sociologist and political economist who directed social analysis to the most important control technology of his age: bureaucracy. . . . Weber was the first to see it as the critical new machinery for control of the societal forces unleashed by the Industrial Revolution.[13]

Although bureaucracy has been prevalent in all major ancient civilizations from ancient China to Rome, it did not assume its modern legal and rational form in the United States until late in the American industrial revolution. The development of the railway produced a complex transportation system in need of control and coordination—that is, administration—to prevent fatal railway accidents and serious economic losses in business.[14] No such administrative systems existed. They were developed as a necessary response to technological change. Weber's conceptualization of rules, rationalization, and their effect on behavior and social relations is as vital today to understanding the modern state as it was nearly a century ago. We have no comparable framework to guide the transformation of the state as a consequence of the information revolution.

Weber's definition of bureaucracy underlies the structural logic of the bureaucratic state in the twentieth century. His delineation of jurisdiction supplies the kernel from which theorists for the past eighty years have developed the normatively and theoretically powerful concepts of division of labor, functional differentiation, and, as a result, clear jurisdictional boundaries in government. Jurisdictional boundaries guide not only agency structure but also the organization of the budget process, oversight agencies, and congressional committees. If the Weberian concept of jurisdiction is changing, what form will jurisdiction take in the virtual state?

Weber's second characteristic, hierarchy, forms the essence of bureaucracy for many theorists. Herbert Simon, a key theorist of both bureaucracy and digital information processing, traces the dominance of hierarchy through a variety of natural as well as social systems.[15] Simon argues that hierarchy as a structural form encompasses and enables the decomposability of complex problems. The ability to factor complex problems, to assign the factors to specialists to solve, and then to recombine partial solutions is the chief reason that bureaucracy supersedes other forms of complex organization. Simon offers as evidence of superiority not only greater efficiency of output, but also the exceptional robustness of decomposable systems to withstand and recover from interruptions and disruptions from a variety of sources. Complex problems might also be factored and decomposed in network structures, although the ordering provided by hierarchy would have to be replaced with significant, perhaps overwhelming, mutual adjustment processes or other rules. A different type of coordination and control would have to replace hierarchy. Although the Internet and the web provide superior communication and coordination capacities, they do not replace hierarchy.

The third chief characteristic of bureaucracy, according to Weber, the "files," constituted an important departure from idiosyncratic, personalized decisionmaking that needed no documentation. As bureaucracy became central to the modern state, for example, tax collectors in England could no longer individually define their operational methods. Written rules and the evolution of standard operating procedures, stored in files, furthered the rationalization of the state and the economy. Consistency of professional behavior through adherence to rules is the basis for complex, wide-ranging financial, legal, political, and social systems. Monitoring and sanctions put force into rules, but most actors most of the time follow the rules out of habit or a sense of obligation, professionalism, citizenship, or other positive norm rather than because they fear the imposition of sanctions if they do not. The absence of widely accepted rule regimes—or widespread failure of actors to abide by rules—constitutes a key reason for delayed development in many societies. As we will see in the chapters that follow, the use of networked computing requires many more rules than are currently needed in government because computers, as binary processors, require rules to work. That more rules, and greater standardization across rule systems, will accompany wider use of the Internet in government is clear. The content and implications of those rules is not.

Weber normatively delineated the bureaucrat as neutral with respect to organizational goals and direction, impersonal with respect to the application of law and administrative regulations, and technically expert in the conduct of a particular, clearly defined office. Although many theorists have discounted the concept of bureaucratic neutrality, it remains normatively powerful in the American state.[16] Indeed, neutrality is a key feature of professionalism within every democratic civil service in the world. It is difficult to imagine a civil service in a democracy without a strong norm of neutrality. In a virtual state, where citizens are as likely to interact with private sector employees as with civil servants in conducting their web-based services and transactions, it is not clear whether the norm of neutrality will be replaced—or can be replaced—by embedded rules or standard operating procedures.

Finally, Weber characterized the rationalization of bureaus and offices increasingly ordered by rules and procedures. He feared the domination of bureaucracy as a form of control, an "iron cage," as much as he appreciated its effectiveness and potential as a rational and legal organizational arrangement of "technical superiority over any other form of organization."[17] Weber's then-radical perspective captured, and abetted, the transition from patriarchal, patrimonial, intensely political, and personal systems of state organization to the rational, impersonal, efficient, rule-based bureaucratic state. Every democratically governed industrial nation organizes as a bureaucratic state following the form delineated by Weber.

The modern American state reflects the ideas of both Weber and Frederick Taylor. Weber might never have held a central role in the development of the modern state in the United States if not for the complementarity between his ideas and Taylor's. In 1911, Frederick W. Taylor published *The Principles of Scientific Management*, a highly normative method of rationalization in industry and government. The essence of Taylorism consists of efficiency gains in production processes through control over the work force and the design of work.[18] Workers were assumed by Taylor to be uninterested and unable to analyze their own task environment, but motivated by money. A reward system based on the number of pieces produced would ensure conformity and speed in the production process. Scientific managers in government eagerly set about the organization of the modern American state as bureaucratic agencies with machinelike, rational, Weberian elements.[19]

Politics and administration would never overlap or compete in such a system. Legislators could pass laws to stipulate ends; administrators would use professional expertise to determine the "best," defined as the most efficient, means toward given ends. The convenient fiction of the policy-administration dichotomy, introduced by Woodrow Wilson, administrative theorist as well as president, helped reassure legislators that a growing state bureaucracy and professional civil service could be developed that would remain utterly subordinate, accountable, and responsive to them and thus to the electorate. According to Taylorists, close observation and rational analysis of any production process would indicate the "one best way"—or the rules—for performing the tasks of a job. Neutrality and rule systems in administration could be combined with neutrality and rule-making in scientific management to produce efficiencies in government. In order for the bureaucratic state to replace a state of parties and courts in late nineteenth- and early twentieth-century America, the relationship of the bureaucracy to Congress had to be clearly negotiated.[20] If the virtual state involves restructuring bureaucracy, this, too, would require considerable political negotiation with Congress and the judiciary to recalibrate the balance of powers.

Taylorism combines two dominant streams in American administrative thought: "the 'good man' approach" and a structural bureaucratic perspective that views people in their positions, or roles, primarily as components of organizational structure. Efficient structures could be achieved through the accurate classification of workers according to demonstrated ability and through coordination of labor: "From positions—abstractly, impersonally defined, in the manner of Weber's ideal bureaucratic type—one can build structures."[21] The deeply entrenched focus on job and position description and complex classification systems, which continued until the 1990s, indicates the institutionalized value within public administration of position, rather than person, as the fundamental structural component of the bureaucratic state.[22] As Gerald Garvey, a historian of public administration, notes: "The Taylorite world was bureaucratic in its very essence. For bureaucracy is, essentially, a means of combining capacity (in circumstances requiring coordination of many different skills and functions) with control. Control is achieved through hierarchical supervision and administrative direction."[23] So we see that Weber's ideal-type bureaucracy greatly informs scientific management and the development of the American bureaucratic state.

Central Elements of Bureaucratic Structure

Weber's ideal type provides a powerful vantage point for examining the bureaucratic state, but his broad conceptual framework requires more detail to be useful for our purposes. If the use of the Internet by bureaucratic policymakers were simply a matter of increasing rationalization in the bureaucracy, the logics would be perfectly aligned. The classical function of organizational structure has been to facilitate the division of labor through departmentalization, task specialization, and standardization. Coordination is achieved through hierarchy, formalization, and socialization. We will hold aside the imperative for bureaucracies to define their boundaries and to formalize relationships with other organizations in their environment. One of the central tasks of public administration and management is the design and maintenance of effective organizations, in part through the repeated reorganization of structural elements as well as coordination, function, and process flows in more or less systematic channels through which move information, activity, production, and decisionmaking.[24]

Coordination

One reason for the powerful potential effect of the Internet is its ability to affect not only production but also coordination. Therefore, this element of bureaucracy is of vital importance if we are going to understand how the use of the Internet by bureaucratic policymakers is mediated by existing structural elements. The division of labor and functional special-ization quickly create requirements for coordination.[25] Formal and infor-mal coordination mechanisms range from mutual adjustment among individuals, to supervision, to rationalization (or standardization) of in-puts, outputs, and even individuals through training, education, incen-tives, and indoctrination. These mechanisms, whose combinations in complex organization are legion, glue together the boxes on the organiza-tion chart, the basic parts of the organization.

Studies of the brain indicate that complex coordination is achieved through the cognitive capacity of one individual working alone. Dyads and small groups use informal means, primarily discussion and nonverbal communication, to coordinate their tasks. A group may informally elect a leader to coordinate its activities through direct supervision. As larger groups undertake more complex problem-solving, however, coordination typically requires standardization.

MUTUAL ADJUSTMENT. Although it is currently fashionable for research-ers to inquire into self-regulating systems and the relationship between the organizing behavior of neural networks and social networks, these ideas, however important, are not new. Economists have always understood the action of "the invisible hand," yet students of government tend to pay short shrift to the role of mutual adjustment as a powerful and ubiquitous means of coordination. This is important to the overall argument of this book because no conceptualization outlines the relationship between wide-spread use of information technology in government and the role of mu-tual adjustment. On the one hand, improved communication and shared information could vastly increase the importance of mutual adjustment. On the other hand, if rigid rules were programmed into information sys-tems, mutual adjustment would lose force as a source of coordination.

In his exploration of the uses of mutual adjustment in governmental decisionmaking, Charles Lindblom argued that "there are no coordina-tors in partisan mutual adjustment; such coordination as is achieved is a by-product of ordinary decisions, that is, of decisions not specifically in-tended to coordinate. *For partisan mutual adjustment, therefore, to study coordination is to study decision making generally. . . . For partisan mu-tual adjustment, therefore, to study coordination is to study rationality.*"[26] If we accept these claims, and I do, then we cannot circumscribe and dis-miss mutual adjustment as an informal mechanism working at the mar-gins of formal rule regimes.

Lindblom's use of partisan mutual adjustment at first glance falls into the pluralist, bargaining tradition in American politics. However, he carefully delineates the interplay among authority, rules, and mutual adjustment—a more sophisticated rendering than accounts of simple bargaining or bureaucratic politics: "The behavior of each participant (including each citizen) in the governmental process is greatly controlled by conventions [rules] about ends and means that have the effect of prescribing behavior conditionally or absolutely."[27] With specific reference to agencies, he argues:

> Each agency possesses and employs governmental authority over some participants in the governmental process (officials, agencies, non-official leaders, citizens), restricted and specialized, however, to its policy-making area. While in its area of specialization each agency makes policy decisions, some agencies also confer governmental authority on other agencies; and, of those that do, all make some decisions designed to coordinate the agencies on which they have conferred authority, and all occasionally prescribe a particular decision to such an agency.[28]

Thus, partisan mutual adjustment, far from a bargaining free-for-all, is always embedded in systems of rules, including rules regarding jurisdiction and authority. Lindblom's analysis anticipates recent scholarly attention to the embeddedness of strategic behavior. When bureaucratic policymakers negotiate the best, appropriate, feasible, or acceptable uses of the Internet in their agencies, their mutual adjustment takes place within nested systems of rules that constrain both the innovations considered and the interests agency actors negotiate for.

SUPERVISION. Although substantial empirical research analyzes the behavior of supervisors, their relationship to operators, and other important characteristics of this role, these things are not relevant to this discussion of bureaucracy because direct supervision requires one person to take responsibility for the work of others by assigning them tasks and evaluating their performance.[29]

Two schools of thought regarding organizational structure coexisted until the 1950s. Classical management theorists, who dominated public administration, focused their attention on the structural properties of direct supervision, the design of official authority and functional relationships, and their optimal organization in the federal bureaucracy. The "principles of management" school provided the central concepts that guided the design of

U.S. military organizations, firms, and public agencies: unity of command (the presumption that a subordinate should answer to one and only one superior), the superiority of the scalar chain (or chain of command), and a preoccupation with the optimal span of control under various organizational conditions. Many government and military officials to this day have been socialized to adhere to principles articulated in the 1930s by classical management theorists such as Luther Gulick and Lyndall Urwick.

Their ideas produced the deeply embedded notion of highly delineated roles and functions circumscribed within a clearly specified authority structure in the bureaucratic state. These ideas transcended their use as principles of management to become norms of good government and professional public management. They are deeply institutionalized in American government. Decisionmakers, analysts, and legislators continue to regard mutual adjustment and the entrepreneurial and political tasks required of every bureaucrat as deviations or problems to be rooted out and remedied by additional controls and rules. So, one finds competing logics and principles that have become values even within the broader logic of bureaucracy. When structural design principles become suffused with value to connote good government and professionalism, they become more difficult to change even when the rational reason for their existence no longer holds.

STANDARDIZATION. A third form of coordination, standardization, was identified by Weber as a form of rationalization essential to bureaucracy. Beniger uses the computer science term "preprocessing" to denote standardization:

> [Coordination] can be increased not only by increasing the capability to process information but also by decreasing the amount of information to be processed. The former approach to control was realized in Weber's day through bureaucratization and today increasingly through computerization; the latter approach was then realized through rationalization, what computer scientists now call preprocessing.[30]

Standardization, then, reduces the variance of inputs, outputs, activities, and behaviors. The current interest in performance measures in public and private management, an exercise in bureaucratic standardization, is part of an effort to improve agency coordination and control and, thus, output and productivity. The Government Performance and Results Act

(GPRA) requires agency officials to identify key measures (standards) and to develop means to monitor their progress. A central feature of the new public management (NPM), a school of thought sweeping through bureaucracies in governments around the globe, recommends linking budget flows to the achievement of performance measures: a most Weberian rationalization exercise. These examples demonstrate clearly the vitality of Weberian rationalization as a means of control and performance improvement in government.

According to March and Simon, who analyzed the development and use of standardized operating procedures and performance programs—or repertoires of routines—in complex organizations as organizing devices: "The coordination of parts is incorporated in the program [for the work] when it is established, and the need for continuing communication [or supervision] is correspondingly reduced."[31] March and Simon focused on the standardization of work processes, but inputs to decisionmaking or production processes, as well as outputs in the form of products, reports, figures, and services, are typically standardized, or preprocessed, as well. Within computer programs and operating systems, the choices made by designers standardize work processes by limiting, or preprocessing, the options and choices of users, and by forcing users to follow decision trees and paths by using the menus and formats provided.

THE STANDARDIZATION OF PEOPLE. Standards may be socialized into people, just as they are into work processes and equipment, through selection methods, training and education, appraisal, and incentive systems that reward standard behavior and punish deviations. An equally strong but more subtle "preprocessing" occurs in professional and university graduate programs where aspiring professionals are trained to focus on particular variables or concepts (and to ignore others), to use standard procedures for analysis, and to use preprogrammed formats for writing and presentation. Socialization, as a form of standardization, provides stability and uncertainty reduction, forms of rationalization that are essential in bureaucracy. Yet the socialization of professionals constitutes a form of "impairment" that constrains inquiry and at times impedes the resolution of complex social problems.[32] For our purposes, it is clear that the socialization of individuals means that new information technologies and their use in government will be perceived through standard lenses that will in many cases bias innovation in unanticipated ways to conform to existing structural and political arrangements.

Hundreds of forms of standardization used throughout bureaucracies, from minute inputs to the regularized flow of information and decision-making to the socialization of professionals, produce not only coherence, stability, certainty, and coordination but also impairment, lack of creativity, groupthink, and resistance to change. Given its predominance in bureaucracy, a rational observer might overstate the degree of standardization in government bureaucracies. Yet in spite of vast efforts at rationalization, mutual adjustment is always necessary to achieve even minimal coordination.

Bureaucratic Functions

Weber had little to say about functions in bureaucracy, but a large body of research in social psychology, industrial relations, and political science analyzes the functional roles of organizational actors. James Q. Wilson organizes his volume *Bureaucracy* in terms of "operators," "managers," and "executives" in order to examine bureaucracy from functional positions rather than from Weberian structure. Studies of bureaucracy usually treat structure and function separately, but separation makes it impossible to examine functions within their structural constraints and divorces actors from the rules that shape their behavior.

In most complex organizations the primary functional actors include: operators at the base of the traditional pyramidal organization; executives responsible for setting direction, strategy, and relations with the external authorizing environment; managers who connect operators with the executive; technical analysts, including auditors, operations researchers, scientists, engineers, and specialists; and support staff with responsibility for activities such as congressional and media relations, human resources, and legal services.[33] The effects of the Internet on all these functional actors will differ. It is likely that operators will lose control over their work because information systems are used to monitor and report exceptional behavior upward. Program, or line, managers traditionally have helped coordinate the work of operators and other managers. Although Leavitt and Whisler's prediction of the demise of the middle manager, made in the 1950s, took nearly thirty years to come to pass, it is indeed the former sorters, collators, and report writers at the middle levels whose numerative tasks have been automated. Executives may gain tremendously from powerful systems that feed them information from throughout the organization. At the same time, if information is widely shared executives lose a form of power. In addition, in a world full of information, executives are in danger of persistent overload. In sum, one can hypothesize that technology use can have either positive or negative consequences, depending on whom it affects. Turning the equation around, one might expect each functional group to try to implement new information systems to benefit their function. At a minimum, this tells us that design and use of the Internet would be a source of negotiation and political contest, the results of which have implications for authority, power, and resource distribution.

The hierarchical distinctions among managers constitute an administrative division of labor in the bureaucracy. Analysts have traditionally been responsible for standardization within bureaucracy. Some analysts rationalize work processes, thus removing discretion and variance from the tasks of operators and program managers. In the U.S. government, the redesign of "business" processes and other efforts to rationalize work processes have been carried out variously by teams of operators and managers, by internal analysts, and to a large extent by private sector consultants—or a combination of all three. Other analysts, such as accountants, planners, production specialists, and logisticians, standardize agency outputs. Human resource specialists and other technical staff standardize employee skills. As these outputs have been further rationalized using information technology, the need for in-house analysts has decreased. Generic functions and tasks are easily outsourced.

Among their other critical functions, analysts design systems that coordinate activities and thus reduce the need for management. Systems analysts, for example, who design computer programs and applications, play a key role in standardization. These distinctions between analysts and other managers are important ones missed in many studies of bureaucracy.

A large proportion of government managers (that is, those with responsibility for functions including research and development, legal affairs, public relations, payroll, maintenance, security, and legislative relations) are considered staff in the traditional production firm because in those firms they are removed from the basic flow of work. In government, however, these functions are central, and so the work of public managers in these functional areas is the central flow of work. Agencies can be distinguished according to whether they perform a service delivery or a "banking" function that includes not only financial responsibilities but also regulation and evaluation. Service delivery agencies typically interact with citizens directly even if through a complex line of contractual relationships. Other agencies are, in essence, the support-staff agencies of the federal government. During the past two decades, generic support functions have been privatized, moved out of the bureaucratic state. Further use of the Internet to link government organizations with the private sector will inevitably increase this trend, with implications for both the size and the nature of government. In sum, from a functional perspective, vertical compression in management brought about by the implementation of information technology has changed the shape of bureaucracy from a pyramid to an hourglass.

Bureaucratic Flows

In the mid-1980s, government managers became particularly interested in process flows in organizations. Total quality management and business process redesign, two leading management ideas from the 1980s, made strong claims that dramatic efficiencies could be achieved by reducing the friction in flows of work across functional, jurisdictional, and other boundaries. Mapping business processes "horizontally" across functional units provides an important source of information about potential efficiencies and promising innovations in the design of work flows. Before the widespread use of the Internet, the development of shared databases across functions and jurisdictions led to the redesign of business processes by automating flows of information so that distributed decisionmaking could occur.[34] This massive shift from linear, sequential processing of information to parallel, shared processing using networked computing has dramatically changed the flow of work, and thereby the structures and roles in government. Yet to date, process redesign has affected operators and managers far more than executives.

The formal organization chart has been a mainstay of federal agency structure. Rules that govern the formal flow of information, work, and decisionmaking coordinate organizational units and functions. Flows of authority, work, control, and staff information circulate in all directions throughout the organization. Though the organization chart reveals some aspects of the flow of formal authority—that is, the flow downward of commands and the flow upward of information—it does not reflect informal influence or power structures or the actual everyday pattern of work and decisionmaking. Formal authority structures are only partial structures, but they guide formal behavior directly, influence informal social and political processes, and require at least the appearance of conformity. In those ways, they structure the agency. Much of the history of federal bureaucratic reform in the twentieth century consists of moving the boxes on the organization chart rather than on process analysis and redesign.

The National Performance Review reforms focused on redesigning process flows rather than on the more political and difficult structural reorganization that typically signals reform.

Command and control, as the term is traditionally understood, comprises a set of largely vertical flows. Decisions made at the top of the organization are decomposed into performance objectives and plans by analysts or managers and then filtered down the hierarchy to the operating levels. As a complement, control systems gather information about outputs and feed this upward to the executive levels for planning. March and Simon's analysis of these social information processes in organizations (though written in the 1950s, before substantial computer use in bureaucracy) explains the intricate interplay between individual cognition and organizational structure. Their concept of "uncertainty absorption" is central to understanding information processing in agencies:

> In our culture, language is well developed for describing and communicating about concrete objects. . . . On the other hand, it is extremely difficult to communicate about intangible objects and nonstandardized objects. Hence, the heaviest burdens are placed on the communications system by the less structured aspects of the organization's tasks, particularly by activity directed toward the explanation of problems that are not yet well defined. . . . The use of classification schemes in communication has further consequences. . . . The technical vocabulary and classification schemes in an organization provide a set of concepts that can be used in analyzing and in communicating about its problems. . . . Hence, the world tends to be perceived by the organization members in terms of the particular concepts that are reflected in the organization's vocabulary. The particular categories and schemes of classification it employs are reified, and become, for members of the organization, attributes of the world rather than mere conventions. . . . Uncertainty absorption takes place when inferences are drawn from a body of evidence and the inferences, instead of the evidence itself, are then communicated. . . . Through uncertainty absorption, the recipient of a communication is severely limited in his ability to judge its correctness.[35]

An equally important system of processes guides the flow of work, information, and decisions in government agencies. The critical notion behind organizational redesign according to process flows—or reengineering—is that productivity enhancement efforts within subunits are stymied if the flow of information and work across subunits and functional areas is ineffective and inefficient. The key design components are not the boxes on the organization chart but the elimination of barriers between the boxes.

Weber Redux

Would Max Weber recognize the current U.S. bureaucracy as a bureaucracy? Undoubtedly. Has jurisdiction disappeared? By no means, although some jurisdictional boundaries have changed character. If we compare the classic elements of bureaucracy with the structural elements that are developing in the wake of technological changes, several broad differences come to light (see table 4-1).

It is difficult to imagine the federal bureaucracy organized into anything but agencies, although their structure and relationships within and outside the government are changing. Similarly, large private sector corporations form alliances and use technology extensively to improve information processing but remain large bureaucracies with characteristics Weber would recognize. In fact, recent antitrust rulings and a more powerful capacity for coordination and control through technology and management systems have led to the creation of huge global firms through a stream of mergers and acquisitions. Professional and operational roles still exist, although many have become broader and more fluid. In spite of some "flattening" of hierarchical structures and loosening of command and control systems, hierarchy remains central to most complex organizations. An important question for students of bureaucracy concerns the optimal, or appropriate, degree and use of hierarchy in information-based organizations. A shorter chain of command in several bureaucracies is evidence of the natural experiment currently under way. The rapid rise of scholarly interest in network forms, both within and between organizations, has obscured the fact that most nodes in networks continue to function within hierarchies. Digital files structured as shared databases make data and information available throughout bureaucracy rather than only to those at particular levels who perform specific functions. A notable result has been the detachment of information from individuals holding a particular role. To the extent that information is power, this fundamental structural shift has important implications for authority and power in government. Much has been written about the assumed democratization expected to occur as a result of information sharing and transparency. But

TABLE 4-1. Comparison of Weberian and Virtual Bureaucracies

Elements of a Weberian bureaucracy	Elements of a virtual bureaucracy
Functional differentiation, precise division of labor, clear jurisdictional boundaries	Information structured using information technology rather than people; organizational structure based on information systems rather than people
Hierarchy of offices and individuals	Electronic and informal communication; teams carry out the work and make decisions
Files, written documents, staff to maintain and transmit files	Digitized files in flexible form, maintained and transmitted electronically using sensors, bar codes, transponders, hand-held computers; chips record, store, analyze, and transmit data; systems staff maintain hardware, software, and telecommunications
Employees are neutral, impersonal, attached to a particular office	Employees are cross-functional, empowered; jobs limited not only by expertise but also by the extent and sophistication of computer mediation
Office system of general rules, standard operating procedures, performance programs	Rules embedded in applications and information systems; an invisible, virtual structure
Slow processing time due to batch processing, delays, lags, multiple handoffs	Rapid or real-time processing
Long cycles of feedback and adjustment	Constant monitoring and updating of feedback; more rapid or real-time adjustment possible

Sources: Author's analysis; Nitin Nohria and James D. Berkley, "The Virtual Organization: Bureaucracy, Technology, and the Implosion of Control," in Charles Heckscher and Anne Donnellon, eds., *The Post-Bureaucratic Organization: New Perspectives on Organizational Change* (Thousand Oaks, Calif.: Sage, 1994), pp. 108–28; James I. Cash Jr. et al., *Building the Information-Age Organization: Structure, Control, and Information Technologies* (Chicago: Irwin, 1994).

most of it ignores the degree of rationalization, the rules, now firmly embedded in digital systems.

Information-based organizations and traditional bureaucracies are equally rule-based, and information-based organizations are perhaps even more highly rationalized. But the rules embedded within information systems are normally less visible and seemingly less constraining to bureaucratic discretion. Embedded rules will increasingly replace overt supervisory control and operating procedures. Indeed often so-called empowerment represents little more than a shift from overt to covert control through embedded rule systems and peer groups.[36]

Rule-based systems are designed to support clear organizational goals. But agencies often must espouse vague, conflicting goals that result from legislative compromise and multiple missions. No amount of rationalization, either through performance measures or new technologies, has altered this fundamental political reality, and the increased rationalization of agencies is at odds with this political fact. After World War II, scholarly attention in organizational analysis turned to the dominance of the manager, a direct outgrowth of bureaucratic development.[37] An equally important though less well recognized recent development is the growth in the number of technical analyst positions required to develop, program, maintain, and service increasingly information-based federal bureaucracies. Because most information technology experts are under contract from private firms, their numbers are hidden from measures of the size of government.[38] Scholarly attention during the next decade may usefully be directed toward the growing dominance and influence of systems analysts within information-based bureaucracy and their role in the policymaking process. The externalities of bureaucratic behavior may be replaced by those of the systems analysts. I take up a number of externalities and unanticipated problems, some hinted at in this chapter, in Part II of this volume.

Clearly, the bureaucracy that formed the foundation of the modern state is now outmoded in many ways. But although modified by information technology, each of its elements remains central. The growth of networks, partnerships, and negotiated collaborative arrangements of various kinds—the subject of the next chapter—presages changes in jurisdiction, hierarchy, boundaries, and agency autonomy. Change that affects the deeper structures of the bureaucratic state will require considerable political negotiation and cultural change. In this chapter I have laid out a mechanical perspective on organizational structure with no mention of political or social organization: culture, leadership, loyalty, socialization. In fact, the characteristics of the individuals who use technology—their values, cognition, motivation, interests—have barely been considered.

In sum, the use of the Internet in bureaucracy is likely to lead to greater rationalization, standardization, and use of rule-based systems. The rules may not be visible because most of them will be hidden in software and hardware. But they will remain and may increase in power. Technology might be enacted to facilitate collaboration, shared information, and enhanced communication. Equally plausible, it may be designed and used coercively to promote conformance and control. But bureaucracy, in either rendering, has not diminished in importance.

Having unpacked the elements of bureaucracy, we can discuss them and their relationship to technology with greater clarity and precision. As we will see in the next chapter, a vast increase in the use of networks has changed but has not diminished the importance of bureaucracy.

CHAPTER FIVE

Interorganizational Networks

ALTHOUGH SOME ELEMENTS of the American bureau-cratic state changed over the course of the twentieth century, most remain firmly fixed. In fact, as Chapter 4 described, the Internet is being used in American culture and the political economy to rationalize and further embed rules rather than to eliminate them. Rules embedded in computer code govern invisibly and powerfully.[1] The prevalence and clear necessity of mutual adjustment in every bureaucracy contrasts with efforts to dampen discretion and to control individual behavior, often through the design of information systems.

This chapter dissects interorganizational networks in order to examine the relationship between networks of organizations and networked computing. What are they? How and why do they form? What holds them together in the absence of hierarchy and a formal governance structure? How do actors in interorganizational arrangements use networked computing? Are networks replacing bureaucracy or coexisting with it? Is the bureaucratic state becoming a network state? Are networks changing bureaucracy as their use increases? What role do digital and interorganizational networks play in institutions? Close examination of interorganizational networks is necessary for researchers and policymakers to better understand how networked organizations and network computing interact. With few exceptions, these interactions have not been examined in previous studies.[2] Finally, we will want to examine the implications of the increasing use of networks for the structure of the state and the policymaking process.

An interorganizational network has been defined as "any collection of actors ($N \geq 2$) that pursue repeated, enduring exchange relations with one another and, at the same time, lack a legitimate organizational authority to arbitrate and resolve disputes that may arise during the exchange."[3] More simply, interorganizational networks can be said to be "the relatively enduring transactions, flows, and linkages that occur among" organizations.[4] In contrast, networks within hierarchies, or intraorganizational networks, subsume relations between and among actors under a governance structure that handles conflict resolution and channels behavior. Interorganizational network forms include "joint ventures, strategic alliances, business groups, franchises, research consortia, relational contracts, and outsourcing agreements," as well as interagency and intersectoral arrangements in government.[5]

Economic relations, as conceptualized in neoclassical economics, exist only for the transfer of goods or services and remain in effect only during the course of that transfer. More enduring relations entail obligation, trust, and calculations that do not overly discount the future and more accurately characterize most professional networks, especially those in government. As Mark Granovetter and other sociologists, economists, and political scientists have come to recognize, economic action is embedded in a rich structure of ongoing networks of relationships.[6]

Neither Market nor Hierarchy?

Organizational arrangements that resemble networks more than hierarchies or markets are becoming increasingly visible, although they have a long history that predates the Internet.[7] During the 1980s, the success of Asian firms relative to that of U.S. firms led scholars and practitioners to examine the networks used in some Asian economies.[8]

Networks came under attack when "markets" and "hierarchies" were characterized as pure forms of organization, combinations of which produced hybrid or intermediate arrangements.[9] Oliver Williamson argued that most organizational arrangements would cluster near the endpoints of a continuum between markets and hierarchies rather than between the two. As an empirical phenomenon, networks have proliferated in the U.S.

economy. Moreover, the growth of strategic alliances among firms has contributed to the visibility and perceived attractiveness of networks in government and between the public and private sectors. Some analysts estimate that by 2002 alliances among the largest one thousand U.S. firms will account for 35 percent of the total revenue of those firms. In 1980 alliances accounted for less than 2 percent of total revenues; in 1997, 21 percent.[10] One report estimates that between 1985 and the mid-1990s the rate of strategic alliance formation increased by 25 percent per year.[11]

A direct connection exists between Williamson's theoretical contributions to economic organization and the burgeoning literature on privatization and new public management. Transaction cost economics and to a lesser extent principal-agent theory are built on the presumption of the dichotomy between markets and hierarchies and neoclassical rational-actor models.[12] Heightened attention to "marketization" in government implied reduced attention to the development of interorganizational networks as a means to promote adaptive capacity, innovation, efficiency, and reduced transaction costs. In contrast to Williamson's approach, some scholars have argued that benefits inherent in the network form led to its prevalence and that the network possesses efficiencies and other benefits not possible within either hierarchy or market. Walter Powell argued that the network should be regarded as a distinct organizational form, conceptually and theoretically equal to hierarchies and markets and possessed of its own logic.[13] The comparative advantage of the network, he argued, is the chief reason for the ubiquity of the form.

The social structure of bureaucracy—that is, flows and networks of informal communication, influence, and advice—is as important to the policymaking process as the formal structure. In major studies of policymaking, Edward Laumann, David Knoke, and other researchers have empirically demonstrated that networks of actors across agencies and in the nonprofit and private sectors are more central to policymaking than formalized governance structures alone. They argue that the state is organized as policy networks.[14] Other researchers have similarly documented the prevalence and importance of social networks in policymaking. Hugh Heclo has argued that both appointees and bureaucrats must build constellations of professional and personal contacts, "the personalized networks that honeycomb the bureaucracy," in order to be effective policymakers.[15] Ronald Burt has demonstrated empirically that power, in the form of social capital, accrues to individuals who straddle and broker among disparate professional networks. Individuals in these positions possess access to especially useful information unavailable to those working within one network and can play a brokering role among structurally distinct network constellations.[16]

Network analyses and ethnographic studies of professional behavior in bureaucracies provide evidence that structured yet informal social networks of communication, advice, and influence have distinctive mediating effects on exchange relations, contracting, and economic behavior.[17] Informal networks operate outside formal organizational flow patterns and are indispensable to professionals. The Internet has strengthened the importance and use of informal networks, although it has not replaced the importance of face-to-face contact or geographic proximity in the building of trust and social contacts.[18]

Central Elements of the Interorganizational Network

Sociologists and anthropologists have long studied social networks of individuals, but the systematic investigation of interorganizational networks is a more recent development. The ability of actors to coordinate activities, to develop a form of governance that is neither market-driven nor hierarchical, and to pursue complex joint initiatives presents a set of conceptual puzzles that challenge bureaucratic notions of organization, rational action, and self-interest. If networked computing enables more extensive use of interorganizational networks, then questions of network management, administration, and governance present challenges of the first importance for government.[19]

As the empirical evidence presented in the following chapters shows, neither the Internet nor the presence of a network of organizations ensures collaboration. Many networks are highly conflictual, mired in contractual disputes and lack of coordination.[20] Indeed, conflict has been the dominant perception of interorganizational "coordination" in public policy and management.[21] However, those networks in which a threshold level of trust and cooperation is developed and sustained generally have lower transaction costs, better resource sharing, increased learning among network partners, and greater levels of innovation.[22]

Interorganizational networks vary greatly by type, environment, and quality of relationship. Although researchers continue to search for the holy grail of productive cooperation and coordination across organizational boundaries, they have not reached consensus on the conditions that promote or discourage network formation and effectiveness.[23] Organizations may develop network relationships for various reasons. The environment in which they exist affects both their likelihood of success and the type of network developed.[24] Many government organizations are required by law or regulation to work across boundaries and develop networks out of necessity. Law enforcement and environmental organizations at the federal, state, and local levels must cooperate under certain specified conditions. Similarly, environmental protection agencies at each level of government coordinate many of their activities by law.[25]

A rational-actor typology of network formation developed by Christine Oliver indicates that individual organizations form strategic alliances and coordinated relationships to overcome asymmetries; for example, community-level nonprofit organizations associate with one another as part of the United Way to organize fund-raising and to gain the benefits of scale the association provides.[26] Firms join industry associations to increase their individual power in negotiations with government, unions, and other interest groups. Rather than leaving the flow of benefits to chance or goodwill, reciprocity ensures that benefits from coordination flow to each organization. Organizations form networks to pool resources and share administrative costs. They use collective action to stabilize resource flows, cycles, and other uncertainties by standardizing procedures. Participation in joint, cooperative associations, federations, and programs also confers legitimacy and visibility on member organizations because organizations, like individuals, are judged by the company they keep.

Continuing this typology, firms enter joint ventures to increase their power in the market; to develop barriers to entry; to share information, skills, and technology across organizational boundaries; to leverage new knowledge; and to pool risk. Trade associations form to increase their individual members' influence in lobbying state regulatory authorities. Cooperation among organizations within such associations both provides benefits to individual organizational members and enhances the image or legitimacy of the member organizations. A joint approach to negotiations with government reduces the uncertainties of the legislative process by maximizing the influence each organization can exert. Economies of scale allow the association to achieve economic benefits for members, including those from procurement, insurance, and pension plans. Volunteer and nonprofit organizations form networks for similar reasons. Collective efforts increase the effectiveness of fund-raising campaigns, save money on advertising and operations, and rationalize funding flows to member organizations. The network increases their visibility in a community and facilitates the presentation of a united front in negotiations with community governments and other organizations.

Despite these rationales for and determinants of networks, it has been shown that relatively few interorganizational networks succeed. Although rationality should lead to many forms of interorganizational networks, the failure rate of networks is reportedly high. One example is strategic alliances between firms, which are formed for the rational reason of "achieving competitive advantage for the partners . . . when any single firm finds it either too difficult or too costly to pursue worthwhile business objectives on its own." In spite of high and growing formation rates, the failure rate of such strategic alliances is also high.[27]

The objectives of interagency networks in government are similar to those of firms, if we substitute superior policymaking for increased capacity for competitiveness. But the structures of incentives, rewards, and risks operate differently within government. Strategic alliances in the economy may be broken when the contractual period expires, not always cleanly or simply but more easily than in the government. Government budget appropriations are more difficult to rescind once they have been used to establish programs. In purely strategic terms, firms enter alliances to maximize gains from other firms by gaining access to otherwise unavailable resources. In this exchange model of network formation, no synergies from the relationships are calculated, nor is social capital, a benefit derived from cooperative productive capacity. Institutionalists find a purely calculative explanation of network formation and persistence inadequate because it fails to account for the embeddedness of economic action in ongoing structures of social relationships and for the benefits of networks typically ignored by simple exchange models.

Policy and politics researchers continue to lament the difficulties of cooperation, although a burgeoning stream of research on partnerships documents either a more optimistic perspective or an actual change in the cooperative behavior of organizations. But social science, policy, and public management research is silent (with a few exceptions) on the question of what would happen if potential network actors could be linked digitally. It is also not known whether tight economic resources during the 1980s led to greater pooling of organizational capacity, whether the example of Asian networked firms traveled to the United States, whether rapid changes in the American economy led to a greater need to pool resources and talent, whether information technologies reduced coordination and communication costs enough to make networks more feasible, or whether some combination of these environmental and technological factors led to behavioral change.[28] It is the case, however, that the use of interorganizational networks has grown dramatically.

Empirical research has established a set of conditions that aid the formation of cooperation. When actors conduct a series of transactions over time and thus form a relationship, they are able to test each other's reputations for fairness and reliability.[29] Elinor Ostrom found that successful cooperative arrangements in governing the commons tend to have a limited number of players and thus allow information about reputations and transactions to be easily shared within the network. The successful formation of cooperative networks requires that actors value the long-run network relationship highly enough to divert resources and attention to network formation and to forgo immediate individual gains. The boundaries and objectives of the network are typically clearly defined, and sometimes it is important for participants to define the rules under which they will cooperate. Well-performing networks develop conflict resolution mechanisms in order to resolve inevitable disagreements.[30] Ostrom found that successful networks develop graduated sanctions, which punish inappropriate actions in ways that preserve the network.

Rational-choice theorists recognize the possibility and stability of collective action. They have been able to do so by expanding their range of vision to encompass the development and persistence of ongoing social relations, extended reciprocity, trust, and the occasional defections that, nevertheless, allow the network to continue and retain its social capital.

Less is known about the process by which individuals actually build and sustain interorganizational relationships.[31] Process perspectives pose difficulties for research. Developmental processes must be studied over time rather than cross-sectionally. Researchers must closely and systematically observe behaviors as they unfold. In sum, research on development uses detailed analysis of cases rather than analysis of large samples. But understanding the processes successful network builders use is of central importance. For this reason, the cases in part II detail the processes of network development. Policymakers and public managers must understand how to develop and maintain networks in order to design incentives and policy instruments that encourage their formation and effectiveness in government. Government officials within interorganizational relationships also must understand key process variables in order to manage effectively in these new structural arrangements. If the virtual state is a network state that uses the Internet as a technological and information infrastructure, policymakers cannot exercise control over its development without understanding both the characteristics of networks and their developmental processes. Central to their development and maintenance is social capital.

Social Capital

Social capital is among the chief benefits of cooperation and a product of well-functioning networks.[32] The stability of relationships in networks allows actors to combine their shared knowledge, experience, and resources in new and productive ways. If the virtual state includes networks, it also will need social capital. Moreover, if networked computing is to become a vital part of the virtual state, researchers will have to clearly articulate how to build and maintain social capital using the web.

Social capital can be defined as the contribution of ongoing productive relationships to institutional effectiveness, measured by economic performance and innovation in policymaking. Relevant relationships include horizontal ties among agencies, vertical ties in supply chains, and multidirectional ties to sources of knowledge. This form of capital, as powerful as physical and human capital, is the "stock" created when a group of organizations develop the ability to work together for mutual productive gain.[33] The concept of social capital is drawn from research that demonstrates the effect of institutional and social arrangements on economic development. It has more recently been extended to explain differences in innovation rates among countries with similar capital, labor, and national resources.[34]

The notion of social capital refines concepts such as "cooperation" or "collaboration" in two significant ways. First, linking cooperation to the economic concept "capital" signals the investment or growth potential of a group's ability to work jointly. Second, the concept identifies the *structure* created from collaborative effort as capital. Well-functioning partnerships, consortiums, and networks are in and of themselves "a form of social capital."[35] Capital is located both in the sharable resources held by individual institutions in a network and in the overall structure among the organizations in a network. For example, a group of scientists who have collaborated on a relatively small scientific project may then use their collaborative ability to propose and undertake larger, riskier research projects. They may further use their network to address the economic revitalization of their community or a global problem such as nuclear weapons proliferation or climate change. Their originally small network may be extended to members of the political and business community: small cooperative ventures may grow into more ambitious undertakings as parties learn how to collaborate productively and develop reputations for trustworthiness. Social capital, like other forms of capital, accumulates when used productively.

Robert Putnam uses the concept to explain why some government institutions succeed and others, designed similarly, fail: like "physical and human capital—tools and training that enhance individual productivity—'social capital' refers to features of social organization that facilitate coordination and cooperation for mutual benefit."[36] The central elements of social capital are trust, norms, and networks. Trust is developed over time as individuals gain confidence in the reliability of others through a series of interactions.[37] A key property of social capital rests on the transitivity of trust: A trusts C because B trusts C and A trusts B. Thus relatively large networks may exhibit generalized trust although there is little close personal contact among all members. Norms of appropriate behavior develop as a social "contract" among actors. The norm of reciprocity is fundamental to productive relationships. In politics and bureaucratic behavior this norm is known colloquially as the "favor bank."[38] Closely linked to reciprocity is a norm that actors will forgo their immediate self-interest to act not only in the interest of the group but in their own long-term self-interest.[39] Thus a reputation for trustworthiness, essential in politics and government, is also essential to actors in collaborative networks. Social capital is preserved through the careful selection of network players and the strict sanctioning of inappropriate (network-destroying) behaviors. A cohesive network develops when a group of individuals or organizations form reliable, productive communication and decision channels and a more or less permeable boundary to define members.

Traditional economic perspectives that focus on short-term self-interest and individual transactions ignore the accretion, or growth, opportunities generated by cooperation.[40] Closely related to accretion is the self-reinforcing cyclical nature of social relations. Trustful relations tend to be self-reinforcing to strengthen cooperation. Mistrust tends to cycle in the negative direction, weakening relationships and cooperation.

In contrast to atomistic perspectives that emphasize individualism, closely held information, and autonomy, social capital is an extension of perspectives in which cooperation paradoxically enhances competitiveness, information-sharing leads to joint gains, and the importance of reputation and trust ensure reciprocity and fair play within a network. Adam Smith and other classical economists of the eighteenth and nineteenth centuries recognized that an individual firm must be embedded in an underlying fabric of shared values and understanding to make division of labor feasible. Networks, partnerships, and consortiums succeed in part through the social glue that holds them together rather than through contracts that attempt to account for every contingency. And cohesion cannot be generated exclusively in digital information systems that link networks of organizations. The glue in cooperative networks includes norms of trust and appropriate behavior underlying exchange.

Economists have contributed greatly to public policy by identifying, clarifying, and sometimes finding ways around dilemmas posed by collective action problems. Although in most situations all parties would be better off were they to cooperate, collective action theory argues that, in the absence of an overarching authority to enforce appropriate behavior or clear mechanisms to ensure commitment, individuals tend not to take the risk of cooperating. None achieve gains from cooperation, and all are worse off. Drawing on the realpolitik of collective action theory, policy analysts and researchers have long argued that the coordination costs associated with interorganizational and interjurisdictional arrangements often exceed the benefits.[41] They have argued for the necessity of clear lines of authority and strong, centralized governance structures to monitor behavior and to enforce sanctions against inappropriate actions.[42]

Over the past decade or so, social scientists from a variety of disciplines, as well as an increasing number of policy experts, have sought to explain the proliferation and success of collaborative arrangements in policy settings. The broad term "social capital" captures many of the salient properties of these arrangements. Development experts note the importance of social capital as a foundation for economic development. They have documented the importance and extent of rotating credit associations—informal collective savings and loan plans—that prosper throughout the world.[43] Others have studied the collaborative stewardship of common-pool resources, such as water supplies and grazing areas, that are managed for long-term collective benefit.[44] Urban development experts in the industrialized nations have made social capital a fundamental element of policies to build and strengthen cities.[45] International relations scholars have documented the extent to which international regimes of many types are developed and adhered to in the absence of overarching authority.[46]

Networks, Technology, and Innovation

Although public-private partnerships are burgeoning, agencies typically find it difficult to work cooperatively within government. Resources are wasted and opportunities to build capacity are forgone. Eugene Bardach, focusing on partnerships in government, argues that serious policy problems go unsolved because of missed opportunities for partnership.[47] Many contemporary policy challenges span policy domains, falling outside the jurisdiction or specialized competence of any one agency. Examples include environmental challenges (air, water, and land quality and use) in large geographic areas; social policy problems (housing, substance abuse, and education and training); and development challenges that include institutional reform and cultural change as well as economic improvement.

Network arrangements in the economy have increased in the face of more rapid technological change, scarcer economic resources, and easier linkage of geographically dispersed actors. As an adjunct to internal restructuring, large manufacturers have turned to external supplier relationships and supply chain integration for inputs to the production process as well as operational and administrative functions.[48] Thus specialized technological knowledge and innovation reside increasingly in small and medium-sized suppliers whose research and development takes place in team-based configurations on the shop floor rather than in corporate laboratories staffed with scientists conducting long-range basic research. The base of technology offerings has outstripped the capacity of single firms to remain competent in the technical fields relevant to their business. In addition, investments necessary to sustain technology development and deployment have increased to the point that single firms usually cannot afford to undertake the level of risk necessary for innovation. For these reasons, networks have grown in importance. For complex production processes, suppliers function both as partners with lead firms and independently to develop and deploy new technologies.[49]

Organizations leverage their information-processing capacity through the use of interorganizational networks. Network structures are more effective than large hierarchical structures at scanning their environment for changes, interpreting environmental change, and responding to change. Better scanning means more timely and accurate problem recognition. Better interpretation enhances policy and problem formulation and decisionmaking. Greater adaptability translates into more timely innovation and better alignment with environmental conditions.

Networks in dynamic industries develop a superior division of labor and task specialization by extending some of the elements of bureaucracy across organizations. Similar logic applies to policymaking networks in government. A major difference between the sectors, however, is the ease and rapidity with which networks may form and reform. Networks in government rely on budgetmaking and oversight processes for funding, support, and legitimation. These institutional structures work too slowly and rigidly to allow network formation to develop in response to opportunities and problems. The Internet as catalyst to network formation simply makes the mismatch of speed between the institutional structures of government and the linkage afforded by the Internet more problematic. As policy environments become more turbulent and complex, the methods of dynamic industries offer intriguing possibilities for policymaking and operations in government. In addition to pooling resources, agencies increasingly require more rapid access to knowledge and stronger innovative capacity.

Access to Knowledge

Many experts regard strategic alliances as the foundation for interorganizational collaboration in the public and private sectors. Whereas large organizations in the past maintained in-house research and development laboratories in order to retain dominance in their core technologies, firms increasingly have externalized this function through cooperative agreements with other firms, government research laboratories, and universities. Most experts explain the rise in consortium activity as attempts to reduce the cycle type of innovation, to reach new markets and technologies, to share risks, and to gain complementary competencies.[50] But these explanations ignore the importance of knowledge diffusion and learning in networks.

Other researchers have argued that when the knowledge base that supports an industry is hard to comprehend, still emerging, and distributed across several organizations, then collaboration among firms, universities, and national laboratories will reflect a strong and fundamental interest in access to knowledge rather than simply strategic calculation, resource sharing, or transaction cost reduction.[51] This argument translates readily to policy challenges that span traditional jurisdictional boundaries. Internal expertise remains necessary to evaluate external research and development, but external relations facilitate access to new information and expertise that is not easily built within the firm. In policy areas that are inherently cross-cutting, in which knowledge is distributed among agencies and other organizations, innovative capacity is located in the network rather than within individual agencies.

A central difference between distributed knowledge in economic and policy environments lies in the incentives for cooperation. Material benefits reward high-technology network actors that innovate well. Agency partnerships gain the reward of solving difficult policy problems that would otherwise fall between the cracks. But the ultimate reward is likely to be budget reductions, not profits, as synergies translate into the consolidation of organizations.

A zero-sum depiction, in which an agency gains only at the expense of others, inaccurately portrays the situation both in competitive industries and in government. It is far more accurate to view external relationships as a positive-sum game in which joint gains are realized and no actor in the network is disadvantaged. For example, few would suggest that the biotechnology industry is not characterized by fierce competition. Nevertheless, the competitors are more accurately described as competing networks of firms than as rivalries between individual firms. The collaboration required to stay abreast of technological and process advances, rather than diminishing competition, merely changes its character. This ability to preserve competition while encouraging cooperation to develop cross-cutting agency and policy capacity is one of the chief challenges underlying the move to G2G (government-to-government) web-based initiatives in the government. The central difference between sectors lies in the incentives and rewards for network formation.

Social Capital versus Informational Capital

Social capital is entirely different from "informational capital." Although open access to information, notably through the Internet, provides a variety of benefits, informational capital is not a replacement for social capital. Social capital provides decisionmakers with information benefits beyond access to shared information on the web. Useful access involves understanding who will benefit from specific information. It also involves screening information for accuracy, importance, and implications. Collaborative social networks perform this critical screening function.[52] Social capital encompasses not only shared access to information but also many positive properties of interdependence, including shared values, goals, and objectives; shared expertise and knowledge; shared work and decisionmaking; shared risk, accountability, and trust; and shared rewards.[53] Social capital increases the ability to build and use informational capital.

Actors in a collaborative network learn about new technologies, opportunities, the outcomes of transactions, and challenges more quickly because of the "density" of interaction within the network.[54] Learning is of a higher quality because it can be discussed and debated horizontally with people whose perspectives and backgrounds may differ. By contrast, vertically organized agencies tend to impede the organization's information-processing capacity. These are the externalities of bureaucracy that have been decried by critics: an inward, insular focus; secrecy and expectations of organizational loyalty that dampen information-sharing; centralized authority; and predominantly vertical flows of information, which tend to be slower, biased, and thus less reliable. The inability of the Central Intelligence Agency to accurately interpret events that led to the collapse of the former Soviet Union and the resistance of the State Department to change are but two of the more notable examples of bureaucratic inflexibility in government.

Understanding the differences in information flows between large, vertically integrated hierarchies and more horizontal structures is critical to understanding how social capital is built and maintained in the latter and how it leads to greater potential for innovation. Better environmental scanning and information flows and a relative lack of bias together amount to a greater capacity to adjust to change and to leverage new technologies in the network than within a hierarchy.

The Internet and Social Capital

Interorganizational networks, partnerships, and consortiums could not function at current levels without an electronic interface. However, the promise of information technologies for bringing about vast changes in structure, systems, and management has yet to be achieved—and may not be achieved.[55] Researchers consistently note that systems and structures resist change even when new information technologies offer the potential to increase efficiency. In order to take advantage of networked computing, organizations must have the ability to cooperate internally and with network partners.

The explosive growth of Internet use prompts another question: Can social capital be built using the Internet, or does it require face-to-face interaction? Currently, experts disagree about whether face-to-face interaction is necessary for the formation of trust and collaboration. Technology researchers celebrate the ability of information technology to make distance and time constraints virtually meaningless. However, most of the research that has been conducted on industry networks notes the importance of geographic proximity. More empirical study is required to understand the potential for developing social capital in geographically distributed networks.

The federal government has been a prime force for investments in information infrastructure that promote interfirm networks.[56] However, these investments have not yet catalyzed extensive cross-agency networks in government. As we learn our way to a virtual state, the more difficult investments in information infrastructure for both the state and the economy will not be hardware but software and institution-building.

The Limitations of Social Capital

It is important to note that social capital—like its constituent elements, trust, norms, and networks—is inherently neither good nor bad. It is a tool that may be employed for legal or illegal purposes, for good or ill. Trust allows actors to engage in productive collaboration, but trust also provides a necessary condition for fraud and other illegal activities.[57] Norms decrease transaction costs and regulate behavior, but may stifle the creativity and diversity of opinion necessary for solving novel and complex problems.[58] Networks of firms collaborating to produce new technologies or applications widely report the benefits of cooperation; cartel members and organized crime syndicates also understand the benefits of network approaches to production and distribution. Social capital is a powerful resource that develops from productive social ties. How it is used depends entirely upon the values and objectives of the actors involved.[59]

Alejandro Portes and Julia Sensenbrenner have pointed out that in some communities characterized by close personal ties and deep norms of family and community loyalty rather than individual achievement, social capital causes economic advancement to be dampened, new ideas from outside the community to be rejected, and adaptation to changing conditions to be slow. Their research focuses on selected immigrant communities in the United States but serves to caution us that social capital is optimally productive when it is combined with critical thinking and competition.[60] When conditions are less than optimal—for example, when trust among network members is either too great or too small, or when social ties restrict sound decisionmaking—some types of productive capacity are diminished (see figure 5-1).

Perspectives that focus on transactions rather than networks alert us to the contingent character of cooperation among organizations in a network. Researchers should also differentiate between the development and

FIGURE 5-1. The Relationship between Social Capital and Trust

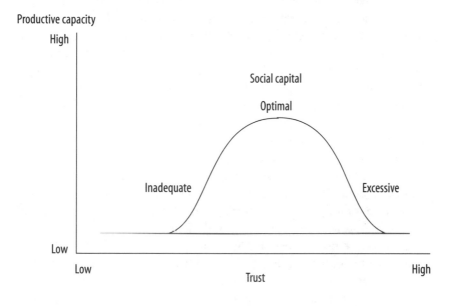

characteristics of voluntary interorganizational relationships and mandated networks, such as those that dominate relationships among levels of government. Power in networks is often conditioned on "organization size, control over the rules governing exchange of material resources and information, the ability to choose a 'do without' strategy, the effectiveness of coercive strategies, and the concentration of inputs."[61] Resource scarcity may lead some organizations to cooperate but leads others to attempt to control organizations that possess the resources they need. Thus although social capital is a powerful positive force in some interorganizational networks, it by no means characterizes all network relationships. The benefits of cooperation exhibited in some networks should not blind us to the enduring problems of power and resource distribution in interorganizational arrangements.

Conclusion

From this dissection of interorganizational networks we can propose that the Internet allows networked organizations to extend control and coordination more easily across organizations. Information technology does not, and cannot by itself, create social capital or cooperation, in the absence of a base of trust; but if easier communication and coordination lead to enhanced trust, then the Internet contributes. The Internet does not, however, substitute for the development of social relations. A government that forces network formation but eschews collaboration may increase, rather than decrease, the costs of coordination. In such a scenario, poor institutional design, not technology, would be the culprit.

Interorganizational networks have emerged in response to large-scale technological, economic, social, and political change. They have not replaced hierarchies, or bureaucracies, as much as they have grown up within them and "sedimented" on top of them. Changes in bureaucracy that are likely to result from its juxtaposition with networks produce what might be called hyperarchy.[62] Hierarchy, in both the state and the economy, "the top-down pyramid, . . . still holds final rule."[63] Bureaucracy, "spew[s] out policies and procedures, rules and regulations."[64] Added to bureaucracy are networks of individuals, small groups and teams at all levels of organizations. Within bureaucracies, networks or teams (small groups) comprise what Herbert Simon called nested levels of activity.[65] Similarly, interorganizational networks are, simply, networks of bureaucratic organizations. This point is often missed by those who claim that bureaucracy is dead, outmoded, and no longer useful. The nation-state will require a large, complex bureaucracy for the foreseeable future. This sedimented view of organizational arrangements has to be reconciled with the simpler and more typical classification of organizational forms into hierarchy, market, and network. In looking at new and old forms in combination and in transition one can more clearly analyze the interaction and development of these forms as government officials work between them and their competing logics.

In many instances interorganizational relationships have been strengthened by the use of networked computing to link administrative systems, to share data, and to rapidly exchange information. In addition, social capital that has been strengthened by digital interorganizational communication can enhance reliability, flexibility, shared understanding, and long-term reciprocity, although these types of benefits are still difficult to quantify. For these reasons, the Internet is more likely to supplement rather than replace the knowledge gained in face-to-face professional relationships.

A rich stream of research has shown that economic relationships are embedded in social structures, or ongoing professional relationships, in which actors often benefit from the credibility, reliability, and flexibility of their professional partners. Spot transactions and arm's-length relationships do not establish the critical social and informal elements that ongoing professional relationships do. Research on networked computing in government must take account of both the formal structures and ongoing social relations in networks.

Government decisionmakers, faced with the design and management of bureaucracy and cross-agency networks and networked computing, face institutional and governance questions of great complexity. Structures are in flux. The tensions between the logics of the bureaucracy, networks, and the Internet must be managed. Those tensions have barely been articulated or recognized. Over the past two decades, public and private sector organizations came under increasing pressure to rationalize horizontal flows of work and decisionmaking—that is, to work across traditional functional boundaries. As those organizations continue to develop new processes and establish cross-functional relationships, their learning will transfer directly to the more challenging tasks of interorganizational network development and governance across jurisdictional and functional boundaries.

Organizations also are under increasing pressure to develop relationships outside their organizational boundaries in order to leverage scarce resources, to capitalize on skills they do not possess internally, and to incorporate new technologies and policy innovations. This emerging trend in government will place pressure on oversight institutions to adjust to more horizontal forms of management. The American state will have to take up the challenge of redefining key institutions to align with networked forms of organization.

Because trust is a key component of successful collaborative networks, mandating the development of social capital is not likely to be a successful executive strategy. Executive orders cannot replace the more gradual development of norms, incentives, and trust that motivate employees and facilitate interagency network formation.

Technology enactment theory says that technology will be enacted to promote interorganizational networks, given their increasing use as an organizational arrangement in government. All networks are established in order to build or improve productive capacity, but networks with productive social capital are difficult to form and to maintain. Some researchers believe that calculations of self-interest and value maximization outweigh social relations as a reason to create networks; others believe that the social relations that undergird some networks provide a necessary form of coherence in the absence of overarching governance. The competing influences on network formation, as well as the variety of interorganizational networks, are reminders that the outcomes of technology enactment are uncertain.

The Internet acts as a catalyst for the formation of interorganizational networks by providing a cheap, powerful infrastructure for communication and shared information. It puts pressure on organizations to form networks, but provides none of the social skills that networking requires. Interorganizational networks are sometimes composed of equals, but may have one powerful central player or a small elite coupled with others who rely on the central organization for resources and exchange. Thus networks vary greatly in structure and in how power and other resources are distributed.

It would be expected that powerful organizations in a network would seek to use the Internet to retain, or even gain, power. In other words, they would seek to perpetuate the status quo in enacting technology. In contrast, less powerful organizations in a network might use the rhetoric of collaboration and the powerful data-sharing capacity of networked computing to try to restructure a network to be more equitable in its resource distribution. These types of power struggles and negotiations characterize the enactment of information technology in government.

Sections of this chapter were originally published as "Social Capital: A Key Enabler of Innovation" in Lewis M. Branscomb and James H. Keller, *Investing in Innovation: Creating a Research and Innovation Policy That Works* (MIT Press, 1998).

CHAPTER SIX

Enacting Technology: An Institutional Perspective

BUREAUCRATIC POLITICS HAS produced the maxim: "Where you stand depends on where you sit."[1] Where a decisionmaker "sits" indicates not only his or her interests, but also how those interests are systematically influenced by institutions and one's structural position. Institutional actors tend to see the world from a particular vantage point colored greatly not by atomistic interests, but by interests and models that derive in part from structural position and ongoing social relations in networks.

In this chapter, I lay out the technology enactment framework. The analytical framework integrates information technology into organization theory and extends related research programs on institutions, social networks, and embeddedness in sociology, economics, and political science to better account for the behavior of bureaucrats in government agencies. The technology enactment framework increases our understanding of bureaucratic politics amid network formation and technological change.

I propose a framework that focuses attention on the relationship between information technology, organizations, embeddedness, and institutions. Before detailing technology enactment, however, I discuss some of the "shadow theories" to which it is an alternative. In each instance, these partial theories cast some light on the subject but are deficient as satisfactory explanatory models.

Perspectives on Technology and Structure

An array of unexamined premises and assumptions, nearly invisible in most discussions of technology and structure but working in the background, form shadow theories that misinform decisionmaking and impede clarity of discussion. They include technological determinism, rational-actor perspectives, incrementalism, systems analysis, and individual and group perspectives.

According to the claims of technological determinism, technology acts autonomously upon individuals, social arrangements, and institutions. By reifying technology and its effects, researchers push to the background of their inquiry both the scope for action available to individuals and the complex interplay between technology, embeddedness, and behavior. Until recently, studies of technology's effects on the economy continually reported that expected productivity gains had not been produced. These discussions implied that information technology, by itself, would somehow lead to greater productivity without organizations having to make structural adjustments to fully integrate and use new technologies. These studies neglected to measure the ways in which technologies have been used by organizational actors, as if the technologies themselves were expected to provide economies.

Equally determinist, some students of technology argue that it has run amok, that technology is degrading society and robbing local communities of their vitality. Ongoing social relations and institutional arrangements are either reduced to passive objects following the imperatives of autonomous technology or treated as exogenous variables.

Several rational-actor theories—including functionalism, natural selection, and other frameworks that assume idealized rational action—have been used to explain the adoption and diffusion of new technologies. Implicit in these accounts is the assumption that, over time and through some degree of trial and error, organizations will choose the "best" technological offerings and learn to use information technologies in better and better ways. Rationality in individuals or collectively in the market will ensure that technological progress continues. Douglass North and others sharply criticize rationality assumptions in neoclassical economics that ignore the role of institutions.[2] A danger in this line of reasoning lies in the assumption that somehow learning will take place and that the "right" lessons will be learned. But actors may learn the "wrong" lessons and act for several years on those lessons. As North argues, path dependence exerts a potent influence on behavior through culture. It is easy to make poor choices because of uncertainty about how to use new technologies, and further, it is unclear that government or any other institution has corrective mechanisms in place that would illuminate them: "The greater the degree of monopoly power, the lower is the incentive to learn."[3] In the United States, the Congressional Office of Technology Assessment (now defunct) was established by Congress to help legislators make sound decisions regarding complex technologies by reducing uncertainties and promoting learning. Its demise removed an important source of learning from the federal government.

Political scientists often invoke incrementalism as a means of avoiding error in the policy process. Charles Lindblom and others argued that in practice policymakers take small, incremental steps or deviations from the status quo because small policy adjustments are easier to analyze, monitor, and correct than comprehensive, large-scale changes.[4] Although incrementalism might offer some degree of protection from error in decisions regarding technology, it does not prevent government actors from moving incrementally in the wrong direction. As a number of studies have shown, so-called path-dependent decision streams are those in which a course (or path), once chosen, is difficult to alter; thus a series of interrelated small decisions may take on a momentum of their own, propelling continued movement in harmful directions.

Research in psychology provides considerable evidence that commitment to a failing course of action often escalates through a series of small movements as decisionmakers become psychologically, economically, and politically committed to it.[5] In these instances, actors find it increasingly difficult to alter course even in the face of negative feedback. In addition, economic sunk costs—time, energy, and money spent on a course of action—make decisionmakers reluctant to change direction. In the case of large, complex information systems, the economic sunk costs are enormous and each subsequent decision is highly path dependent. It is costly and difficult to reconfigure, rebuild, modernize, or otherwise substantially change information systems.[6] Thus incrementalism offers only limited guidance for constructing a digital government.

Systems perspectives have offered useful analogies for the exploration of technology and complex organizations.[7] Yet an often-employed term from systems analysis, "institutional lag," implies that social systems must—and should—somehow catch up to new technologies. To say that institutions lag behind changes in technology implies a normative judgment that actors and structures should adjust more swiftly and efficiently to technological advancement, as the cart should follow the horse. An additional implication is that new developments in technology should always be adopted and as rapidly as possible. Several social lags on change may be identified. Human cognition requires some degree of stability and so tends to lag behind environmental changes in an effort to retain cognitive balance. Political regimes resist changes that would alter the power of those in control. A fine mesh of institutional entailments envelop and create structural inertia in large organizations.[8] Their number and interdependencies render change complex and necessarily slow. A systems perspective on technological change ignores these and other social structural processes.

The high failure rate of business process reengineering—a management movement that directed rapid, deep structural change to leverage new technological potential—exemplifies the need to attend to social and political structures, organizations, and networks.[9] Paradoxically, many researchers conclude that technology has failed when expected improvements in productivity or organizational design fail to take place. Other analysts invoke organizational lag to explain a similar absence of the hypothesized direct effects of technology.

The scale of government organizations is enormous. The relative scale and complexity of the tasks performed by the federal government renders integration of new information technologies exceedingly difficult. Government procurement of new information technologies remains slow and cumbersome despite legislation designed to streamline information technology (IT) procurement and to provide technology leadership within agencies. Scarce resources in government make IT-based innovation difficult to undertake. Systems perspectives fail to account for the mediating links in the chain that presumably connects information technologies to organizational change.

Early studies that attempted to explain the effects of IT on organizational structure drew strongly from social psychology and communications research. One stream focused on the hypothesized effects of information technology on individual-level variables such as employee satisfaction, performance, and discretion. Other studies have attempted to measure the effects of individual variables, such as the level of user involvement during implementation of new information systems, on the probability and degree of success.[10] This individual-level perspective is meant to yield models that build upward from the effects of technology on organizational actors to structural change.[11] Research results employing this approach have been inconclusive and contradictory. At times, research designs have been weak. Different, noncomparable technologies have been compared as if they were similar. But most important, the models have not conceptualized the processes by which change occurs.[12] The assumption that technology works autonomously has plagued causal studies of this type.

As a result, several students of information technology and organizations began to focus on structural analysis at the level of the organization. These studies attempted to measure the direct effect of IT on structural attributes such as authority relations, task structure, and employee autonomy. But early studies of every hypothesized direct relationship between technology and structure also have produced contradictory findings. Both streams of research indicated that detailed examination of the dynamics that link technology and structure might generate more fruitful results. A small number of researchers began to reconceptualize the study of technology and structure by drawing from other theoretical perspectives. These more structural approaches began to point to flexibility in both the design (architecture) and use of information systems and organizational arrangements that challenged more determinist perspectives.[13]

Stephen Barley argued that the typically weak and contradictory findings of contingency theories could be explained by an alternative conceptualization in which "technologies are . . . viewed as occasions that trigger social dynamics which, in turn, modify or maintain an organization's contours."[14] Barley's account expanded on the popular reengineering theme that information technology is an "enabler" of organizational change. Thus the same information system implemented in similar organizational contexts may contribute to the implementation of different structures. Barley used interpretive and institutional perspectives to redefine the key concepts of technology and structure. Technology is an entity whose attributes are at least partly socially constructed. Structure is a set of processes more fluid than previous definitions had allowed. Barley traced the effects of a digital radiology system on analyst and operator tasks and skills and, as a consequence, on relations between functional roles.[15] According to the model, technology either modifies or reinforces role relations and through these relations occasions either structural change or maintenance. His project, though highly useful, leaves key questions unanswered. Although Barley theorized role change in detail, he left open the theoretical details of structural change. In focusing on roles and role relationships, the model left the examination of organizational mechanisms, such as performance programs and operating procedures, to other researchers. Finally, the model ignores the political or strategic behavior of actors in the context of new technologies. Technology enactment theory contributes partial answers to some of these unanswered questions.

Each of these perspectives contributes to an understanding of technology and structure, but each omits critical elements that are included in the technology enactment framework. Institutional and embeddedness perspectives, extended and refined to account for information technologies and their interrelationship with organizational and institutional arrangements, point toward a more complete and powerful explanatory framework than the partial theories summarized here.

Enacting Technology: An Analytical Framework

The technology enactment framework invites us to reverse the direction of the causal arrow that lies between technology and structure to show how the embeddedness of government actors in cognitive, cultural, social, and institutional structures influences the design, perceptions, and uses of the Internet and related IT. Individuals perceive, and therefore define and use, IT in subjective ways. Most individuals and organizations use only a few of the functions and features of their hardware, software, and telecommunications capacity. Consider those who use their personal computer only as a "smart" typewriter—that is, as a word-processing machine. And most people use groupware such as Lotus Notes, a sophisticated group problem-solving software package, as a tool merely for sending and receiving electronic mail.

It follows logically that information technology may be described in its objective sense, that is, in terms of the capacity and functionality of hardware, software, telecommunications, or digital devices. But the material components of technology represent a potential capability that is of little practical value to an individual or an organization until knowledgeable agents use them. Organizations are just beginning to formulate designs and uses that incorporate the Internet and web into their operations and structures. Organizations rarely use the full capability of their information systems, and they do not often leverage their strategic potential.[16]

Indeed, many organizational actors are scarcely aware of the potential of their technological systems. It is not surprising, therefore, that similar organizations may use identical information systems in vastly different ways. It follows that the capability and potential of an information system are enacted by the users of the system. Individuals and organizations enact information technology by their interpretation, design, implementation, and use of it in their organizations and networks. The flexibility, decomposability, and functionality of the web and related information technologies mean that a system's objective characteristics may differ substantially from those that are actually used.

Technology enactment is the result of cognitive, cultural, structural, and political embeddedness. Enactment is similar to "the definition of the situation," or the subjective representation of a problem that reflects an actor's perception and boundedly rational reasoning rather than the situation itself. Social scientists from W. I. Thomas to James March and Herbert Simon and, more recently, Douglass North, have employed the concept to connote the selectivity with which individuals perceive and frame, or make sense of, stimuli in their environment due to cognitive and social constraints.[17]

Organization theorists have used the term *enactment* to refer to the selective attention paid by individuals to environmental stimuli; the propensity to represent, act out, or enact institutionalized (or routinized) performance processes and standardized organizational arrangements; and the construction of organizational life that results from conflicting, competing, and sedimented enactments.[18] The Internet, and decisions regarding its use in organizations and institutions by nontechnical decisionmakers, is a quintessential example of decisionmaking under uncertainty. Uncertainty pertains to the technology itself as well as the future effects of its use on individuals, organizations, and institutions.

The analytical framework details the ways that individuals in institutions tend to enact new information systems to reproduce existing rules, routines, norms, and power relations if institutional rules are clear and no salient alternative uses are visible in the environment.[19] This conceptual framework illuminates the critical role played by sociostructural mechanisms in organizational and institutional arrangements as public managers struggle to make sense of, design, and use new IT.

The technology enactment framework extends the logic of embeddedness to the issue of the Internet and organizations. Cognition, culture, social networks, and formal rule regimes shape perceptions, interests and behavior.

Individuals often enact existing performance routines and network relationships in the way they design and use web-based information and communication systems. But the unintended consequences of these enactments occasionally lead to subtle modifications of structure to accommodate new technology. The accumulation of unintended, subtle modifications may lead to more dramatic shifts in structure and power, but actual outcomes are indeterminate in the enactment framework (see figure 6-1).

Three general propositions of the technology enactment framework are explained and illustrated below. A set of more specific propositions follows later in this chapter. The three propositions follow from the initial observation that enacted technology differs from objective technology. The process of enacting technology refers to the tendency of some organizational actors to implement new IT in ways that reproduce, indeed strengthen, institutionalized sociostructural mechanisms even when such enactments do not use technology rationally or optimally. Organizational actors tend to enact technology to preserve ongoing social, or network, relationships and to maintain performance programs: the routines, scripts, frames, and patterns that constitute the typical "organized set of responses" within organizations. More entrepreneurial or visionary professionals might use the Internet to develop new networked organizational forms or new capacity typically through a mimetic process that operates within social networks.[20]

Knowledgeable actors try to pursue their interests in enacting technology. However, their interests are influenced by their organizational tasks, incentive structure, and ongoing social (network) relations. Finally, institutional actors tend to enact new technologies in ways they hope will sustain or strengthen what I call "deep institutions," history and culture encoded in the existing norms and values of an organization.

Chapters 2 and 3 examined enactments of IT in American government in the 1990s. Chapters 4 and 5 analyzed the central elements of two predominant organizational forms, bureaucracy and interorganizational networks. But what of institutions?

Institutions and Embeddedness

In *TVA and the Grass Roots*, a case study of a new government organization in a complex political environment, Philip Selznick examined from an institutional perspective how a complex organization must adapt to its environment in order to secure the legitimacy and resources needed to

FIGURE 6-1. Technology Enactment: An Analytical Framework

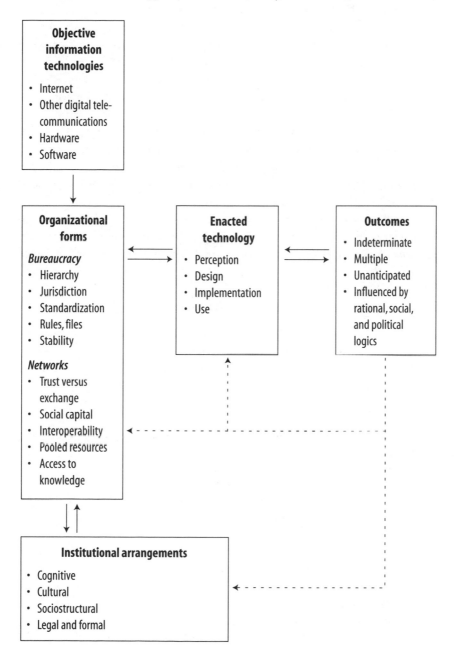

survive. In the process of adapting, organizations may shift their mission or objectives. The Tennessee Valley Authority, a newcomer to the federal government, "adopted strategies that decisively affected its capacity to uphold standards of environmental protection and, in the early years, its willingness to reach out to poor blacks and farm tenants."[21] Building on this study of the development and character of organizational competence, Selznick distinguished "organizations" from "institutions," noting the propensity of some organizations to take on a particular character or competence over time. He defined the process of institutionalization as "the emergence of orderly, stable, socially integrating patterns out of unstable, loosely organized, or narrowly technical activities."[22] In some instances the patterns that emerge are highly productive; in others, a learned incapacity or blinders may develop.

How would a decisionmaker know when a pattern had become institutionalized? The traditional test, according to Selznick, is expendability, or the ease with which an organization or practice could be modified or given up when environmental shifts or changes of circumstances demanded. Institutions typically grow out of social commitments made by people acting within social networks. Selznick observes:

> The underlying reality—the basic source of stability and integration—is the creation of social entanglements or commitments. Most of what we do in everyday life is mercifully free and reversible. But when actions touch important issues and salient values or when they are embedded in networks of interdependence, options are more limited. Institutionalization constrains conduct in two main ways: By bringing it within a normative order, and by making it hostage to its own history.[23]

Interrelated norms and social relations form a context within which choice and problem-solving take place. This context influences choice, as well as every step preceding choice: the recognition and formulation of problems, the development of preferences and interests, which problems are put on the agenda for attention, the criteria for analysis, the participants in the problem-solving process, and the roles they will play. Rational-choice perspectives drawn from neoclassical economics paint a portrait of atomized choice apart from its context. Institutions are constraints on choice and frame how those constraints operate.

Sharon Zukin and Paul DiMaggio classified the constraints and rule regimes that form institutions, or embeddedness, into four types, which are highly interrelated and distinct only analytically.[24] At the micro level, procedures, habits, and cognitive patterns are institutional instruments when they are widely shared and largely taken for granted. Cultural elements—including stories, myths, symbols, rituals, and worldviews—function as sources of embeddedness when they form part of the belief systems of actors and shape behavior, preferences, and calculations of effectiveness or efficiency. My framework employs culture not only as belief system but also as a "'tool kit' of symbols, stories, ritual and world-views, which people may use in varying configurations to solve different kinds of problems."[25] Thus "multiple and competing versions of institutionalized belief systems" can be selected and used strategically by organizations and policymakers.[26] The environment in which agencies operate consists of interorganizational systems that include other agencies, other branches of government, economic actors, and other interest groups. Although some relationships at this level are formalized, many are less formal ongoing social relations. Granovetter argued that economic action is embedded in ongoing social networks. His argument may be extended, at least hypothetically, to technology enactment. Finally, all organizations function in legal, regulatory, and political environments that consist of hundreds of rule systems, some of which are contradictory. So, the behavior of bureaucratic decisionmakers is embedded in four ways, through cognition, culture, social structure, and formal government systems.[27]

Related research streams in institutional analysis and embeddedness leave several questions unanswered. To what extent and in what ways does structure constrain action? How do constraints change over time? Who or what changes them? What is the role of power in the creation and maintenance of institutions? Do constraints differ systematically for actors depending upon their power? How or why do some individuals and organizations conform to rules while others either innovate, skirt the rules, behave strategically, or otherwise transcend conformity and habit?

During periods of stability, institutions are taken for granted. But when environmental shifts occur, including economic, political, or technological "shocks," crises, or revolutions, institutions are less resistant to change. Communism in the former Soviet Union gave way in a peaceful revolution after a long period of weakening within, catalyzed by environmental shifts. Career ladders in professions have given way to the portable assets of professionals increasingly moving from one organization to the next. Marriage, certainly a deep social institution, falls apart nearly 40 percent of the time in Western society. Myths, symbols, and rituals such as family, religion, patriotism, cooperation, partnership, innovation, standardization, and efficiency constrain action but also are tools that political actors manipulate with regularity and skill.

The Interplay of Action and Structure

Early studies in the institutional perspective were unable to account for organizational and institutional change and strategic action by individuals. Structure and institutions were viewed as both "fixed" and "external" to social actors and thus as a constraint on cognition and choice.[28] More recently, institutions and structure have been conceptualized as enablers of, as well as constraints on, behavior. This "duality of structure" thus links action and structure. In other words, individual action is constrained by structure, but it is action that maintains and modifies structure.[29]

In this sense, institutions can be defined simply as "reproduced practices" that are both flexible and remarkably stable. Giddens, followed by some new institutional theorists, argued that "a sophisticated understanding of agency" is necessary to comprehend structure. The reflective capacity of agents, their constant monitoring and indexing of behavior against standards of appropriateness and the pursuit of interests, for example, diminishes the unshakable constraints of institutions. In this view, "even the most enduring of habits, or the most unshakable of social norms, involves continual and detailed reflexive attention." Routinization, as we saw in Chapters 4 and 5, is of "elemental importance in social life; but all routines, all the time, are contingent and potentially fragile accomplishments."[30] Informal rules, in particular, remain in effect only to the extent that, and as long as, people decide to follow them.

Others have explained the duality of structure using cognitive science to characterize some institutions as production systems—that is, sets of production or if-then rules that structure standardized interactional sequences.[31] The value of the production system model for representing institutions as rule regimes stems from its ability to explain how departures from accepted rules are treated. A routine may be said to be institutionalized only when "departures from the patterns are counteracted in a regulated fashion, by repetitively activated, socially constructed, controls—that is, by some set of rewards and sanctions . . . [I]nstitutions are those social patterns that, when chronically reproduced, owe their survival to relatively self-activating social processes."[32] This account allows for organizational change only through external shocks to the system or through collective action organized to block reproduction of an institutionalized process.

Other theorists allow greater scope for organizational change. Giddens emphasizes the key role played by the unintended consequences of behavior in modifying institutionalized structures. March and Olsen and others have noted the contradictions in collective and individual behavior that result from multiplicity and conflicts among complex systems of rules within organizations. Granovetter and other researchers focus on behavior influenced, but not determined, by institutions and network embeddedness.[33]

Insights from cognitive science help to explain adherence to routine and norms, as well as deviations from them. Insights including selective attention and search; limitations of perception; the centrality of scripts, schemas, routines, and performance programs; and the variety of unanticipated consequences of rule-based behavior explain departures from rationality and, ironically, departures from institutional constraints as well.[34]

Drawing from cognitive psychology, organizational analysts have advanced an understanding of the relationship between action and institution using the distinctly cognitive organizing structure of scripts but using "grammars" to portray flexibility within scripted behavior. Research in this stream reiterates the critical position of routines as intermediate structural elements mediating between institution and action but details the use of "rule-based, grammatical models" of routines to capture both structure and agency and to convey the stability of rule systems as well as the flexibility of each performance of a routine. In this view, "Members enact specific performances from among a constrained, but potentially large, set of possibilities that can be described by a grammar, giving rise to the regular patterns of action we label routines."[35] Similarly, researchers have reconceptualized the bureaucratic notion of communication channels as elements of formal structure to be more fluid "genres of organizational communication."[36] Repertoires of meetings, forms, memos, correspondence, and training formats simultaneously constrain and enable action. Their enactment reflects and reconstitutes the ongoing accomplishment of structure. New institutional economists tend to ignore these fine-grained sources of flexibility and change, focusing instead on the pursuit of interests with constraints.

The important insights of the Carnegie school that stem from viewing organizations as interdependent and partially consistent production systems complement negotiated order theory's view of the fluidity of structure and the processual nature of scripted behaviors. Together, these images yield powerful insight into stability and change within organizations and networks. They also provide us with the "hooks" upon which organizational actors hang elements of enacted technology.

Even theorists who emphasize rational choice in social networks note the fluidity of structure. In this view, institutions also shape choice through a series of "social mechanisms" or "processes that are built into ongoing social relationships—the domain of network analysis in sociology." Nee and Ingram argue that "by structuring social interactions . . . institutions produce group performance" from the micro level of the family, to the large organization, and the economy as a whole: "Networks of social relations are always in flux insofar as individuals respond to perceptions of costs and benefits in exchanges, and invest or divest themselves of particular social ties. The production and monitoring of norms, standards of expected behavior that enjoy a high degree of consensus within a group or community, are rooted in such elementary forms of social behavior."[37] Norms relate directly to incentive structures, the rewards and sanctions that further influence social behavior. Formal norms operate explicitly through rules and are reinforced through the monitoring and enforcement efforts of, for example, individual organizations and the state. Informal norms, the rules adopted and adhered to by a group, may be explicit but are often implicit. They are enforced through social mechanisms, including approval, acceptance, disapproval, avoidance, and shunning.

The institutionalization of key elements of organizational structure helps to explain its surprising resilience in the face of disruptive information and communications technologies. The stability of organizational forms demonstrates the importance of an institutional perspective in a terrain that remains dominated by the assumption that information technology determines structure. Society has entered the information age with major structural changes attending technological change. However, it is erroneous to attribute structural change directly to technology. Organizational, network, and institutional arrangements—and the embeddedness of behavior in them—play key roles in technology enactment.

Embeddedness and Technology Enactment

Those who celebrate the integrative power of the Internet rarely consider the complexities required to develop and manage interorganizational networks, including the intricate balance between trust and interests and between cooperation and competition.[38] Most discussions of digital government do not adequately take account of research on social and interorganizational networks. Yet it follows as a logical consequence of these research findings that technology enactment and organizational change, catalyzed by the Internet and related technologies, must follow similar patterns. Absent theories that connect the logic of networked computing with that of institutions, researchers and practitioners are left without sufficiently realistic analytic frameworks. The decoupling of embeddedness and its effects on action and institutions from models of technological change produces an erroneous, overly simplified view of the Internet and its likely uses in a society of complex organizations.

In the public sector, as in the private, three aspects of technological change have contributed to an increase in network formation. First, there has been significant growth in the base of technologies that agencies might use. Many new government services and policy instruments combine disparate technologies. For example, a geographic information system (GIS) requires large capital expenditures and technical experts. But the benefits of data generated by a GIS spill over to environmental regulation, economic development, housing, law enforcement, and other policy areas. Second, single agencies cannot maintain proficiency in all the technical fields relevant to their policy domain. Moreover, it is not feasible for single agencies to attempt to develop those proficiencies in-house because, as policymaking becomes more complex and uses combinations of new technologies, agencies will increasingly face pressures to coordinate with other sources of expertise and knowledge. Third, the rapid pace of technological change makes it increasingly difficult for any single agency to keep up with all relevant technologies.[39]

The Internet creates far-reaching possibilities for interorganizational networks. Although technologically determinist, Mark Ackerman emphasizes the potential of the Internet to allow new types of networks:

> Software can construct more flexible expertise networks than society could sustain previously. This new flexibility can change the way we produce, disseminate, and store society's knowledge. Within these networks, moreover, we have the flexibility to include information databases, documents, agents, and people together as resources. And as interesting, the same software allows emergent networks to be used for political action, hobbies, a sense of community, and other forms of social life that we can barely imagine. The standard forms, and even the vocabulary we use to describe the forms, will blur even more.[40]

But even Ackerman allows that "Our ability to design technically far exceeds our understanding of what socially needs to be incorporated into a design."[41]

In sum, objective technology includes the Internet, other networked computing systems and telecommunications, hardware, software, and digital devices. Enacted technology is the perception, design, and use of objective technologies. Organizational and institutional arrangements, dissected in this and the previous two chapters, include the bureaucratic and network forms of organization and the institutional logics discussed here. The bureaucratic form, whose logics—particularly standardization, the primacy of rules, and control—remain robust, exhibits some changes due to technology, as we saw in Chapter 4. In contrast, because interorganizational networks follow different internal logics, they find coherence and governance in norms, trust, and the structure of network ties rather than in hierarchy and command-and-control systems. Some network forms appear to offer greater flexibility, access to knowledge, and adaptability than bureaucracies.[42]

Thus institutions influence and are influenced by enacted information technologies and predominant organizational forms. Institutions enter the technology enactment framework in the form of cognitive, cultural, sociostructural, and formal embeddedness. The outcomes of technology enactment are therefore multiple, unpredictable, and indeterminate. Outcomes result from technological, rational, social, and political logics.

The Virtual Agency

As a concrete application of the technology enactment framework, I focus on the virtual agency. The virtual state, as I noted in the first chapter, denotes a government in which information and communication flow increasingly over the web rather than through bureaucratic and other formal channels. The restructuring of agency services and information in portals sometimes makes it difficult for citizens to know which agency they are dealing with. Moreover, the distinction between government and business may be blurred on the web because both the public and the private sector provide government services, increasingly through the same portals. My analysis focuses on structural change in the federal bureaucracy, a relatively neglected but vitally important area of governance and policymaking. The technology enactment framework could be applied, with modification, to the Internet and its uses in electoral politics, Congress, the judiciary, state and local politics, intergovernmental relations, and international affairs. The virtual state is one in which the organization of the government increasingly resides within networked computerized information systems and within interorganizational networks rather than in autonomous bureaucratic agencies. A virtual state consists of virtual agencies overlaid on a formal bureaucratic structure. Such a state will depart from the bureaucratic state as the formal institutions that structure oversight and the budget process are modified to align with the logic of web-based policy networks.

The term *virtual agency* has been given to a number of innovative agency arrangements. These range from agency websites to interagency websites organized by client group or policy domain—such as financenet, Access America for Students, and the U.S. Business Advisor—to more complex cross-agency systems such as the International Trade Data System. The virtual agency, in its many forms, represents an emergent structural change in the American state that roughly parallels structural changes in the economy, including the growth of interfirm networks.

The term *virtual agency* describes at least four different enactments of the Internet and related technologies by government agencies. For a graphic depiction of the relationship between virtual agencies, operational complexity, and institutional barriers, see figure 6-2. First, agencies have produced single-agency websites that make government information available to anyone in the world with an Internet connection and web browser. In most cases, these websites have had little impact on internal agency structure, culture, and power.

Second, groups of agencies linked by common clients, such as students or senior citizens, have developed virtual agencies. These virtual agencies use the connectivity of the web to co-locate the information and transactions of several agencies on one website. So, for example, a senior citizen using the Access America for Seniors website will find information from several agencies and can download forms or perform simple transactions with them.[43] A visitor to the Wilderness Information Network will find the resources of five federal agencies with jurisdiction over wilderness management as well as information from a host of other organizations in the public, private, and nonprofit sectors.[44] The integration of information across agencies in these examples consists of website design decisions only. Each website makes it easier for users to find information, regardless of its actual agency location. But the agencies themselves have

FIGURE 6-2. Virtual Agencies and Ease of Implementation

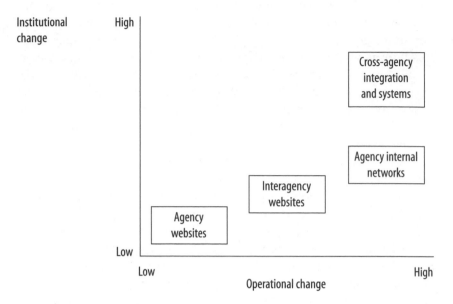

not modified or integrated what designers call "back channels," their procedures or systems.

A third type of site is the intranet within an agency. This type of integration and networking is often more complex than the interagency website because of the requirement to integrate performance programs and other internal structural arrangements. Chapter 9 analyzes the development of a complex intranet enacted in a traditional command-and-control organization, the U.S. Army.

Fourth, a virtual agency may consist of a group of agencies that integrate some of their activities both on the web and "behind" the website, within and across the structures of the agencies themselves. At this level, the Internet is a catalyst and an enabler for restructuring agency processes, information systems, and procedures to achieve partial integration within the network of agencies involved. Clearly, this fourth level requires a great deal of operational, political, and institutional change. It is at this level that institutional barriers to interagency networks become evident and significant.

Virtual agencies are nothing more than organizations connected by networked computers and linked on the screen by means of a web-based user interface that presents a seamless image to the outside world. For example, the customer of Acme Advertising (a fictitious virtual agency) may not realize that the "firm" is nothing more than an individual and several contractors. The Virtual Department of Business, an important innovation of the National Performance Review examined in Chapter 8, is in one sense nothing more than a website that includes all the government information and services for business, spanning several agencies located "virtually" in one website.

In the federal government, virtual agencies operate in a heavily institutionalized setting where historical, cultural, and professional norms of good government, sound administration, and efficient public management are formalized in legislation and rule-making; in the structure and processes of the federal budget process; in oversight arrangements within the Office of Management and Budget, the Congressional Budget Office, and the General Accounting Office; in relationships between the executive and legislative branches; and in the socialization and reward systems of career public servants. Agencies are embedded in an institutional environment that discourages horizontal cross-agency initiatives and that encourages competition among autonomous agencies for resources. Thus, in contrast to the economic firms in the market, government agencies face strong institutional constraints on network formation in the form of oversight relationships, the budget process, and a long tradition of adversarial bureaucratic politics. The incentive of profits and economic success that accrues to firms that form wise strategic alliances in the private sector is not available in government. On the contrary, efficiency gains from networking across agencies are likely to result in the loss of budget, staff, and even agency jurisdiction. These disincentives to the development of cross-agency networks contrast sharply with the networking logic of the Internet or the logic of networks of organizations that benefit from cooperation.

Although the technological logic of networked computing suggests that networks of organizations are a logical and natural outgrowth of the Internet, this claim ignores the embeddedness of economic action in social, political, organizational, and institutional life. Technological logic must be connected to, and integrated with, the logics of the institutions and social relations that constitute interorganizational networks. Virtual agencies succeed only when the agencies involved can develop and maintain social capital. Although the Internet provides the potential for vastly improved communication across organizational boundaries, these benefits are realized only when embedded in appropriate cognitive, cultural, social, and formal norms, rules, and relationships.

The technology enactment framework suggests a set of guiding propositions for interactions among technology, organizations, institutions, and individuals. I offer additional propositions here as a scaffolding to support research and theory-building. These propositions are "tested" in an exploratory manner against the case studies that follow.

Proposition 1: Government agencies will resist the potential for dramatic efficiency gains if those gains translate into loss of resources (budget and personnel) for the agency. As I noted in Chapter 1, agencies are highly likely to lose budget and personnel through their enactment of the Internet. The logics of technological advancement and rationalization conflict with the logics of bureaucratic politics.

Proposition 2: Federal interagency networks will be difficult to build and maintain because the formal institutions of the federal government reward agency-centered activities and discourage cross-agency activities. There are few processes in place for evaluating or advancing cross-agency activities (action channels, templates, models, rule regimes).

Proposition 3: Agencies lack resources for learning to use IT. The current cost-cutting environment in the federal government, which demands immediate cost savings from information technology expenditures, makes it difficult for agencies to develop prototypes and to pilot new information systems. The learning curve government managers must climb in any new initiative is steep, as are the costs of organizational restructuring. The requirements for agency learning suggest that some IT appropriations should be viewed as investments rather than expenditures and should not be traded off in the budget process with other classes of expenditures.

Proposition 4: Intergovernmental and public-private networks will overshadow cross-agency IT-based networks because the institutional context favors those arrangements more readily than cross-agency federal networks.

Proposition 5: Agencies are likely to focus reform efforts on constituents, or "customers," who also are potential or actual strategic allies in the appropriations process. Large interagency initiatives have redistributive effects; and some constituencies are likely to benefit more than others, depending upon the enactment of web-based interagency networks. Such a bias toward serving the public interest is an unanticipated outcome of customer service norms in government.[45] Customers with little political influence are likely to receive fewer benefits of the Internet from government restructuring.

Proposition 6: The nature of changes necessary to develop a network will affect the probability of success of the effort. Cross-agency IT efforts that require standardization of data are more likely to succeed than projects whose success requires structural change in the agency or its network ties. This proposition follows from the dissection of technology, as well as from organizational and institutional logics.

Proposition 7: The culture, history, mental models, and standard practices of a policy domain or agency will affect technology enactment—that is, whether and how an agency uses the Internet. Agencies involved in science and technology activities are more likely to engage in network arrangements than agencies with less exposure to science, technology, computing, or cross-jurisdictional collaboration. This proposition follows from our discussion of culture, history, and professional practice as elements of embeddedness.

The technology enactment framework can be used to address a broad range of research questions and to develop a much more elaborate set of expectations. The initial sketch of propositions is limited to those that explicitly explore the data that follow. As noted previously, the analytic framework could be used to analyze a variety of policy networks at the transnational, federal, state, or local levels of government. Similarly, it extends to the judiciary and the Congress.

What difference does networked computing make to these propositions? Networked computing acts to pressure political entrepreneurs to seek out uses of the Internet that ultimately involve networked agencies because networks economize on time, resources, and information. This pressure may be in the form of external actors in the authorizing environment who promote the use of the Internet. Through the reinventing government effort, the Clinton White House played a chief catalytic role in fostering certain enactments of information technology. Congress might play a similar role. The federal government tends to imitate the private sector, particularly when influenced by outside contractors, consultants, political appointees from business, and the popular media. As networked computing becomes a bigger part of the government infrastructure, more and more policy entrepreneurs will take its growing acceptance as an invitation to increase their agencies' resources, capacity, or responsiveness. As institutional, technological, social, and political logics collide and are negotiated, so the virtual state will be built.

PART TWO

Practice

CHAPTER SEVEN

The International Trade Data System

> Even the boldest ideas, like . . . one trade data system rather than 40, are within reach.
>
> *Vice President Al Gore,* Access America, *February 3, 1997*

THIS CHAPTER TURNS from conceptual analysis and dissection of organizational and institutional arrangements to the far messier empirical world. My first objective is to illustrate technology enactment at work. At a more ambitious level, the cases presented in this and the following three chapters are meant to test whether the framework is supported. If the technology enactment theory were disproved, we would expect to see technology directly leading to organizational and institutional change without mediation. We would also be able to predict outcomes of technology adoption or implementation. The International Trade Data System (ITDS) represents an ambitious, visionary use of the web to enable deep integration across agencies. In these ways, it represents a second phase of Internet use in government, moving beyond the development of web portals to the integration of back channels among agencies. As such, it represents the potential for institutional transformation of the policy domain for international trade.[1]

The reinvention of international trade through ITDS was the largest, and perhaps most important, IT (information technology) initiative of the National Performance Review. The system was designed to use the Internet, as well as existing agency computing systems, to create a network of the large number of federal agencies involved in international trade. In the broadest terms, ITDS represents the federal government's attempt to modernize international trade processing in order to close the growing gap between the state and a global, digital economy in which international trade now flows at a volume and rate beyond the organizational capacity of the government to manage. This chapter chronicles the modernization of international trade processing from about 1994 until the end of 1999. The history and culture of the U.S. Customs Service, the dramatic change in its environment, and the rise of the Internet all focus attention on the institutional factors whose confluence influenced the politics of enacting the ITDS.

Firms that transport goods internationally are required by law to obtain licenses and permits meant to protect national security, public health, and the orderly flow of international trade. All imports are "processed" to check the accuracy of customs declarations; to collect fees, duties, and tariffs; and to examine international cargo before its release into the commerce of the United States. The Bureau of Export Administration regulates the export of high-technology goods. The Bureau of Alcohol, Tobacco, and Firearms monitors the import of firearms. The Department of Agriculture oversees imports for a variety of agricultural products. The U.S. Constitution prohibits taxation of U.S. goods that are exported. Therefore, outbound shipments are not generally subject to large amounts of regulation and paperwork except in consideration of goods deemed a threat to American military or technological superiority or in defiance of trade and foreign policy objectives. For example, the Bureau of Export Administration regulates the export of high-technology goods. The Departments of State and Commerce cooperate to restrict export of goods to Cuba, Iraq, and Libya.

Government analysts and statisticians compile and study international trade data as an essential basis for the development and enforcement of trade policies. The International Trade Commission and the Office of the U.S. Trade Representative use international trade data gathered from a variety of agencies to negotiate and monitor trade agreements. The Department of Commerce, the International Trade Administration, and the Customs Service analyze data to evaluate trends and practices in trade. Businesses rely extensively on government trade data as part of their strategic and planning processes. Accurate and immediately available country- and industry-specific trade data are vital for export promotion, especially in a world of digital order placement. Traditionally, however, international trade data analysis required compiling information from several different agency databases whose construction and data elements over-lapped and often were incompatible because data were defined and measured differently by each agency.

The current system for processing international trade and transportation data exhibits the highly segmented patchwork quality of many federal policy domains. Nearly two hundred years of legislation has responded to specific trade problems identified by committees and subcommittees in Congress and has accreted to form incompatible, fragmented, duplicative reporting and record-keeping requirements. Business and government data flow through subsections of this byzantine structure at every crossing of the border. Trade and traffic flows meet a serious bottleneck at the borders that grows tighter as the gap between government and business organization and professional practice grows larger.

The cost of international trade, estimated at 4 to 6 percent of the value of goods, represents the cost to business of managing and providing the documentation required for transacting trade across borders.[2] The average rate of duty collected in the United States is about 3 percent of the value of goods. Not surprisingly, the administration of international trade is a profitable and complex industry that comprises a long, complex, and costly chain of brokers, forwarders, insurers, and other agents. Many intermediaries exist primarily to manage government regulations.

The ITDS was envisioned as a way of integrating and standardizing U.S. government international trade and transportation data and processes across the federal agencies with jurisdiction over international trade. By building a single, standardized interagency database, ITDS promised to reduce the time and costs of trade processing for both business and government; eliminate unnecessary and duplicative reporting requirements; improve the timeliness and quality of information to promote informed compliance by the trade community; standardize import and export data to allow more accurate, complete, and timely analysis of trade-related issues; provide more accurate and complete trade statistics; improve financial control throughout the trade administration network; and create partnerships with international trade agencies by developing one global standard for shared data and the technology platform on which to manage it.

The organizational and institutional changes needed to implement such a vision require a transformation of work within public agencies. In addition, the integrative network assumes a shift in mind-set from the logic of largely manual inspections performed individually by each agency to a different logic: more abstract analysis of patterns in trade data to develop

Departments and Agencies with Jurisdiction over International Trade

Department of Agriculture
  Agriculture Marketing Service
  Animal and Plant Health
    Inspection Service
  Economic Research Service
  Farm Service Agency
  Federal Grain Inspection Service
  Foreign Agriculture Service
  Food Safety Inspection Service
  National Agricultural Library

Agency for International Development

Central Intelligence Agency

Department of Commerce
  Bureau of Export Administration
  Bureau of the Census
  Economics and Statistics
    Administration/Stat USA
  National Marine Fisheries Service
  National Oceanic and Atmospheric
    Administration
  National Environmental Satellite
    Data Information Service
  National Technical Information
    Service
  Patent and Trademark Office
  Office of Textiles and Apparel,
    International Trade Administration
  Trade Information Center, Interna-
    tional Trade Administration
  U.S. and Foreign Commercial
    Service

Consumer Product Safety Commission

Department of Defense
  Army Corps of Engineers
  Defense Logistics Agency

Department of Energy
  Committee on Renewable Energy,
    Commerce, and Trade
  Energy Information Administration
  Fossil Energy Office

Environmental Protection Agency

Export-Import Bank

Executive Office of Management
  and Budget

Federal Communications Commission

Federal Maritime Commission

Federal Reserve Board

Federal Trade Commission

General Accounting Office

Health and Human Services
  Center for Disease Control, Public
    Health Service
  Center for Disease Control-Quarantine
  Food and Drug Administration

Department of the Interior
  Fish and Wildlife Service

International Trade Commission

Department of Justice
  Immigration and Naturalization
    Service
  Drug Enforcement Administration

Department of Labor
  Bureau of Labor Statistics

Library of Congress
  Congressional Research Service
  Copyright Office

Nuclear Regulatory Commission

Overseas Private Investment Corporation

Department of State
  Office of Export Control Policy
  Bureau of Political and Military
    Affairs
  Office of Defense Trade Controls
  Bureau of Political and Military
    Affairs

Department of Transportation
  Coast Guard
  Federal Highway Administration
  Volpe Institute, Federal Highway
    Administration
  Federal Railway Administration
  Maritime Administration
  National Highway Traffic Safety
    Administration

Department of the Treasury
  Bureau of Alcohol, Tobacco and
    Firearms
  Internal Revenue Service
  Office of Foreign Assets Control
  U.S. Customs Service

U.S. Trade Representative[3]

risk management profiling and a data-driven approach to inspection. The technical logic of an integrated information system assumes a high level of cooperation among the key agencies and the willingness of agencies to develop more integrated, cross-agency trade enforcement, analysis, and promotion.

ITDS would alter business and government relations along several dimensions, including increased electronic exchange of data between business and government; disintermediation, with the potential effect of changing the business structure and strategy of key intermediaries such as brokers and forwarders; and simplified, less costly trade processing, which would not only reduce the cost of trade to businesses but also effectively lower barriers to entry into the international trading arena for small and medium-sized firms. In sum, the argument for fundamental restructuring of international trade data and management is clear; yet the organizational and institutional transformation required to align the state with a digital, global economy is difficult to achieve.

The Transformation of International Trade

Without substantial modernization of trade administration and analysis, neither the United States nor other countries with significant trade flows can hope to accurately, efficiently, and safely process goods at national borders in the twenty-first century. In 1970 international trade flows into and out of the United States totaled $82 billion. By 1994, the year ITDS was initiated, international trade flows had grown to more than $1 trillion.[4] Although historically trade has been less important to the U.S. economy than to many other countries, it rose in importance from 9 percent of gross domestic product (GDP) in 1960 to 25 percent in 1998.[5] Internationally, trade flows also are increasing significantly. The total volume of goods and services traded internationally constituted approximately 25 percent of the world's GDP in 1970. By 1990 it had risen to 45 percent of world GDP.[6] Not only has the total volume of trade increased, but the number of different products, components, trade agreements, and trading partners has proliferated. As a consequence, the administration of trade policies has become vastly more complex and consequential to the flow of trade in an increasingly global and networked business environment.[7]

The transformation of business practices, fueled largely by technological change, has meant that supply and manufacturing processes themselves are increasingly carried out across borders.[8] Moreover, these flows have become temporally constrained by just-in-time practices in manufacturing, inventory control, and distribution, which are meant to minimize the use of buffers in production and distribution channels through sophisticated, networked planning and management between units and firms. A related development, supply chain integration, formerly denoted the use of electronic data interchange and increasingly denotes use of the web to rationalize flows of information and materials among firms within a supply chain. Both developments restructure the geographic configuration of industries and have increased the pace, or metabolic rate, of business.

Information technologies and the operations methods that use them are inadequate on their own to rationalize such complex flows. Management practices have also begun to incorporate collaboration within supply chains in order to gain the efficiencies that social capital and mutual adjustment mechanisms in complex, interdependent systems can provide.[9]

The macroeconomic and industry-level developments outlined here will continue to strain the capacity of the state until it, too, uses not only technologies readily at hand but also new organizational and institutional practices that promote networked approaches and productive collaboration to restructure outmoded and inefficient programs, procedures, and agency relationships. A rapidly changing, tightly integrated, and automated business environment stands in stark contrast to the bureaucratic and technological logic that has guided the agency with the most visible responsibilities at the border: the U.S. Customs Service.

The Changing Role of the Customs Service

Congress created the U.S. Customs Service in 1789 to collect duties on imported goods in order to generate revenue for the federal treasury— even before the Treasury Department existed.[10] Today 19,000 customs employees inspect and clear tens of millions of people and $1 trillion in imported goods entering the United States each year through 301 land, sea, and air ports of entry. In addition to its commercial activities, the Customs Service polices the nation's border. Customs officers enforce the rules and regulations of many other federal agencies, each of which has some statutory purview and responsibility over imports and exports— including the Food and Drug Administration, Fish and Wildlife Service, Environmental Protection Agency, and Consumer Product Safety Commission. During the 1980s the Customs Service acquired a principal role in the nation's drug control effort, which is exercised largely at the border. In addition, it has long been responsible for providing the Commerce Department with data on the flow of the nation's imports and exports.

For more than 200 years the basic tasks of the Customs Service, the structure of international trade and the business of ports, remained essentially unchanged. Many procedures in use through the twentieth century were deeply institutionalized in the byzantine body of law that former Customs Service commissioner William von Raab once observed was only "a slightly updated version of what the British left us, designed for an era of sailing ships and physical handling."[11] A freight carrier—for example, a steamship—carrying a load of textiles from China to Seattle was required to file a manifest with the Customs Service that listed its cargo, where the items were bound, where they came from, and their value. On shore, a customs broker—someone licensed by Customs and hired by the importer to expedite cargo through port clearance procedures—was required to file an "entry" that described the goods his client intended to import from the shipment. With the manifest and entry in hand, Customs decided whether to inspect the shipment or clear it for entry and determined the duties and taxes owed. All this happened after a ship docked and could take hours, days, or weeks.

At the beginning of the 1980s, the Customs Service had a $521 million budget and generated $8 billion in duties, fees, fines, and taxes.[12] But its environment changed rapidly and significantly thereafter. Imports increased 50 percent from 1980 to 1985.[13] In 1980, with 12,804 staff at headquarters and in the field, the Customs Service processed 4 million brokers' entries (covering 2.2 million cargo containers) and processed 30 million air passengers for U.S. entry.[14] The resulting oceans of paperwork erected a classic nontariff "paper barrier" to trade. Port clearance delays were common and costly, bills went unpaid, and cash flows were halted until goods actually reached their distributors. Even so, import inspections were rare and commercial fraud common. By 1987 customs inspectors opened fewer than two of every 100 oceangoing containers that entered the country.[15] To make matters worse, heroin, cocaine, and marijuana began entering the country in large quantities through land, sea, and air ports.

Determining how to balance the demands for law enforcement and trade facilitation was difficult, a twist on the traditional customs dilemma: to facilitate trade or to detect and deter violations of trade laws and import quotas and stop drugs at the border. Incorrect labeling of origin, false invoicing, undervaluing the contents of a package, and false reporting of the weight of products such as steel were common ploys. East German steel, for example, might be stamped as a product of West Germany to receive lower tariffs. Sweaters woven in the People's Republic of China were relabeled "Made in Japan" to bypass textile quotas.

At the busiest ports of entry on the southern border, customs officers inspected only 3.7 percent of the laden trucks entering from Mexico.[16] Contraband such as counterfeit parts for aircraft, cars, and electronics amounted to an "epidemic" that cost American industry $20 billion annually, according to one concerned legislator.[17] Airfreight officials complained that air cargo spent 10 percent of its time in the air and 90 percent on the ground waiting for clearance.[18] Oceangoing carriers complained that from 30 to 35 percent of their costs reflected administration, largely redundant paperwork.[19] The Big Three automakers, General Motors, Chrysler, and Ford Motor Company, faced with strong foreign competition, were eager to institute just-in-time inventories that required keeping only an hour's supply on hand. "We have to schedule our assembly plants and docks hour by hour," one Ford manager pointed out. "You can't do that with paper."[20]

In the new global trading environment the provision of trade data to other agencies from Customs became unacceptably slow. Customs provided the Census Bureau with trade data each month. Federal policymakers and negotiators relied on the data to develop the U.S. position in international trade discussions and to monitor violations of trade agreements, including antidumping legislation. At the height of one set of bilateral textile negotiations, a Customs official claimed that three major American ports were so backed up with entries that data were being sent to the Census Bureau two to three months behind schedule.

In 1985, Customs Commissioner von Raab declared: "The real solution to the problem of trade facilitation is to automate the entire process as much as possible."[21] A Reagan appointee and champion of smaller government, von Raab was determined that Customs would perform its mission with fewer staff and an automated system that would accept information directly from the computers of trade businesses. Electronic submission of manifest and entry data, performed largely by the brokers who handled this paperwork for importers, could then be used by computerized models to develop risk profiles of businesses based on their record of compliance. "Ultimately," he said, "the system will permit Customs, through the use of preprogrammed [standardized] criteria, to process and liquidate selected entries with absolutely no hard copy documentation."[22] Von Raab's vision for Customs reflected the radical reengineering movement of the 1980s, which was committed to using information technology to restructure business process flows within and across firms.[23]

As early as February 1970, the consulting firm Booz-Allen & Hamilton had advised the Customs Service to replace its many nonconvergent information systems with "a single nationwide system." Instead, Customs built the Automated Merchandise Processing System (AMPS). AMPS was composed of individual functional units that had been developed over several years, with different data and application programming styles. It was assumed that it could be integrated into one functioning system at a later date. This assumption of cross-functional integration proved bureaucratically and politically impossible for Customs to implement. In addition, AMPS was premised on the infeasible idea that Customs officials would manually enter all data from carriers, brokers, and importers at ports of entry. By the late 1970s, only about 20 percent of trade businesses were automated, but this 20 percent accounted for 60 percent of the import entries. More than half the data Customs would have entered, using its own staff, already existed in digital form. It could be submitted electronically directly from trade firms' computers to the computers at Customs. When von Raab arrived in the early 1980s, Customs began testing the Automated Broker Interface. The strategic use of IT began to have leadership and focus at Customs.

In 1981 the drug war was looming. Imports were surging by 8.3 percent annually, rising from 2.8 million entries in 1970 to 8 million in 1987.[24] Within the year, von Raab had launched a three-pronged effort to drive Customs toward automation using what would become the Automated Commercial System (ACS). The first step was to design an integrated system that would link the trade to Customs nationally and that would link all Customs systems from stand-alone "stovepiped" systems to an integrated whole. The second was to fund it. The third was to build it. But the success of ACS would require changing the way the whole industry did business, moving it from a paper to a digital environment. Using a phrase popular during the radical reengineering period in American business, von Raab told the broker community, "Automate or perish"—in effect: "Change or die." The businesses that filed international trade transactions electronically would receive more rapid processing from Customs. Those firms that fell behind would lose business and likely fail.[25]

"Armed with the necessary information, Customs will be able to tell you, up to 48 hours before sea borne cargo arrives, which cargo we will want to examine," von Raab asserted to port authority executives. "This gives shippers who use your port a tremendous advantage in planning the use of their resources."[26] During von Raab's eight-year tenure as head of the Customs Service, imports increased by 50 percent, and revenues from duties and fees climbed to $20 billion annually.[27] The budget for Customs grew to $1 billion, due largely to von Raab's dogged pursuit of the drug war, his insistence on developing information systems for processing imports, and strong relationships on Capitol Hill.

The Automated Commercial System (ACS), a successor to AMPS, was the first nationwide automated system for processing multiple Customs functions. Robert W. Ehinger became its acting head. The system focused on reprogramming the import entry or declaration processing modules and networking the nation's ports for processing all commercial goods entering the United States. Each ACS module automated an important segment of the importing process. These included an electronic manifest, an electronic entry (declaration), an automated cargo release, electronic funds transfer for payment of duties to Customs, an automated data transfer of import statistics to the Census Bureau, and an automated notice of completed transactions, called Notice of Liquidation.

An automated broker interface (ABI) system, connecting brokers' data to Customs, was widely publicized among customs brokers who were encouraged to participate and promised "front of the line" treatment for all declarations submitted electronically. Customs brokers reacted to this pressure by using their national association to threaten a boycott of the automated interface unless Customs paid for each electronic transaction. Customs responded that electronically filed declarations benefited importers, who received faster and, therefore, cheaper service. Customs also provided electronic filers with client representatives who successfully tested and interfaced hundreds of electronic filers in less than four years. Moreover, competitors to traditional brokers began to offer faster, cheaper service to importers by filing their declarations electronically. The inducements had the desired effect. In 1985, 20 percent of the declarations were filed electronically. By 1988, 57 percent of customs brokers were online and 40 percent of all declarations were filed electronically. Customs reported that its costs-per-transaction had fallen from $28 in 1984 to $3 in 1988. By 1990, *American Shipper* reported that 90 percent of all entries were handled electronically.

But the rapid processing achieved by these automation efforts provided no gain to other agencies tasked with trade processing responsibilities at the borders. Half of all imports cleared by the Customs Service also required clearance by one or more other federal agencies. The Food and

Drug Administration (FDA) itself had jurisdiction over 25 percent of all import transactions. For example, when an importer filed a declaration with the FDA, the broker filled out a paper form, stapled it to a copy of the invoice, and hired a messenger to deliver it. When a second or third agency, less automated than Customs, had to clear an import, delays could add three or four days to processing times.

During the late 1980s, Customs began to electronically connect the network of agencies centrally involved in trade. Brokers wanted all inspections agencies linked to ACS so that they could key in information once and take advantage of the automation investments they had already made to speed cargo through ports. Customs wanted all information to be transmitted to ACS, where the agency would then sort it and send trade data to other agencies who would respond electronically. Any message to and from federal agencies would flow through one Customs system, ACS.

But each agency performed its trade inspection or data collection mission using different organizational logics, its own set of routines for inspections and risk analysis. For example, the FDA, with responsibility for health and safety standards, wanted to perform its own inspections. Moreover, it did not want to receive information through the Customs Service's information system, filtered by Customs programs. Because the FDA wanted its own system businesses had to file with two government systems.

Other agencies had reason for concern. Customs had a reputation for sacrificing other agencies' interests at the ports when they conflicted with Customs priorities to collect revenues and clear cargoes at low cost to the Customs Service. Complained one U.S. representative: "When safeguards required by other agencies, pursuant to their statutory responsibilities, conflict with the highly questionable policy of the Customs Service to cut personnel while expediting the entry of goods into this country, those safeguards are removed."[28] Among the offending past practices, for example, the Environmental Protection Agency accused Customs of delaying the issuance of port directives that would have subjected imported chemicals to the same controls as U.S. chemicals, a directive that meant more work for Customs inspectors and slower clearance of goods. The FDA furiously accused Customs of directing its field offices that an FDA "notice of sampling"—an announcement of FDA's intention to sample an import—was insufficient reason not to clear cargo.

Meanwhile, domestic producers and drug control advocates pressed for more and tougher inspections. In the late 1980s, Congress took frequent testimony that Customs staffs were severely shorthanded, as one

General Accounting Office (GAO) investigator explained to a House committee:

> There's a huge facility called the Miami Free Zone near the Miami airport. The whole thing has two or three Customs people in this little office where the phone is ringing constantly. The day we visited them, they were almost in tears. The vaunted computer system was down most of the time, and when it wasn't, it was almost worthless because the categories of cargo that it identifies for inspection are obvious anyway and too broad: "Goods from Taiwan." They have not the slightest idea what goes in and out of that place, nor do they have the ability to do any kind of auditing of that place. It's wide open.[29]

ACS fell under increasing scrutiny from government and industry watchdogs.[30] The GAO and the trade both noticed that ACS had quietly fallen behind on its implementation schedule; delays on the delivery of promised modules and new functions raised the first questions about the ability of Customs to develop an integrated system. GAO noted, in addition, that Customs had rolled out ACS so quickly that it had failed to plan for or publish the documentation required to update and modify the system. Industry officials complained to Congress that because the system was developed rapidly it required constant reprogramming and manual systems to back it up. "ACS has changed almost daily, without testing and certainly without informing the users," congressional subcommittee staff reported.[31] Customs, meanwhile, was charting a course for the 1990s. In 1988 Customs released the results of a study by the consulting firm McKinsey & Company to define the Customs Service's role in the future of global commerce. The McKinsey report urged von Raab to eliminate the paper backup of manifest and entry forms, as required by law, and to migrate to ANSI X12, the electronic data interchange (EDI) syntax that many American corporations had adopted. As a result of the report, Von Raab committed Customs to migrating to EDIFACT, an international syntax that was unfamiliar to most American producers, and to modifying ACS accordingly. EDIFACT offered tremendous global advantages over the American standard, von Raab argued, and represented an "opportunity for the world's customs organizations to interact with the trading community and with each other in a more efficient and less disruptive fashion through computer-to-computer communication."[32]

A second implication of the McKinsey report recommendations was the standardization of trade-related data across business and government, a completely new concept. The government had always used trade data that were different from the commercial information generated in the course of international trade. The translation from commercial to government data naturally led to inaccuracies. The shift to a commercial data standard and an international electronic data exchange standard was a remarkable rationalization of the international trade processing system.

Von Raab left government at the end of 1989. In 1991, U.S. Representative Philip Crane (R-Ill.) introduced the Customs Modernization Act (H.R. 2589), the first major revision of the Tariff Act since 1978. The "Mod Act," as it became known, gave the Customs Service authority to use electronic processing for all its transactions, eliminating requirements for paper documentation of manifests and entries. The Mod Act provided the legal institutional framework for a digital international trade environment.

Harmonizing Trade in North America

In 1992 the United States, Canada, and Mexico signed the North American Free Trade Agreement (NAFTA), which opened the continent's borders for trade, establishing the largest free-trade zone in the world.[33] In signing NAFTA, the three nations agreed to "exchange statistics on international trade, harmonize documentation used in trade, standardize data elements, and accept an international syntax for the exchange of information" (Article 512). Work soon began to standardize these trade processes and test them in the design and operation of the North American Trade Automation Prototype.

In the midst of changing international agreements, the growing digitization and globalization of trade—in short, fundamental shifts in the environment of the Customs Service—the service continued in incremental fashion to develop the Automated Customs System. As trade barriers fell, could the Custom Service's automation effort keep pace with even faster growth in imports and the increasingly complex demands of global trade? Could its strategy, systems, and performance make good on the promise of both speed and quality—hastening the pace of goods through ports by reducing the number of shipments that required inspections, while also detecting and deterring illegal shipments that violated import quotas and other trade laws? Could Customs integrate other federal agencies' requirements into its border control mission without slowing trade? Could it develop the systems it required and at the same time satisfy skeptics, earn government and trade support for new investments, and pave the way for seamless, paperless trade in the global economy?

FACET: The Future Automated Commercial Environment Team

At the end of the 1980s, as the Customs Service's aging information system, ACS, began to fall behind more advanced technologies, Deputy Commissioner of Customs Michael Lane convened an internal task force, the Future Automated Commercial Environment Team (FACET), to examine the state of business practice, automation, and government and to make recommendations for modernizing the system. In part echoing past recommendations from external consultants, and in part responding to an internationalized trade administration regime, the FACET report included three operational recommendations: first, that original commercial information be used as the basis for government processing; second, that imports and exports be processed within the same system, using standard data and, where possible, the same application processes; and third, that trade data be shared across relevant government agencies. In other words, the report called for integrated government oversight.

The Customs Service's response to the recommendations was tepid at best. Some executives and program managers, particularly within the operations and information resource management groups, maintained that, for purposes of collecting tariffs and duties, the tariff number, a Customs classification, was adequate. Customs felt that it was unnecessary to collect original commercial information for each transaction before or at the time of the transaction. But FACET members, some of whom had decades of field experience as inspectors and examiners, knew that although the tariff number was used in the automated system, ACS, customs agents used the commercial invoice to determine tariffs. The practice used by agents was to check invoices against the cargo to determine whether the two corresponded.

Traditionally, tracking exports had not been part of the mission of the Customs Service. The United States had not monitored exports carefully because it had always been the world's largest exporting country and routinely had a positive balance of trade (more exports than imports). Although the trading environment had changed significantly since the 1970s and the consumer appetite for foreign goods had quickly changed the country from the world's leading creditor nation to the world's largest debtor nation, a U.S. capacity to monitor exports accurately had not been put into place. This inaccuracy affects exchange rates and balance of trade. Shortly after the release of the FACET recommendations, the Customs Service, working with the U.S. Census Bureau, began to design a new information system, the Automated Export System (AES). However, they ignored the recommendation to make the import and export systems compatible and thus made the transition to an integrated North American trade administration process much more difficult.

One of the central conceptual changes, integrating government oversight of trade, related both to the potential efficiency gains of cross-agency integration and to the growing realization that, as one government official put it, "an international trade transaction is not any one thing. Obviously you have to clear the goods, but you also have to clear the conveyance and you have to clear the person. Now any system that is designed to only do one of those functions is not doing the job properly."

The Customs Service "officially accepted" but in practice rejected and ignored the recommendations of the FACET report and began to develop the next version of its overburdened information system. Only incrementally different from ACS, the Automated Commercial Environment (ACE) was premised on the same theory of trade administration that Customs had held for many decades.

NAFTA and the Internationalization of Customs

At the beginning of the 1990s, Commissioner Carol Hallett formed several working groups to prepare for the implementation of NAFTA through the Customs Office of International Affairs. The chief implementation task involved Article 512, which required the customs administrations of the United States, Mexico, and Canada to standardize, harmonize, and implement processing procedures and to provide an institutional, organizational, and technical infrastructure to support the free-trade agreement. Commissioner Hallett also formed an international working group among the NAFTA countries to advance international standardization efforts. The group, the Heads of Customs Conference, quickly designated several trilateral working groups to take responsibility for issues under Article 512. The Trilateral Coordinating Committee managed the working groups and helped prepare policy. Another of the working groups, Automation and Information Exchange, was supported by the Intradex Office, a U.S. Customs automation group.

Many members of the Intradex Office were also members of FACET, set up to explore how Customs might modernize its aging automated system for trade administration. With overlapping membership, it is not surprising that the recommendations to the Trilateral Coordinating Committee of the NAFTA countries were similar to the recommendations in the FACET report. The legal requirement for standardization under Article 512 logically and technologically led to many of the same outcomes arrived at independently by FACET in its exploration of trade administration in an increasingly automated global trading environment. FACET and the Information Exchange Automation Working Group produced the same three recommendations.

With these recommendations in hand and already developed within U.S. Customs, although not without disagreement, the heads of Customs eventually adopted them. Working groups in the NAFTA countries began working together in December 1992 at their initial meeting in Ottawa. Several subcommittees were formed, with participation from members of the trade community: operations and procedures (responsible for the data elements), technology, border modifications, systems architecture, trade software package design, statistical needs, cost benefit, and financial. The subcommittees were jointly governed and worked in consultation with the trade community. A trilateral report, whose details had been developed and negotiated from 1992 to 1994, was written and then finalized during 1994 and 1995 detailing how the trade data requirements and trade administration border processes in North America would be harmonized and standardized. The three countries reviewed, edited, and agreed to the final trilateral report, which was issued in June 1995. But from 1992 onward the Trilateral Coordinating Committee worked at odds with the U.S. Customs project to develop the next-generation ACE. The FACET group, now joined together in a separate office, called Intradex, and later ITDS, was following a vision of international trade data processing that would electronically join trade agencies within the U.S. government and then among the other nations with whom the United States trades.

The North American Trade Automation Prototype

The working groups of the NAFTA signatories agreed to design and test a prototype system, called the North American Trade Automation Prototype (NATAP). Its purpose would be to test the concept of a seamless, digital, integrated, pre-arrival processing system and many of the critical technologies and processes that would be required. Shortly after Carol Hallett stepped down as commissioner of U.S. Customs, the new commissioner, George Weise, approved the plan to develop a prototype.

Article 512 of NAFTA and international pressure to harmonize trade data and processes made it difficult for U.S. Customs to disapprove the trilateral recommendations. It was thought that harmonization and more advanced use of technologies could be explored as part of the long-range planning by the Customs Service.

The trilateral working groups constructed the prototype to test the concepts of operation as well as the technologies that would be used in an international trade data system. The intent was to determine whether a system of this type was feasible and whether it could become operational. Although Mexico rapidly decided that the NATAP system would become its automated trade system, the United States and Canada planned only to test the concept. The objective would not be to construct a working system. Rather, a project staff member explained: "It was a prototype . . . it's like the car that you see at the auto show. I can drive it around the showroom floor, but I can't drive on the beltway at 75 miles an hour. It's not designed to do that, and NATAP really wasn't." A prototype made sense for several reasons. During one of the five large public meetings held by the trilateral working groups with the trade community, business leaders asked for a prototype so that the software could be tested before the government required businesses to adjust their trade systems. The benefits were clear, but a prototype would require that the legal systems for trade data processing continue to operate in parallel during the prototype development process. Thus participating firms would have to use two different trade processing systems in order to participate in the test of NATAP.

During the early 1990s the aging Customs information system, ACS, collected trade data for 95 percent of U.S. import transactions.[34] Using this automated system, Customs had developed information sharing capabilities with agencies including the Internal Revenue Service, the Food and Drug Administration, the Department of Transportation, and the Fish and Wildlife Service. By 1993 Customs was in the process of developing information exchange capacity with the Bureau of Alcohol, Tobacco, and Firearms; the Food Safety Inspection Service; and the Environmental Protection Agency.[35] As the central computer system for initial collection, processing, and dissemination of trade data, ACS was used by brokers and importers. The trade community had increased its use of ACS from 8 percent of all data entered into the system in 1984 to 93 percent in 1993. Customs estimated that 1,324 brokers and importers used the system in 1993 for the release of cargo, duty payments, and updating data. During this period, more than 350 million requests for information and 600,000 transactions daily were processed.[36] With the trade community using ACS and with the competing demands on Customs intensifying even more acutely in the 1990s than in the decade before, the leadership of Customs decided to move forward with the Automated Commercial Environment (ACE) project by developing the system incrementally rather than adopting a revolutionary, transformative approach to international trade.

ACE differed conceptually from NATAP in three respects. First, ACE was designed as a single-agency Customs information system. No provision for integrated trade oversight was made. Second, in keeping with the core mission of the Customs Service, ACE was designed to process goods imported into the United States. The system ignored the NAFTA mandate to standardize data and processes across North America in order to create a seamless border process for three countries. A seamless system would, of necessity, process imports and exports similarly because, for example, goods imported into the United States from Canada are processed as exports by the Canadian government. A unified system would allow two countries to use the same standards, data, and procedures. Finally, ACE was not designed to completely eliminate paper processing at the borders. As an incremental step forward from the older ACS environment, it represented little conceptual modernization. For these reasons, both philosophically and technologically the two efforts continued to diverge from each other.

Reinventing International Trade

In 1993 when Vice President Gore launched the National Performance Review it was heralded as a major government reform effort to build a government that works better and costs less. During the spring of 1993, on the assumption that important ideas for improving government are likely to be found within the operating ranks of agencies, the NPR invited agencies to submit proposals for reinventing government to their government departments for review; each department then forwarded its best proposals to the White House. The FACET report was an official submission from the Customs Service to the Treasury Department. The Treasury Department reviewed it among several proposals submitted by the Customs Service and selected it, as one FACET member recalled, as "one of the more mega-projects, the wider-ranging projects." According to one author of the FACET report:

> At the time that [the FACET report] was first done and first written and proposed, it hadn't sunk in yet what it meant. . . . And there was

a group of philosophers and thinkers in Customs at that time that believed that this was at least an idea which should be investigated. And so long as it's studied, it was not much of a threat. It made it through the process of being proposed.

Reinvention teams were enthusiastic about the proposal to transform international trade. The project promised to better serve "the customer," defined as the trade community, with more efficient, streamlined processing. It used information technology to reduce waste, redundancy, and overlap in the federal bureaucracy. The project fit the rhetoric and goals of the National Performance Review and played well in the press as a major breakthrough in the modernization of the government.

The vice president ordered that all the NPR initiatives move forward immediately. Listed as IT06, the project was rechristened the International Trade Data System. It became one of thirteen information technology initiatives of the National Performance Review. In June 1993 the Office of the Vice President issued a report that identified international trade as one of seven key policy areas in which information technology should be used to modernize government.[37] The original recommendation to establish ITDS clearly stated its rationale:

> Existing agency databases and computer systems are limited in their ability to integrate and disseminate trade data since none were designed to support such a broad community of interest. For example, limitations to ACS include difficulty in retrieving information, costly hardware expansion, and 10-year-old software programs that are difficult and expensive to maintain. Customs has established a Future Automated Commercial Environment Team (FACET) to address these shortcomings and chart a course for a future system.[38]

Its multiple identities brought visibility. As one of the architects of the idea put it: "We decided that . . . we would do NATAP as a proof of concept for the same ideas expressed in the FACET report which are expressed in the ITDS concept of operations." Several members of FACET became the ITDS group. The same prototype, NATAP, served as a proof of concept and technologies for both the NPR initiative and the implementation of Article 512 of NAFTA. Scrutiny of and support for an integrated international trade data system came from international actors, from meetings with the trade communities and governments of Canada and Mexico, and from the NPR initiative in the White House.

Understanding the need to move quickly and decisively, the NPR directed the secretary of the Treasury to begin developing the International Trade Data System by April 1994. The Treasury Department was to seek technical support from the International Trade Commission, the U.S. Trade Representative, and the Departments of Commerce, State, Agriculture, and Labor. Treasury was to complete an implementation plan by January 1995 and submit it to the Government Information Technology Services Working Group for approval.[39]

As evidence of the cross-cutting nature of international trade policy and administration, fifty-three agencies participated in the task force that created the detailed plans for ITDS. All committee members served on a voluntary basis. The FACET report, an internal Customs document, was revised and issued during the summer of 1995 as a National Performance Review document, "Concepts and Recommendations for an International Trade Data System." The initial common statement defining the goals of ITDS provided a compact focusing device for the large task group:

> The U.S. Government in concert with the international trade community will develop and implement an integrated systems approach for the collection, use, and dissemination of international trade data. This effort will provide a vastly improved service to U.S. businesses, increase U.S. competitiveness, reduce Government burden, and coordinate and streamline Government operations. . . . Agencies will cooperate to: establish standard international trade data requirements; eliminate collection, processing, and reporting inefficiencies; provide more accurate and timely information for trade analysis; and more effectively disseminate international trade data for both Government and private sector purposes. . . . Through cooperative Government and international trade community efforts to eliminate redundancies, streamline processing, and share information, the U.S. Government and the private sector will achieve a significant step toward a "Government that works better and costs less."[40]

As the implications of an integrated trade oversight system became clearer, support from Customs for the interagency NPR initiative plummeted. Customs recognized the futility of attempts to control a governmentwide international trade data system. But ITDS had the attention of the White House and the wider trade community.

Departure from Customs

The philosophical and professional differences became untenable between those at Customs who advocated an incremental, agency-centered approach to trade processing modernization and those who had developed a fundamentally different perspective on the role of Customs in an international, networked trading environment. As it became clear that the concept of a cross-agency trade data system was now a serious consideration, and that Customs could not effectively dampen or control the architects of that concept, the schism between the two Customs groups became serious. Customs made it clear that it would not support ITDS as it was conceived under the National Performance Review. But as one ITDS project staff member recalled: "As we heard more and more about the go-it-alone ACE approach . . . it became more and more unacceptable. . . . If you'd worked on this thing and done eighteen months of real hard analysis and come to these conclusions called FACET, there was no turning back for us. And so several people just stepped out of the mold and separated ourselves from them."

In September 1995, Vice President Gore signed a memo to remove the ITDS project from the purview of the Customs Service and detailed the project to the Treasury Department. The budget for the ITDS project was set at $5.4 million per year for three years with a sunset provision. Vice President Gore appointed an interagency board of directors to govern the project and a senior executive from the Treasury Department to chair it. The board of directors was authorized by the vice president to implement the ITDS initiative according to the recommendations of the IT06 Task Force. The ITDS project office would be responsible for implementing ITDS. One of the key recommendations of the task force that first proposed the creation of ITDS was the appointment of an interagency board of directors with the authority to "recommend and, if necessary, direct individual agencies to modify their processes and systems to conform with the principles for an integrated International Trade Data System." Further, the task force report warned that vesting the authority to make multiagency decisions would be the only way to ensure the cross-agency reengineering required to develop ITDS.[41] It was clear to members of the task force that an interagency governance structure with authority to direct, rather than simply to advise, was critical to sustain the momentum of such a large, cross-agency project.

The next chapter details the development of the prototype process, the standardization required for agencies to integrate under one "front-end" information system, and the political struggles of public managers puzzling about new forms of policymaking, information processing, and power.

The development of the International Trade Data System explores not only the potential of the Internet to transform institutionalized policy domains but also the circuitous, highly mediated route that that transformation will have to follow. This case also provides insight into the potential for the governance of interagency efforts by an interagency board of directors, an intermediate layer above agencies but below other oversight bodies, the White House, and Congress. It raises questions regarding the authority such bodies would need, their accountability, and the changing nature of jurisdiction as interagency networks increase in importance and begin to formalize their activities beyond temporary projects for which informal mechanisms of governance and conflict resolution typically suffice.

CHAPTER EIGHT

Enacting
the ITDS

ALTHOUGH NOW INDEPENDENTLY managed, the North American Trade Automation Prototype (NATAP) could only be demonstrated effectively at ports of entry with the cooperation of Customs personnel, who would need to execute NATAP and the traditional process.[1] Before the project was separated from Customs, the International Trade Data System (ITDS) staff had secured agreements and commitments from six ports of entry managed by Customs. Port directors, all Customs executives, had promised time, equipment, and field personnel in order to conduct limited experimentation at their ports with the technologies, software, and processes of NATAP. The border crossings selected were Otay Mesa, California; Laredo, Texas; Nogales, Arizona; Buffalo, New York; and Detroit, Michigan. Staff at ITDS chose several ports of entry because each port was organized and managed differently according to local circumstances, leadership, and history. An integrated system would have to work equally well at all ports of entry.

Several complex tasks had to be accomplished during the prototype period. Among the many challenges, negotiations with transportation and immigration authorities are detailed here for the insights they provide into the efforts required to develop interagency standardization and coordination. A series of apparently technical challenges in software and hardware design carried significant political and institutional implications. Although many of the details of these challenges lie beyond the scope of this case analysis, the number and complexity of networks and institutionalized practices affected by NATAP made the task of enacting digital, networked governance on the scale and at the structural depth envisioned by ITDS a difficult one.[2]

At a minimum, the logic of a seamless border for trade in North America, as envisioned in NAFTA, required the standardization of data definitions, practices, and information systems both within and across the three member countries in three policy domains: customs, transportation, and immigration. Before the prototype was launched, there was very little cross-border contact by transportation or immigration inspection regimes. Indeed, an arm's-length relationship was preferred and perceived as appropriate. The NATAP working groups forced a dialogue among the transportation and immigration administrations in North America. Without such negotiation, a seamless border could not be implemented.

Under NAFTA, trade agencies were required by law to begin adopting a networked approach to trade. Civil servants in enforcement roles found the new internationalist stance particularly difficult given their culture and professionalization. In contrast, the ITDS perspective, to quote one staff member, was strongly international: "When you're in this together, you're in this as a NAFTA country. You should be working towards the same mutual goals, better imports and expediting trade. And you can't do that on your own because remember, if you have the swiftest, fastest Customs system coming into the country, but if Mexico slows down their export system, what good is it? There's a backup."[3]

Interagency Integration

In addition to Customs, the agencies that required international coordination included the U.S. Department of Transportation (DOT), the Federal Highway Administration, and the Immigration and Naturalization Service. These agencies—responsible for cargo, vehicles, and drivers, respectively—became increasingly engaged in the core of the developing network of trade administration.

Standardizing Transportation Practices

In spite of NAFTA, advances in automation, and a marked increase in the volume of cross-border trade, deep institutionalized differences persisted between the vision of NAFTA held by some government actors and the values and practices of many agencies.

In the early 1990s when NATAP working groups began discussions with transportation authorities, the major issue centered on the use, standardization, and compatibility of transponder technologies to be used in North America. The objective was to allow trucks, their drivers, and cargo to be "read" electronically as they arrived and departed in the United States, Mexico, and Canada. Although standardization of this type is increasingly commonplace, at the time transponder technologies were not widely used and few standards existed. Moreover, the three policy domains lacked coordination at the borders. According to an ITDS project staff member: "The Customs officers at this point do nothing whatsoever to transportation. They don't know if the truck is safe. They don't know if the driver has a DWI [drunk driving record]. They have no idea about that. So that is a function that was completely ignored in the current environment."

A subset of the NATAP implementation team, having virtually no expertise in transportation technologies, quickly delegated the issue of transponders to the department and ministries of transportation. In retrospect, noted an ITDS staff member:

> That was a mistake. . . . We assumed that the transportation officials would have enough expertise to arrive at an interactive, flexible solution to the transportation piece. That didn't happen. We also thought they'd have the money to do it. Which they did have. So one of the reasons we went to the Department of Transportation was that they were doing various studies in land borders anyway about employing this type of technology. But they were doing it alone. . . . [For the purposes of NATAP] it would be completely inefficient.

The NATAP team quickly learned the institutional differences between ITDS and the Department of Transportation. The federal transportation authorities award money to the states and allow each state to administer federal programs within broad guidelines. California might administer transportation programs differently from Arizona, for example, tailoring its programs and spending to local conditions. Under the Intermodal Surface Transportation Efficiency Act, DOT was interested in experimenting with transponders and, more broadly, electronic technologies. Technology promised to improve the transportation of goods into the United States by relieving congestion at the ports of entry.

Officials from DOT had already begun to work with local Customs authorities, each of which organized its port of entry in a different way. As DOT experts envisioned the future, transportation technologies would have been adopted to fit each local setting. But the local, decentralized approach that characterizes DOT worked at odds with an integrated approach to border processing for North America. An ITDS staff member from the Customs Service explained:

> Trucks do now go from Laredo to Detroit. . . . And if you have a methodology to use in Laredo, and that methodology is incompatible with what you're doing in Detroit, well then, what the hell are you doing it for?
>
> . . . One of our inspectors . . . is really the one who brought this to a screeching halt because they brought him in as a Customs opinion regarding the experimentations to be going on in Buffalo for transponder technologies. He happened to be a field representative to the FACET group, so he knew what was going on in Washington. And he said, "I'm not making a decision here. You have got to really bring a national perspective into this whole thing of transponder technologies. You can't have Laredo doing something different from Buffalo doing something different from Detroit. Because these are the same trucks crossing the border."

In order to bring coherence to the transportation technologies that are fundamental to the international trade data system, the working groups for NATAP became one of the approval authorities for transponder contracts that were being negotiated in Buffalo and Detroit. The ITDS staff were able to amend contradictory contracts for technologies that were to be deployed in Otay Mesa, California, and in Nogales, Arizona.

U.S. transportation authorities had little interest in negotiating standards and practices that would create a cohesive, interoperable North American transportation system. The Department of Transportation had decided to pursue different strategic policy objectives on the northern and southern borders. A uniform strategy did not follow from their history, culture, relationships with state governments, or their decentralized approach to transportation policy.

In order to preserve coherence at all the ports of entry that would be part of the pilot, the ITDS Project Office acted as the catalyst and broker for a difficult negotiation involving the Canadian government, local governments in Buffalo and Detroit, the New York and Michigan State

Departments of Transportation, the Peace Bridge (between Buffalo, New York, and Fort Erie, Ontario), the Ambassador Bridge (between Detroit and Windsor, Ontario), the Ontario Ministry of Transport, U.S. Immigration, and Canadian Immigration. The group negotiated with two major suppliers of transponders to ensure interoperability with the transponder technologies that had already been negotiated for the U.S.-Mexican border. After protracted negotiation, the entire group had to vote on the contract award. An objection raised by one member meant that the negotiations had to begin again.

Unfortunately, the need for negotiations with transportation authorities became clear only after the trade community and ports of entry had been signed up to participate in NATAP. A delay of more than a year ensued while the transportation technologies to be used as part of the prototype process were agreed upon. This delay cost ITDS valuable time and support. A project architect lamented:

> We went out to the public with NATAP, and said, 'Come on, let's do NATAP.' And then we hit this snag with . . . that transponder technology. That just slowed the whole process down, it took us over a year, a year's delay. . . . We were piquing interest in the public, and we couldn't do it for a year. And the interest went right down, and we weren't able to generate it back to where it was.

Strengthening Network Ties with Immigration through Technology

An international trade database implies that there should be a standardized way to identify drivers. But commercial drivers' licenses are state-controlled. Truck drivers typically do not carry passports. A standardized system required being able to check the status of drivers through the computer systems of all three countries to determine whether the driver should be allowed to cross international borders.

The U.S. Immigration and Naturalization Service had its own initiatives in play to respond to increases in cross-border movement after the implementation of NAFTA. As part of the trilateral dialogue built by Customs Commissioner Hallett, the Information Exchange and Automation working group arranged to bring together immigration authorities from all three countries for a discussion of how to adapt to a changing business environment. One of the lead staffers during the trilateral meetings recalled:

> [We] would pool our immigration folks together and make them sit down at the table and start discussing how they're going to accomplish this electronically . . . And that took place in Mexico City, and it was wonderful because they'd never done it before. . . . The results were a standard application form for a person to fill out . . . in order to obtain a driver registration number, and the sharing of that information so that each country would be able to make its own determination as to the admissibility of that person into the country.

The standard application form was approved for use in the prototype. Variations among countries were allowed, although the basic application was standardized. During the prototype process, immigration authorities in North America also developed a photo register, which allows border inspectors to view a picture of the driver when a truck arrives at the entry point. For the first time, inspectors would be able to verify a driver's identity by comparing a visual image on a computer screen with a driver. Customs inspections at the land border are "cross-designated," meaning that, for commercial transactions, Customs officers can perform both Customs and immigration inspections. But the primary interest of Customs officers is determining the requirements for Customs fees rather than immigration inspections:

> Most of us in America don't realize this. . . . One of the biggest single holes, the illegal entry to this country, is through the commercial lines because there's virtually no immigration treatment of the driver. And we don't know whether this guy's a [legitimate truck driver] or who he is. . . . All the time is spent on the cargo stuff. . . . And so ITDS will give [INS] an operational opportunity they'd never have.

Although there were delays and detours, the prototype succeeded. Among the other complications during enactment was encryption, which ensured the privacy of commercial data that would travel over the web from traders to ITDS. In addition, directors at some ports of entry, such as Detroit, refused to cooperate with the prototype team. The auto industry in Detroit had well-developed bilateral arrangements with Customs giving them a dedicated lane at ports of entry and expedited cargo clearance with almost no data required. At the port of entry in Laredo, Texas, the political nature of broker-government relations in Mexico made testing difficult. But the feat of integrating information technologies, trucks, procedures, agencies, and countries in the prototype was demonstrated. Its success illustrated the feasibility of the concept of integrated trade management even as it revealed the immense political and organizational challenges of its full implementation.

> When we had the first experiment where the truck approached the border, the reader picked up the signal from the vehicle. It read the number accurately. It brought it quickly to the computer. The computer pulled up the right record from its massive database and put it on the screen just as the truck arrived. . . . That was just absolute euphoria . . . because the integration of all of these different pieces [Customs, Immigration, and Transportation] that had not been tried ever before in this combination was really leading-edge stuff. And everybody said we couldn't do it. Even our engineers had said we were not going to be able to do this.

Beyond the Prototype: Building Support for an ITDS Pilot

The prototype and its evaluation, completed in 1997, supplied proof of the ITDS concept and evidence of the feasibility of automating many of the processing functions at the border, including inspections of shipments, transportation, and drivers. Continuing ITDS would involve linking trade-related data in a single, standardized database among more than sixty federal agencies and bureaus with responsibilities for trade policy and administration, a challenge of a different magnitude entirely. Following the prototype of the system, ITDS was officially announced at a hearing in Washington, D.C., in November 1998. At that hearing, the trade community expressed its support for the project. James Clawson, secretary of the Joint Industry Group, a consortium of 130 Fortune 500 firms, trade associations, and individuals, and president of JBC International, a trade consulting firm in Washington, testified that "the role of the ITDS in coordinating and integrating all of the U.S. import and export requirements in a single system is important and has the potential to save U.S. traders billions of dollars."[4]

The International Trade Data System, when built, would collect and store standardized trade data from all federal agencies. Moreover, ITDS would provide a single point of entry for all trade data. The commercial data currently submitted to the government in the conduct of business would form the foundation for ITDS. The ITDS project leadership did not envision a new system but modification of agency systems to conform to a new, unified, and consistent set of data standards.

For example, trucks crossing into the United States from Canada over the Peace Bridge at Buffalo, N.Y., and Fort Erie, Ontario, must often wait in long lines because forms required variously by Customs, the Immigration and Naturalization Service, and other agencies are not in order. ITDS would reduce the data and paperwork required by each agency to one format that would serve all agencies. It would enable importers to file all trade-related data, according to John Simpson, the chairman of the ITDS board of directors, "through a single electronic gateway. ITDS would funnel to each government agency the particular information it needs. ITDS will reduce the information collection system for the public and improve the quality of data needed for government statistics."[5]

The ITDS project staff identified approximately thirty core trade data elements needed by the entire federal government and obtained agreement from all relevant agencies to develop standard, uniform data definitions for these elements. ITDS allows firms to file trade administration and enforcement data over the Internet using "highly sophisticated encryption."[6] All government fees charged to a firm would be billed together once a month. To build consensus for the prototype, ITDS decisionmakers decided that if the data elements required for a shipment were for Customs only, meaning that data for other agencies were not required, and Customs did not need all thirty data elements for that shipment, then the trader could file only those elements required by Customs through the ITDS system. In spite of this agreement, importers and brokers feared that a proliferation of data entry and filing requirements would change the scope of their work and increase their costs. But at the beginning of 1999, the future for ITDS seemed promising. The government had estimated the cost of trade in 1997 at $3.2 billion for the entire trade community, including importers, exporters, intermediate-level actors, and carriers.[7] The ITDS Project Office estimated that, given the total cost of the project at $256 million through 2005, the system would save $2 billion over the same time period. Media reports confirmed this optimism. As one report noted: "ITDS officials project the system will need $19.6 million for the fiscal year starting October 1. . . . Advocates of a federal proposal to allow importers, exporters and intermediaries to file all trade documentation through a single, electronic gateway say they have wide support to build the $256 million system."[8]

Competing Enactments

Critics of ITDS argued that modernization of the broader automated system for inspections, ACE, was more important and urgent. The massive information system, ACS, was nearly fifteen years old and arguably at the end of its life. Ironically, as international trade had burgeoned, stressing all aspects of the system, Congress had underfunded its modernization.[9] Congress had suggested that the private sector help fund system modernization through user fees, which would force the trade community to pay for approximately half the costs. This suggestion was fiercely resisted by the private sector. Traders argued that fees had been used in the past and had been channeled to the general fund rather than targeted for improvements in Customs administrative and inspection systems. Moreover, the Canadian government formally criticized the Clinton administration for its proposal to adopt a fee structure.

In a February 1999 report on Customs Service modernization, the General Accounting Office criticized the management and technical elements of ACE, arguing that Customs was constructing ACE in the absence of "a complete and enforced enterprise systems architecture," investing in ACE without thoroughly vetting its cost effectiveness, and "building ACE without using engineering rigor and discipline."[10] The Clinger-Cohen Act, as well as guidance from the Office of Management and Budget (OMB) and the General Accounting Office (GAO) prescribe that agencies first identify and analyze alternative system solutions; second, develop reliable estimates of the costs and benefits of those alternatives and invest in the most cost-effective; and, third, structure major projects incrementally to ensure that each incremental investment is judicious. The GAO argued that Customs followed none of these steps in the planning of ACE.

Specifically, GAO charged, Customs had not evaluated the relationship between ACE and ITDS,

> including considering the extent to which ITDS should be used to satisfy needed import processing functionality. . . . The [ITDS] system is expected to reduce the burden federal agencies place on organizations by requiring that they respond to duplicative data requests. Treasury intends for the system to serve as the single point for collecting, editing, and validating trade data as well as collecting and accounting for trade revenue. At the time of our review of ACE, these functions were also planned for ACE.[11]

In response to this strong criticism, Customs Commissioner Raymond Kelly agreed with the GAO findings and resolved to implement GAO recommendations for improvement. As part of its response to GAO, Customs hired a contractor to strengthen the cost-benefit analysis of ACE "including the use of ITDS as the interface for ACE."[12]

In March 1999, following the announcement of ITDS, the National Customs Brokers and Forwarders Association of America (NCBFAA) met for their annual meeting. As the implications of ITDS became clearer to intermediate actors in the international trade industry, opposition to a networked, distributed approach grew: "Importers and exporters have feared that by speeding the flow of information to those many agencies, the system will give the agencies more excuses to stop goods at the border. Mr. Simpson, in essence, confirmed those fears."[13]

Several actors in the trade industry made it clear that they lacked a clear cost-benefit analysis of the consequences of an interagency regime for international trade. Customs brokers, historically the key intermediaries between import/export firms and the government—and thus the stakeholders with potentially the most to lose from a disintermediated, digital system—raised concerns about the confidentiality of their data on the Internet and the potential of an integrated trade management system to generate added costs and additional requirements. Brokers and forwarders supported ACE because they decided that their closely developed relationships with Customs were more likely to result in fewer, faster, and more targeted inspections for their businesses. The influence they had established with Customs would diminish if more government agencies could review a shared set of data during the federal government processing of their transactions.

John Simpson, chairman of the board of directors of ITDS and a senior Treasury official, reported that ACE and ITDS do not compete for funding because ITDS forms the broader computerized environment of which ACE would be a part. ITDS assumes the existence of ACE.[14] In fact, Simpson argued, ITDS will manage some of the "front-end" functions that ACE would have handled, thus reducing the cost of ACE.

Customs continued to press for funding for ACE during hearings held in the spring of 1999. They argued that ACE would improve and modernize the enforcement of import trade laws and regulations, including the assessment and collection of import taxes, duties, and fees, which totaled $22 billion in fiscal year 1999. The estimate given by Customs for the cost of ACE was approximately $1.05 billion, although the General Accounting Office reported that that amount would be increased. In May 1999, Commissioner Kelly testified again to emphasize that the continuation of sharp increases in international trade and travel additionally stressed the capacity of Customs at the borders. He noted that in 1998 Customs had "processed over 19 million trade entries, close to 2 million more than 1997, and approximately $955 billion dollars' worth of goods. Four hundred and sixty million passengers moved through our inspection areas last year, 13 million more than the prior year."[15]

In spite of the ban on lobbying federal agencies, Customs marshaled strong support from powerful international trade businesses in its battle for appropriations. Its "customers," the recipients of bilateral arrangements for expedited cargo processing under the account management strategy Customs had adopted, testified on behalf of ACE and began to express concerns that the cross-agency system was framed not as a complement to the Customs system but as a competitor. As the international trade community grew more tightly linked in its own emerging Internet-based systems, the need for rapid processing at the border became even more acute.

The president of the Joint Industry Group (JIG), one of the most powerful trade associations, who was also a representative of Caterpillar, Inc., described in his testimony to Congress the increasing time constraints on trade processing and the potential impact of a nonfunctioning automated Customs processing system:

> For Caterpillar . . . a one-day shut down of ACS will cause disruptions. A prolonged ACS blackout of more than a day or two would halt production lines and cause serious delays in shipping needed replacement parts to our customers. An inactive assembly line is a scenario that will face many of JIG's manufacturing company members. General Motors, DaimlerChrysler, and Ford Motor Company will be forced to shut down production lines at a much earlier date than Caterpillar because of their high-volume just-in-time delivery procedures. In fact, miles of idling trucks strung across the Texas, California, New York, and Michigan borders is certain to occur during a major shut down of ACS.[16]

The Air Courier Conference of America (ACCA), a trade association that represents the air express delivery industry, includes members such as Federal Express, United Parcel Service, DHL, Worldwide Express, and other large firms with international delivery networks. The interest group also includes smaller firms with regional delivery networks such as Midnite

Express and Global Mail. Various measures of the size and scope of this trade association help to convey the magnitude of global trade and its implications for American businesses. ACCA members employ approximately 510,000 American workers and more than 800,000 people outside the United States, operate in at least 200 countries, ship more than 25 million packages daily, and generate revenues of more than $50 billion per year. James Rogers, president of ACCA, testified in May 1999 in support of modernizing the Customs Service's automated systems:

> The express transportation industry specializes in time-sensitive, reliable transportation services for documents, packages and freight. We are a relatively new and rapidly expanding industry, having evolved during the past 25 years in response to the needs of global international commerce. Express delivery has grown increasingly important to businesses needing to use "just-in-time" manufacturing techniques and supply-chain logistics in order to remain internationally competitive.
>
> The express industry has revolutionized the way companies do business worldwide and has given a broad-based application to the just-in-time concept. Producers using supplies from overseas no longer need to maintain costly inventories, nor do business persons need to wait extended period of time for important documents. In addition, consumers now have the option of receiving international shipments on an expedited basis. Increased reliance on express shipments has propelled the industry to average annual growth rates of 20 percent for the past two decades.[17]

The testimony reveals the tight interconnection that is growing between international trade data management and rapid, international, web-based supply chain management:

> [The] Customs administration play[s] a critical role in ensuring expeditious movement of goods across borders and consequently [is] critical to our industry's ability to deliver express international service. To give you a sense of the size of our industry in U.S. trade—and as a customer of U.S. Customs—the express industry accounts for roughly 25 percent of all Customs formal and informal entries. In addition, express operators enter more than 10 million other manifest entries on low-value shipments, plus millions of clearances on letters and documents. In short, American business is dependent upon

our industry, and we are dependent upon an efficient and effective Customs service.[18]

As the conflict between ITDS and Customs became increasingly public in 1999, the uncertainties of a new, relatively untested concept, ITDS, and the lack of strong constituents for the new project turned the tide of support against cross-agency trade reform. The benefits of streamlined, digital trade processing through ITDS as the front end for trade agency systems could not offset the creeping realization—emphasized by Customs in its close contacts with constituents in the industry—that superior, faster data collection for other agencies would provide them with the capacity to fulfill their legal mandates and thus potentially to conduct more inspections.

Uppermost in the interests of the trade community were the costs of compliance. In other testimony, the costs of the system were raised:

> With respect to the International Trade Data System (ITDS), ACCA supports the general objectives and theory underlying ITDS, i.e., elimination of redundancy in government reporting requirements related to trade, confusion in data requirements, and incompatible data exchange methods. However, we have numerous concerns about the practical implementation of such objectives—for example, with respect to potential delay in express operations and burden on the industry in collecting all the ITDS required data elements.
>
> We have held several meetings with the ITDS team to discuss these issues and plan to continue this process. ACCA is especially concerned with the apparent lack of coordination between Treasury's work on ITDS and Customs' development of its next-generation automation systems.

Industry representatives also raised the specter of the potential for proliferation of competing technological systems and their cost to business:

> One noteworthy aspect of this applies to exports. The existing automation program for reporting exports—the Automated Export Reporting Program, or AERP—expires this December 31. Customs has announced that it will be replaced by the Automated Export System, or AES. The trade community is now being asked to bear the costs of reprogramming commercial systems for AES, at considerable expense. At the same time, the ITDS team is informing the trade community that it could be required to reprogram its systems once again

to accommodate the ITDS-based export reporting program as early as 2002.

Both U.S. Customs and ITDS officials privately acknowledge that this redundant reprogramming would be a waste of private sector resources, yet they also indicate that, because Customs and ITDS are unable to agree on an appropriate joint approach, they fully expect that industry will face this double reprogramming expense. ACCA urges the Trade Subcommittee to exercise its oversight authority to prevent the U.S. government from imposing this needless cost on U.S. industry simply because of the government's inability to work with itself.[19]

Testimony before Congress during this period also made it clear that the business community was growing increasingly concerned about the aging Customs system. Weekly warnings from Customs about system overloads and several notable interruptions of ACS processing frightened the trade community and increased the probability that system failures could shut down retail and manufacturing supply chains.[20] Several trade association representatives were cautious about the additional requirements for data that an integrated system might generate, as well as delays that might occur in trade processing if Customs and ITDS could not agree on procedure and jurisdiction:

[The Joint Industry Group] supports the concept of a front-end interface to serve as a single data collection point between government and industry. We support the Treasury Department's mission to reduce the amount of data required by the government prior to importation. However, as we have come to understand the design and enforcement nature of the Treasury ITDS system we are concerned with its true role in the clearance process. Therefore, at this point JIG cannot support the proposed ITDS system. We do agree that a front-end element is necessary for ACE, but the ITDS proposed to us today is not the solution.[21]

Business has been negotiating with trade agencies to adopt new risk management methods to reduce inspection of shipments from "low-risk, highly compliant importers."[22] An interagency risk management system changes the nature of these negotiations because the criteria that trigger inspection differ from agency to agency. Some agencies, such as Customs, are viewed as responsive to the needs of the business community for rapid processing of shipments. However, other agencies, such as the Food and Drug Administration, view citizens as their "customers" and are considered less responsive to business concerns.[23]

Finally, the competence of the ITDS board of directors to carry out the project came under attack. Some intermediaries in the trade community questioned the experience of the members of the interagency board to handle international trade data processing, "an area long dominated by Customs and the Census Bureau."[24] Thus powerful interests, categorized euphemistically as the "customer," increased the intensity of their support for state capacity structured bilaterally through "corporate accounts" or bilateral agreements with specific large firms or powerful industries. A governmentwide, robust, and equitable regulatory regime for international trade serves broader, but unorganized, interests.

A Return to Tradition

In September 1999, John Simpson, deputy assistant secretary of the Treasury, Office of Regulations and Trade Enforcement, and chair of the ITDS board of directors, abruptly resigned from the board after a Treasury Department announcement that the development of ITDS would shift from the ITDS Project Office to Customs on October 1, 2000. The Customs Service and representatives of the major trade associations supported the decision. Simpson reported: "The burden will be on Customs to look beyond its own interests and develop ITDS so that the needs of all government agencies are addressed. Customs will have to be bigger than it was in the past. The key is, does Customs have the maturity and comprehensiveness of vision to do this?" One journalist referred to the development as "a return to tradition."[25]

As the ITDS board prepared to launch the operational pilot projects to test the new system, the assistant secretary of the Treasury for management recommended several changes to the ITDS project. Responsibility for ITDS would be transferred, effective immediately, from the ITDS interagency board of directors to the Customs Service. The board of directors would become an advisory committee to Customs and the ITDS project office would return to the Customs Service where it had begun. Customs would define the architecture for trade data systems and would henceforth design, develop, and implement ITDS. Further, ITDS was to become part of the Automated Customs Environment, the ACE system.

At the end of the twentieth century, during the final months of 1999, it was not clear what role the interagency board would be allowed to play in the development of ITDS. ITDS had been funded for fiscal year 2000, but Customs had yet to be appropriated funds for ACE. A networked inspection and enforcement regime, one that would be interagency in scope and data-driven, was a threat to key actors in the trade community. One of the key information technology initiatives of the National Partnership for Reinventing Government appeared to have succumbed to the status quo.

Conclusion

In a simple version of networked governance, entrepreneurial political actors would find uses of the Internet that would achieve efficiencies, including uses that require restructuring and reorganization. But even in the private economy the massive failure of thousands of dot-coms and the slowing pace of the Internet revolution reveal that the organizational and interorganizational restructuring necessary to develop information-rich channels for production and distribution is difficult. The efforts in government mirror some recent events in the economy. The use of the Internet for efficiency gains at structural levels deeper than the web interface is difficult, slow, and painstaking political work. The political struggles and negotiation engaged in by the public managers with responsibility for ITDS are emblematic of the types of political challenges involved in using the Internet to build a virtual state. These second-stage activities differ significantly from the easier first-stage development of web portals for the public that involve little integration "behind the screen."

Second, the case described here provides little evidence for technological determinism and strong support for enactment influenced by organizational and institutional arrangements. The Internet is a catalyst and enabler of change. Its potential led to more rapid development of the project than would otherwise have occurred, but the final design, implementation, and use of ITDS will be enacted by public managers and political actors influenced by their institutional setting. At the same time, however, enactment of ITDS will modify institutional arrangements, including the concept of trade data management in government, interagency relations, and reporting to oversight and budgetary authorities.

In retrospect, it is not surprising that Customs could essentially exercise veto power over the project. In the international trade network there is no more powerful actor than the U.S. Customs Service. In this case, the influence of the Customs Service was strengthened by its powerful con-

Table 8-1. National Interests Enforced at the Border

Interest	Issue (Customs jurisdiction noted in parentheses)
Traditional revenue	Duties, taxes, and fees on imported goods (Customs)
Prohibited contraband and transactions	Drugs, narcotics, and controlled substances; child pornography; money laundering; export of stolen vehicles (Customs); fraud
Entry controls	Quotas, dumping (Customs), immigration
Supplemental revenue generation	Additional special taxes and fees
Environmental protection	Insect and pest control, toxic wastes, production inputs and processes, manufacturing emissions, endangered species
Health and safety	Food safety, drug and medical device safety, consumer goods safety, animal disease, plant disease, genetic safety, vehicle safety
Communications systems	Frequency and radio emission controls, radio wave compliance
Labor protection	Children, prisoners
International safety	Antiterrorism, gun controls, arms trafficking, weapons of mass destruction (nuclear, chemical, and biological)
Intellectual property	Patents, trademarks, copyrights

Source: ITDS Project Office, "The International Trade Data System: Transforming International Trade and Enabling Global E-Commerce," 1999.

stituents in business. Large firms strongly favor the preferential treatment they receive from Customs under the "account management" strategy by which large "customers" of Customs are rewarded with faster processing (meaning fewer inspections) at the borders. None of these political relationships were developed for ITDS. This alone would have ensured its demise in the politics of international trade in an era of global supply chain management and just-in-time business processes. ITDS lacked both cognitive and political legitimacy. The iron triangle of Customs, its key congressional committees, and international trade partners in business does not diminish in a networked governance arrangement.

It is clear that the role of Customs relative to that of other agencies is changing at the borders as product safety, food safety, intellectual property, antiterrorism, and other inspection regimes gain in importance (see Table 8-1). Given the present volumes of trade, individual inspections become infeasible as a regulatory mechanism. Data-mining and modeling capacity will have to be developed in Customs as well as in other agencies such as the Food and Drug Administration and the Consumer Product Safety Commission. The implications for the type of information systems that would integrate these modeling and risk management efforts are not yet articulated. But they are more political than technical in nature. The development of the virtual state, although its contours are indeterminate, is also political in nature.

Finally, the case raises questions about the nature of accountability, jurisdiction, control, and more broadly, governance in a virtual state. Would lines of accountability be clear in a networked interagency system? Would jurisdictional authority be clearer or more muddy in an ITDS world? Would an interagency board of directors possess sufficient clout to govern a governmentwide system in which political conflict is high? These questions, and others like them, must be addressed if networked computing is to foster institutional transformation of the kind envisioned by ITDS.

In the next chapter, I take up the simpler case of web portal development, a stage-one Internet activity. The creation of the U.S. Business Advisor, the first virtual agency developed during the National Performance Review, set the pace for several similar projects across the federal, state, and local governments.

CHAPTER NINE

A Virtual Agency for Business

I N ORDER TO PROVIDE web-based information and services, many government agencies have simply added these
innovations at their boundaries with the public. Such innovations require
neither substantial integration of the new technologies with agency processes and procedures nor any changes in agency culture or structure. For
this reason, some argue, interagency linkage and coordination at the level
of a website designed for public access is relatively simple organizationally and politically. The case of the U.S. Business Advisor challenges that
view.[1] Web-based information and service provision are high-leverage
initiatives. They have the potential to influence relationships within networks of agencies as well as relationships between agencies and their
constituents.[2]

This chapter examines the efforts of public managers, executives, and
White House staff to design and develop an interagency website for small-
business owners and managers. The case traces the development of the
initiative from its beginnings in 1994 to 1999. The U.S. Business Advisor
served as a template for several other agency and interagency "advisors,"
as government information and services—from education to housing, aging, and parenting—have been extended to the web. The development of
this site illustrates the challenges, as well as the opportunities, faced by

federal agencies as they are increasingly pressured to enact technology to provide web-based information and services. The design and implementation of cutting-edge technology-based services remain subject to all of the traditional bureaucratic logics, which impede technology-based interagency initiatives in the government. Moreover, although these virtual agencies provide access to a wealth of information and services, problems of massive information overload, search, and the interpretation of arcane, complex government information found on the web are emerging as challenges to digital government efforts of this type.

The National Performance Review and the rapid diffusion of Internet use during the 1990s raised expectations that government, eager to be more responsive to the public and to be "run like a business," would reach out to the public through the Internet and the web. The U.S. Business Advisor represents one of the earliest efforts to create a virtual agency. Integration across agencies and other organizations occurs at the level of what technologists call the GUI, the graphical user interface, rather than through deeper structural coordination across a network of agencies. Even in this case integration at the virtual level requires cooperation and coordination outside the scope, culture, networks, mission, and formal norms of agencies and the government officials within them.

The Role of the Small Business Administration

In 1997, during the implementation of the U.S. Business Advisor, tax forms indicated that there were about 24 million U.S. businesses. Approximately 6 million of those businesses had employees. Of that 6 million, 99.7 percent were small firms; 75 percent were independent proprietorships. Large firms, those with more than 500 employees, numbered only 15,000. According to the Small Business Administration, in 1997 small business, defined as any firm with fewer than 500 employees, employed 53 percent of private sector employees, contributed more than half the nation's gross domestic product, and accounted for almost half of all sales by U.S. firms. Seventy-five percent of new job creation was attributed to small business, as well as 55 percent of innovations.[3]

Between 1982 and 1997 the number of small businesses grew 49 percent. In 1997 alone, 3.6 million firms had been created, 75 percent of which were start-ups. Most small businesses are indeed "small." U.S. legal institutions make business creation easy. At almost no cost, using a telephone or a fax machine, an entrepreneur can register a new business. Two-thirds of new small businesses begin in the home. The average investment at the time a small firm is created is $4,000. Twenty percent of small firms began in 1997 with an investment exceeding $50,000, often raised through credit card debt. Capital accumulation at the level of the small business is not difficult. Only 25 percent have employees other than the owner(s).

The fastest-growing firms in the United States, defined as firms that have doubled their revenue in four years and have a compound growth rate of at least 20 percent, are known as "gazelles." According to David Birch, an economist who studies job creation and small business and whose research results are used by the Small Business Administration, there are slightly more than 355,000 gazelles, and they operate in every industry and state in the country. Although gazelles represent only about 5 percent of small firms with employees, they are the job creation engine of the U.S. economy, generating 70 percent of new jobs. About one out of three such companies is in the technology sector; many gazelles are commercialization efforts that began with government research and development funding. In all cases, a gazelle gained access to capital in amounts and types that allowed it to prosper in early stages of growth. The economic importance of gazelles provides the rationale for the role of the federal government as a catalyst for the creation of new firms, and thus the creation of jobs and revenue.

The failure rate of small business is also high. Although one out of twenty-two Americans will start a business, only half will be in business four years later. But aggregate statistics fail to show the reasons for business "failure." Some owners find other opportunities; others retire. More than 67 percent of small-business owners who fail are employed within a month. Many begin other businesses. Of those businesses that closed their doors in 1997, 20 percent were sold. Business owners terminated more than 1.1 million firms in 1997. During both 1995 and 1996, their owners terminated 1.6 million small firms in each year. In 40 percent of terminations, owners report that their firms were profitable during the lifetime of the business whose median lifespan was between three and five years. Only 10 percent of small firms survive for twenty years or more. Bankruptcy laws in the United States, another formal institution, allow business owners to make a fresh start. A failed business's assets must go to creditors, but remaining claims are forgiven.

During the mid-1970s, Congress established the Small Business Administration Office of Advocacy to provide a voice for small firms in the federal government. The office addresses four primary public policy concerns of small business: the contribution of small business to the economy; the effects of regulatory changes on small firms and providing solutions to inequitable regulation; legislation to assist and protect the interests of small business; and major initiatives to assist small business.

As part of its advocacy role, the Office of Advocacy within SBA saw the Internet as a powerful means to develop "matchmaking" products and services to connect small-business owners with sources of financing and contracting services. As the globalization of the economy has continued, the SBA has worked to assist small businesses adjust to a global environment by promoting exports and providing country-specific and industry-specific information about the laws, procedures, regulations, and businesses of other countries.

Developing a Web Portal for Small Business

The idea of web portals was "in the air" during the early 1990s. The attractiveness of portals aligned with some of the major features of the National Performance Review, detailed in Chapter 2. Two hundred and fifty career civil servants working on reinvention teams began reviewing agencies and governmentwide systems such as budgeting, procurement, and personnel, in search of ways to create a government that would work better and cost less. Following the template used in the private sector during re-engineering efforts in major corporations, the government promptly reduced the number of federal positions by 252,000. In many cases, privatization and outsourcing were used to "reduce" the size of government. Rather than become bogged down in agency restructuring and reorganization, the NPR focused on cutting red tape through an intensive effort to streamline and rationalize government regulations and services. Moreover, agencies were required under executive order to identify their clients as "customers" and to systematically provide better "customer service" through the use of surveys and feedback measures. Finally, information technology was to be used vigorously to create an electronic government. Thus, in an environment of scarce resources, cutbacks in staff, and heightened attention to responsiveness, the Business Advisor was an idea whose time had come.

Both National Performance Review staff in the White House and public managers at the Small Business Administration understood the potential of the Internet for networking information and services across agencies via web portals. Client-centered portals not only would post government information on the web in the fashion of electronic bulletin boards but also could be used as a platform for problem-solving and interactivity between citizens and government. The U.S. Business Advisor took flight as a powerful means to reinvent the relationship between government and small business through the use of the Internet.

Two primary factors led the Small Business Administration to initiate the Business Advisor in 1994: the web's potential for broad-based use and the demands of small-business owners for easier access to business-related information and services. Federal agencies were beginning to become interested in establishing an Internet presence and in using the web to improve service delivery and operations for the public. More specifically, the Small Business Administration wanted to respond to small-business owners who continually told the agency that it was too difficult to find business-related information, too complicated to receive essential Small Business Administration services, and too burdensome to undertake the paperwork necessary for receiving these services.[4] A website customized for the needs of small business would provide twenty-four-hour access, seven days a week, 365 days a year. The ability to index and search huge volumes of information on government regulations on the web promised significant benefits to business.

The Magic Kingdom

In an effort to develop greater responsiveness to business, in 1994 public managers from six federal agencies with major responsibility for business regulation (the Justice Department, the Internal Revenue Service, the Environmental Protection Agency, the Food and Drug Administration, the Occupational Safety and Health Administration, and the Department of Transportation) held a series of meetings with the business community. Business representatives wanted clearer regulatory language, easier interpretation of regulations, and the ability to identify more quickly the laws and regulations relevant to their firms. Increased accessibility and clarity would, they claimed, promote voluntary compliance and reduce the cost of regulation for government and business. An SBA lawyer, Ron Matzner, determined to use the web to build an easily searchable, comprehensive, business-oriented database of regulatory information that would allow people to search across the regulations of different agencies within one website. He called his idea the Electronic Regulatory Information Network (ERIN).

Even before the Internet, the idea of a single point of contact for a client, "one-stop shopping," had become a central management initiative in the private and public sectors. Government agencies had developed toll-free telephone numbers that allowed the public to dial one number for information and services within agencies. Organizing by customer or client rather than producer was also an important part of the "customer service" and reengineering movements. Technology was to be an enabler. When Internet use exploded, the potential for service integration by co-locating information on the web and using a mouse to "click" across enormous amounts of information located virtually anywhere brought concepts like client-based service to a new level. Agencies that had begun to think cross-functionally rather than vertically were already moving in the direction of the connectivity made feasible by the Internet and web. At the time, however, the co-location of government services meant being located in the same building. In sum, the Internet made it possible for agencies to connect—internally, across agencies, and with the public—much more easily. The management concepts were already in use.

Matzner thought of ERIN as a "Magic Kingdom" of the regulatory policy areas. His vision was to organize business regulation by function rather than by agency. Jim Kallenborn, a partner with Matzner in the development of ERIN's architecture, observed: "When you had to deal with the government, it would be a lot more intuitive. . . . If you went to 'law land' or 'regulation land' everything would be there to help you deal with that area of a problem."[5]

A public manager in the Department of Energy, Jerry DiCerbo, was leading a similar effort to make a database of environmental regulations available on the web by developing a client interface for the public. This project, called Envirotext, combined with ERIN, formed the basis for a demonstration of the interagency website of regulatory information. At the EPA, two staff were developing ways to increase public access to agency information using the Internet. Beyond these three independent efforts, however, support for the idea of interagency regulatory websites was scarce. Matzner found it difficult to gain the support of other agency managers for ERIN.

Enacting a Business Advisor Prototype

The prototype of the U.S. Business Advisor was launched two years after the first web browser became available to the public in 1993. In 1995,

FIGURE 9-1. The Business Advisor Interagency Network

Source: Author.

following the lead of business, several federal agencies had primitive websites, which offered little more than basic information about the agency. But a handful of public managers were beginning to envision the use of the web as a means for government to interact with the public in an entirely new way, providing information that would have been difficult and costly to access otherwise. But few government officials had conceived of virtual agencies at this point in time.

To address these issues, the Small Business Administration—with the support of Vice President Gore's National Performance Review—began to conceptualize a "virtual department of business" the goal of which was to make government information and services available electronically in an integrated, accurate, and easily understandable fashion.

Business complained vociferously about the difficulties of finding the regulations and laws that governed them. As David Barram, deputy secretary of commerce, noted: "It's hard for big companies and it's hard for smaller entrepreneurs. Sometimes you don't even know what to ask."[6] The complexity of regulation and its dispersion across several agencies, many with overlapping jurisdiction, made it nearly impossible for businesses to understand the regulations they were responsible for complying with. Moreover, state and local laws and regulations added further layers of complexity. Using the Internet and the web, a virtual agency—in this case, a virtual department of business—could organize under one site the regulation, incubation, and administrative information and services of the major federal agencies tasked with business regulation, including but not limited to the SBA, IRS, EPA, OSHA, and DOT (see figure 9-1.)

A senior adviser within SBA, James Van Wert, viewed ERIN as the beginning of an answer to the NPR's desire to become more responsive to business through regulatory reform and the use of the Internet to restructure the relationship between government and the public. Van Wert understood that ERIN could provide client-focused, one-stop shopping to business in keeping with the customer focus of the National Performance Review. Simultaneously, Van Wert estimated, sponsorship by the NPR for ERIN would ensure the support of other agencies for the interagency initiative. A White House conference on small business, planned for the summer of 1995, would be an ideal platform for a virtual agency for business. In spite of its small size, SBA would be able to focus at the center of a high visibility, cross-agency Internet effort.

During the winter of 1995 the SBA built a prototype of the site, using an informal network of federal experts from several agencies and the tools they had developed: the Department of Energy's Envirotext System and a search engine, designed by a faculty member at the University of Massachusetts to access regulations electronically. The prototype was limited to regulatory information and tax assistance.

In April 1995 the NPR, making it a White House initiative, formally adopted the Business Advisor. The Small Business Administration formally invited NPR to take the lead for the project under its reinvention mandate and to expand the objectives of the Business Advisor site beyond the provision of electronic access to business regulations. To accomplish this expansion, the SBA recommended that the NPR involve other agencies in a collaborative partnership. NPR wanted a far more ambitious undertaking that would provide assistance to business in finance, labor issues, and trade. The White House also wanted the site to offer current business news items and press releases in order to bring visitors to the site repeatedly.

Strengthening the Interagency Network

The original builders of the Business Advisor—federal technical specialists, information systems analysts, and website builders from several agencies— on the whole engaged enthusiastically in such a creative, cutting-edge, technology project. The potential to organize an enormous volume of information was intrinsically exciting to information specialists. As one put it, it would allow you to "just touch your computer and you're grabbing stuff anywhere in the world and bringing it together." For some technical specialists the participation, and lead, of White House staff, however, dimmed their enthusiasm for what had been a technical, rather than political, project. One specialist recalls the beginning of NPR involvement: "From then on, it was an NPR thing—driven by NPR. Jim [Van Wert] realized that this was a way to make it happen, but the rest of us all viewed NPR with a great deal of skepticism."[7] As Van Wert had told his group, the "good news" related to NPR leadership would be increased support, visibility, and influence. The "bad news" was working on the NPR timetable.

Acknowledgment of the intrinsic value of the project also was tempered by the reality of bureaucratic life and the vicissitudes of collaborative problem-solving. One government official, whose agency decided not to participate, described the early meetings:

> There were interminable meetings talking about, arguing about what technology to use and what should be there and who should be responsible. . . . The meetings never got anywhere. I would take some of my staff to them and they would sort of beg me not to go to the subsequent meetings because they found them to be frustratingly inconclusive. I just think you have a lot of people with good ideas and nobody could settle on one strategy. . . . Which search engine? What was going to be in it? Who was going to be responsible? Things like that. And there was more of a focus not necessarily on content but rather on image. . . . We operate on a self-supporting basis. We would have liked to have had the job. . . . Given that we are self-funding, every time I go to a meeting I know that it's costing me $100 an hour to sit in the meeting. I get worried that I'm sitting here with a lot of my staff tying up time that's not being used productively. I have a private sector focus because of the nature of my budget process.

In June 1995, the prototype of the Business Advisor was unveiled at the White House Conference on Small Business before 2,000 delegates from around the country. The site was given a cool reception by the conference delegates, who upon viewing it "wanted to change practically everything" about the prototype.[8] In response to this clear criticism, President Clinton and Vice President Gore issued a directive that formalized the development process under the joint chairmanship of SBA Administrator Philip Lader and Deputy Secretary of Commerce David Barram.

The Small Business Administration and the Department of Commerce revised the service during the ensuing six months, responding to suggestions made by small-business owners in a series of focus groups on the Business Advisor. Business owners wanted the site to provide increased access to information and services using features that had become available in private sector web design, such as search engines and tools, guidelines to move users through business transactions, clearer classification of information, FAQs (frequently asked questions), and a space for current items of interest to the small business sector. They requested that the SBA publish online current items of interest to small business. In addition, the business community asked the Small Business Administration to minimize the use of graphics so that visitors to the website could easily download forms and conduct transactions online.

In February 1996, Vice President Gore unveiled the new Business Advisor site as a "beta version" with a new and improved mandate: small business would have "one-stop Internet access to every service and every bit of information that government provides to business."[9] As an initiative of the White House under the National Performance Review, the site received strong media visibility.

Adding to expectations for the virtual agency at that time, SBA Administrator Philip Lader announced that the U.S. Business Advisor was hoping to make compliance easier for small businesses, promising that "businesses will be able to find applicable laws and regulations through keyword searches and will be walked through the compliance process step by step."[10] But it is not clear how to, or if agencies can, organize websites for compliance. A regulatory agency official expressed frustration with the mismatch between the information access promised by the Internet and web and the current construction of the regulation: "Let's say you go in and click on safety and health. Do you realize how broad safety and health is? Mine safety and health, occupational safety and health, railroads, aircraft, transportation in general, Transportation Safety Board. I mean how do you organize something like that?" It was easy enough to list agencies and provide their telephone numbers. But providing information on a "deeper" level was much more complicated. Legal interpretations of legislative acts, for example, were extremely complex and often case-specific.

One government executive noted that integrating agency regulations and information using the web oversimplifies regulatory regimes: "Our website is immense and complex. Now you've got somebody else's website that's immense and complex. How do you sit up here on high with the technology we have today and do anything to make that kind of a unity?

Our country has got an immense organization, and to be able to put that together in a computer so a business person comes in being ignorant of all this stuff and finds the things they want, that's the problem."

Between February 1996 and April 1997, the task force led by the Small Business Administration and the Department of Commerce continued to focus on creating the capacity for small-business people to conduct transactions with government on the web. Because of staff turnover within the Small Business Administration and the Department of Commerce, the operational management of the Business Advisor was subcontracted to FedWorld, part of the National Technical Information Service (NTIS) within the Department of Commerce. FedWorld had been assigned the role of "the official source for government-sponsored scientific, technical, engineering, and business-related information."[11] As a contracting agency, FedWorld responded best to relationships with single agencies. It had no clear point of contact for an interagency, interactive website that was breaking new conceptual ground. Moreover, as a contractor FedWorld lacked the incentive to act simultaneously as an advocate or participant in the development of the site.

The scope of the site grew in other ways as well. In December 1996, the SBA proposed redesigning the international trade portion of the site to include an interactive, query-driven system that would provide both information and financing for small businesses seeking to enter the export market. By March 1997 the Government Information Technology Services (GITS) Board had approved the proposal, and the new system, now known as the Export Advisor, went forward.

The Business Advisor was relaunched in June 1997. This version provided links to 300 government databases and offered electronic information and service delivery via the Internet. Users could access the most frequently asked questions about business development, download Small Business Administration loan applications and other business forms, and access more than 500 types of business software. This version and its new features were warmly received. In August 1997 Vice President Gore awarded the SBA and several other agencies a Hammer Award for their role in developing the U.S. Business Advisor. The award had been initiated by the National Performance Review to recognize significant government reform. This version of the U.S. Business Advisor was also lauded by government reinvention pundits David Osborne and Peter Plastrik, who praised it as one of the most useful sites operated by the federal government. They singled out its comprehensive nature as one of the key features. At that time, the Business Advisor offered links to 106,000 web addresses containing, it was claimed, virtually everything a person might need to know about doing business. Osborne and Plastrik marked the advent of the Business Advisor as the beginning of government services online.[12]

Although the site was seemingly securely positioned by White House approbation and media accolades, the leadership found that the challenges of developing and launching the site were rapidly eclipsed by the lack of incentives in an interagency network of participants to maintain the site in order to keep information current. By the first quarter of 1998, the site was seriously out of date and lacked the responsiveness to the public that was one of its key strategic features. E-mail to agencies sent through the Business Advisor was never responded to because staff in the agencies involved had not been assigned to this task. The news items of interest that small business owners had requested as part of the website were in some cases out of date by nine months or more. Links to other sites were not checked periodically, resulting in "dead" links that led nowhere. Critics commented that the site offered little interactive communication and that announcements posted on the website lacked dates, making it impossible to know how fresh the information was. As more and more features were added, increasing the scope of the Business Advisor, the main homepage and search mechanisms obscured, rather than clarified, what resources were on the menu.

Most important, the site continued to be organized by agency name rather than by the type of information or service, making it difficult to find information or services without knowledge of the agency regulatory structure.[13] No technological fix, or "logic," could overcome the autonomy of the network of agencies involved in the development of the web portal for small business or their embeddedness in agency-centric institutional structures including agency budgets, jurisdiction, and interests. Ownership of the Business Advisor was never clearly negotiated. The National Performance Review staff in the White House could shepherd the project, add to the urgency of its development, and provide visibility. But the NPR was not in a position to manage the Business Advisor or to ensure its long-term survival and health. No one agency perceived it in their interest to take responsibility for the Business Advisor, and no funding for an interagency portal had been sought or appropriated.

The politics and management of sustainability of large web-based networks differ fundamentally from those during the exciting start-up period of development and launch of a new effort. Federal managers are well aware of the shift in dynamics from one phase of networked organization to the next. One early participant in the process captured the agency-centered culture and incentives of the federal government:

> I have yet to see agencies that are wanting to cooperate in a long-term relationship. . . . They may get together in the spirit of doing something short-term, but keeping it going past version one is really tough. . . . Agencies want their name in lights and to get credit for things because of course they think that it ultimately comes back to them via appropriations. . . . I think you need to get agency buy-in and real strong commitment, and that's enormously difficult.
>
> In many respects it may require the force of law. I mean I think that that's what really made the National Trade Databank success-ful. . . . We'll go back to our participating agencies and say: "The law says you have to do this." . . . Whereas if you just do this volun-tary thing, then you volunteer as long as you view it as in your ben-efit. But if it's not viewed that way or people change or priorities change, then it just dies of inertia. So I think the key to this is having a long-term, high-level commitment to make something like this happen. And let's face it, that requires that you give something to everybody so that when they say "What's in it for me?" or "What's in it for my agency?" they can answer that question relatively easily.

In spite of these challenges, the site has continued to survive and im-prove, largely through ongoing social ties among committed public man-agers. In June 1999 the Small Business Administration announced that it had created a partnership with the Internal Revenue Service to help small businesses manage tax issues and had issued a CD-ROM called "What You Need to Know about Taxes and Other Products."[14] The Business Advisor site was again relaunched in December 1999, after an eighteen-month review period in which private and public sector designers built the new site architecture.

This version of the Business Advisor is divided into several separate areas: A "frequently asked questions" (FAQs) section provides links to documents of various government agencies. A "how-to" section provides tools and guides for visitors to the website about topics as diverse as busi-ness financing, getting a passport, Social Security regulations relevant to small businesses, and obtaining venture capital. A "search" function helps visitors search government databases for health, safety, and environmen-tal regulations, and other information. A "news" section posts items of interest from agencies other than the Small Business Administration. Finally, a "browse area" allows people to peruse information on federal agencies by subject. The site includes significant technical improvements as well, incorporating more powerful, better focused search engines, database-driven web page development, and a correspondence tracking system to provide better customer service. In addition, it provides a fully developed administrative interface for federal webmasters.

The Business Advisor continues to rely on public-private partnerships as well as interagency collaborations to provide services to its users. For example, the SBA and two private sector partners, Network Solutions and inc.com, recently announced the creation of "On-Line Business Resources," an area now available through the SBA Small Business Classroom. These pages provide small businesses with information and resources for current business challenges, especially e-commerce.[15] This is part of a stated SBA interest in making the benefits of e-commerce available to small businesses.[16]

The Challenges of Interagency Websites

Challenges associated with the design and implementation of the Business Advisor point to the difficulties of fitting a bureaucratic government to the tools and classification schemes that are becoming institutionalized on the web. SBA policy adviser James Van Wert indicated that forming the necessary network of public managers to develop the site was among the biggest challenges. When the idea of a "virtual business department" was developed, the Department of Commerce was in the process of developing its own website for business, STAT-USA. In its review of the project, Congress had required the Department of Commerce to charge business owners a fee for using the site, which would then be used to fund the site. The Department of Commerce also had discussed with NPR building a business and economic node on the Internet, using STAT-USA. Van Wert says that the Department of Commerce made overtures toward working together on such a project but eventually dropped out, largely because of interagency disagreement about user fees.

The challenges posed by interagency ownership of the project did not appear to limit its ability to collaborate with stakeholders outside the federal government, at least for brief periods of time on specific tasks. For example, the SBA has consistently worked with agency subgroups on the decision-tree logic and functional specifications for improving the Business Advisor. When designing the Export Advisor, the SBA worked with the Florida Small Business Development Center network. Together they conducted focus group sessions and hired a contractor to build a more interactive system that profiles businesses as they enter the system and offers them the trade information and financing that they need.

Nonetheless, challenges have continued to emerge. The very concept that has made the Business Advisor responsive to the varied needs of business owners—its interagency approach—make the project difficult to sustain politically and organizationally. Although the site was designed to be functionally driven, the limitations of interagency cooperation have constrained its ability to be fully responsive to the needs of its users. Some critics claim that it has reverted to the organizationally driven, agency-based structure of the federal government. The leadership of the project has changed, and no significant new leadership has emerged. Former sponsors such as the NPR no longer exist.

Knowledge Management in the Virtual Agency

The organization of all government information and services related to small business poses complex problems. Although some federal websites have limited information in an effort to simplify their website, this is not currently the norm. An agency manager involved with the project noted that the desire to place all government information on the web as a form of public service has unexpectedly led to new problems of information overload.

The complexity of an interagency website, the central concept behind a virtual agency, multiplies the problematic nature of information overload and accessibility. A different participant in the development process analyzed the incentives to tailor information:

> Part of the problem is that every agency sort of has [the attitude], "Well, it's on my website, why do I need to do anything for you?" It's a not-invented-here kind of problem. And yet, the frustration from the public side [is that] every place is different, every place requires a different searching technique, every place does their own thing. And it's frustrating for somebody to try to figure out the subtleties of every single individual site.

Epilogue: Interagency Websites as Virtual Agency

The Business Advisor laid the groundwork for a stream of governmental and nonprofit "advisor" websites. As of February 2000 the list of federal interagency websites was growing. These websites were established initially by agency entrepreneurs rather than in response to any overarching plan from the National Performance Review or other central decisionmaking bodies. However, the NPR launched Access America with the goal of creating interagency portals organized by customer rather than by agency.

A second high-profile effort of the NPR, Access America for Students (AAS), an interagency website, was designed to capture the enthusiasm of Generation Xers for electronic government. Vice President Gore unveiled the site, which operates under the aegis of the Department of Education, in January 1999 at the Global Forum on Reinventing Government. The site's stated goal is to "[deliver] federal electronic services across agency boundaries to better serve the needs of post-secondary students."[17] AAS's first initiative was a project that allowed students at seven pilot campuses to use an electronic "smart card" to access a website and conduct transactions, including paying tuition and student loan fees.[18] This project does not change the basic structure of financial aid applications and awards but makes it easier for students to conduct financial aid–related business online. In addition, commercial services—such as banking and textbook purchasing—will be bundled with government services.

The goals of the project suggest that it has been designed to be a "next-generation" electronic innovation for the agencies involved. The pilot will investigate two possibilities for financial transactions, both of which are also being tested in the private sector: the implementation of a common account structure (with the goal of consolidating students' educational loans) and the establishment of consistent account management through the commercial electronic payment infrastructure. In addition, the pilot will also explore ways to ensure the privacy of the information provided by students.

Eight campuses were involved in the first phase of the AAS initiative: DeVry Institutes of Technology located throughout the United States, George Washington University in Washington, D.C., Iowa State University, New York University, Tarrant County Junior College in Texas, Tennessee State University, the University of Florida, the University of Missouri–Kansas City, the University of Northern Colorado, and Western Governor's University in Iowa. The second phase offered increased services for the 2000–01 academic year and involves up to fifty colleges and universities.[19] The colleges and universities have various reasons for participating in the project. For example, the University of Northern Colorado was chosen by the Department of Education because it already provides financial aid for eligible students within forty-eight hours of applying for help. School officials were enthusiastic about the pilot project because they anticipated that it would improve the school's existing electronic infrastructure and put "UNC on the leading edge of 21st century technology."[20]

The AAS initiative is working closely with all of the federal agencies involved in student financial affairs. In October 1999 AAS collaborated with the IRS to make electronic tax filing available to students, as well as information on the tax rules associated with loans, scholarships, and fellowships. This program helps AAS improve student services and furthers the IRS goal of getting citizens to file electronically.

The AAS has private sector partners as well. A Minneapolis-based company, National Computer Systems, which has a long-standing relationship with NPR and the Department of Education, has several contracts with DOE, including one to provide services and systems for calculating student eligibility for financial assistance. In August 1999, NCS implemented the Student Account Manager project as part of the AAS initiative. The firm also developed web-based programs that allow applications to be filed electronically. In addition, NCS handles more than 5 million telephone calls and 200,000 pieces of written correspondence from the public each year on behalf of the department.[21]

At this writing, the primary problems with AAS are ensuring privacy and security. To address those issues AAS has assigned students personal identification numbers, or PINs, so that they can access more federal government services, complete transactions online, and ensure privacy and security for both the user and the government. This is no small undertaking. Some critics in the higher education community have publicly questioned whether the agency has the capacity to undertake these initiatives.[22]

Conclusion

Following Access America for Students and Seniors, the General Services Administration launched FirstGov, a portal designed to simplify search for any government information and services regardless of agency. FirstGov is meant to be the point of entry for anyone who wants to interact with the U.S. federal government on the web. A "cross-agency portal" effort in the federal government was born with the Access America projects and, more recently, with FirstGov. But fundamental institutional and governance questions are raised by these efforts. Experience in developing the U.S. Business Advisor and subsequent cross-agency G2C portals raises questions about institutional enactment of web-based technologies in addition to those we encountered in the last chapter on the enactment of international trade using a G2G initiative. Are web portals on their own likely to lead to deeper structural changes in American government? Are interorganizational networks at this more modest G2C level governable through informal networks? If so, are jurisdiction, accountability, and control adequately provided? The case also raises questions about the development of incentives for cooperation across agencies. Where are these likely to lie in the virtual state absent market-based incentives? And in a government in which bureaucracy and interagency networks possess contradictory internal logics, what logics will guide the behavior of public managers?

The challenges of enacting networked government differ substantially from popular rhetoric that celebrates collaboration, creativity, openness, and an end to the externalities of stifling bureaucracy. A dual system is growing in the American state that combines pockets of networked creativity and openness with large areas of traditional command and control. It is not clear how a hybrid hierarchical and networked government will operate as networked arrangements move beyond informal undertakings to ongoing operations. Among the most challenging questions is how to build appropriate levels of social capital where relationships have little history of trust or shared culture. What forms of leadership will be most effective? How much participation and collaboration is optimal? How should the porous boundaries with society and economy created by web-based government services and information be managed? What are the tradeoffs between stability and coherence in programs versus inventiveness and entrepreneurship? How will the relationship between the bureaucracy and the Congress evolve during the next decade or so as cross-agency networks proliferate? All of these are open, pressing questions to which celebrants of "digital government" have few answers.

One administrator involved in the development of the Business Advisor traced the design issues of interagency websites to the separation of powers in the federal government: "You bring something up that's terribly important, say, to the nation and to the government, but right now Congress hasn't done anything about it." So, he continued, an administrator has little incentive to deviate from an agency mission, agency reporting requirements, or testimony before Congress to justify agency appropriation levels. To deviate from agency-centered activities, an administrator typically waits for legislative or administrative direction. In addition, administrators fear the expectations that may be raised by cross-agency portals: "Because everybody wants an answer, and you can give legal answers to questions they have, but [you can go] only so far. We can point you to the regulation, but the interpretation of that at the time that we're considering a violation on your part has to deal with all the facts at that moment, and we can't see into that."

Putting aside for the moment the politics of the Business Advisor's association with the White House–led National Performance Review, the interagency network that developed the Business Advisor never had clarity regarding budget, authority, accountability, or linkage to the legislature. Similar cross-agency portal efforts—that is, the development of virtual agencies—are proliferating both in the United States and globally. But interagency interactions are still largely ad hoc, informal professional networks that rest on a thin base of collegiality and support for the appealing and intrinsically logical idea of providing value to the public. Mutual adjustment is not enough, regardless of rhetoric about self-organizing systems, to sustain such interagency efforts over the long run, particularly when these networks are embedded in institutional rules oriented to hierarchies. This case and the development of the International Trade Data System make it clear that social capital is a necessary, but not sufficient, underlying element of interagency networks in government.

It may appear that construction of an interagency website involves simply placing the information and services of several agencies together on the web. The case reveals the difficulties involved in building the types of websites that can render coherent the amount and complexity of information in the federal government. By contrast, compare shopping sites or other commercial sites. These are far simpler. Most private sector B2C projects are not nearly as complex as making vast amounts of government regulations reasonably clear and accessible to the public. Moreover, the costs of maintaining government websites have not yet been well estimated in dollars or staff.

Stephen Skowronek's analysis of state-building during the period 1870 to 1920, the beginnings of the modern bureaucratic state in the United States, reminds us that the struggle by politicians and other powerholders to retain their status during government reform is a long-standing one:

The expansion of national administrative capacities in the age of industrialism became contingent on undermining the established structure of political and institutional power and on simultaneously forging an entirely new framework for governmental operations. The state that now supports so prominent a central bureaucracy is the product of this precarious politics of negotiating an internal governmental reconstruction. . . . These political struggles are intervening and mediating variables in the administrative response to industrialism.[23]

Skowronek's illuminating account of the political development of the bureaucratic state ignores technological change. The cases I examine in these chapters cast light on and examine not only political negotiations but also the enactment of technology, institutional constraints, and the interdependence of their logics as individuals engage in the process of building new state capacity and reformulating state and society relations in the information age.

The politics of developing and maintaining the U.S. Business Advisor are trivial in comparison with the deeper structural integration required to leverage the coordinative capacity of networked computing. Although web-based innovations allow agencies to build Internet-based capacity rapidly and visibly, these efforts at the boundaries of organizations do not replace, but merely delay, difficult internal and interagency structural and political adjustments that will be central to building the virtual state.

CHAPTER TEN

Command
and Control
in Cyberspace

"Everyone on the battlefield can interact at anytime using all the
tools necessary to convey thoughts, orders, or plans to any
system, mounted or dismounted, on the battlefield in real time."
U.S. Army, C4I Integrated Idea Team

THIS CHAPTER DEPARTS slightly from the interagency
focus and the Internet to examine an internal organizational use of networked computing. It probes how some micro-level institutional features interact with new information technologies. In all instances
of interagency network formation, internal change is being enacted at the
same time. The case described in this chapter highlights the differences
between networked computing and information flows and the vertical
structures within a traditional Weberian bureaucracy, a division of the
U.S. Army.[1] The case reveals that, just a few years before the Gulf War, the
army was struggling with basic issues of organization, roles, and performance programs. Behind the dazzling rhetoric of net-centric warfare lie
fundamental questions of institutional and organizational behavior in an
increasingly formalized cyberspace. The army continues to struggle with
the gross mismatch between networked computing and its embeddedness
in cognitive, cultural, structural, and formal institutions designed for traditional battlefields.[2]

The development of the command-and-control organization for the high-
tech army that began in the late 1980s dramatically exemplifies a bureaucracy enacting networked computing. The experience of the army details
how the introduction of networked computing into the very fabric of

167

division operations, staff, and command affects task structure, communication patterns, hierarchy, jurisdiction, norms, and authority relations—every essential element of bureaucracy. The institutional transformation of command and control in the army, as well as in the other branches of the military, constitutes a critical challenge for military organizations and provides lessons for other government organizations. The speed and accuracy of contemporary weapons systems, largely computerized, have outstripped the organizational capacity of military decisionmakers to manage and plan their use and to react to an enemy similarly equipped. This case illustrates and tests the technology enactment framework; but it also raises a larger question for government: Have the logics of information technologies, including the Internet, outstripped the capacity of government to use them effectively for democratic purposes?[3]

This case details closely the experiences and sense-making of organizational actors in a bureaucracy working across the logics of technology, organization, and institutions. Most civilian government organizations operate at a slower pace, with lower stakes and considerably more slack than a division of the army does during battle. I was eager to learn firsthand how army professionals and soldiers were changing decisionmaking processes and organizational practices as a consequence of the introduction of networked computing. My field research with the Ninth Infantry Division at Fort Lewis in the state of Washington offered surprising lessons.

The Ninth Infantry Division (Motorized), designated in the 1980s as the design and implementation site for the Maneuver Control System (MCS2), is a light division.[4] Light divisions, forces armed with rifles and trucks rather than tanks and armored vehicles, are organized for contemporary perceived threats to national security, such as "low-intensity" conflicts in developing countries rather than large-scale European conflicts modeled after the world wars.

Units and Their Functions

The major hierarchical levels of a division divide units into three parts: headquarters units, which provide staff support to the division commander; lower-echelon support units, such as the signal battalion and the engineering battalion, which provide support in areas other than battle planning and management; and operating units, comprising maneuver brigades as well as cavalry and air defense brigades.[5]

In addition to the command staff, located in headquarters units, lower-echelon support units and operating units contain staff whose functions parallel those of the headquarters staff units—that is, battle planning and management. These lower-level staff are designated S1 through S4; the designation parallels the G1 through G4 functions of the headquarters staff. Staff across the division therefore constitute a functionally distinct and coherent group who communicate with each other primarily by sending information up the chain of command for planning and decisionmaking and plans and orders down the chain of command for dissemination and refinement.

Staff Functions

CHIEF OF STAFF. Located at headquarters, the chief of staff coordinates the efforts of five staff functions: personnel, intelligence, operations, logistics, and civil-military operations. The division commander usually delegates command of the staff to the chief of staff. Members of the coordinating staff hold titles such as assistant chief of staff, deputy chief of staff, and director, with the greatest responsibility and authority delegated to directors.

At the brigade and battalion levels (as well as others not relevant to this discussion), headquarters staff are smaller but organized in the same fashion as those at division level. The executive officer (or XO) coordinates the smaller unit staff and has responsibilities paralleling those of the chief of staff. Special staff, also under the command of the chief of staff, work with specialized groups. Of interest to this study are staff officers of engineering, communications and electronics, and air defense artillery. Often these staff officers also function as the commanders of, for example, an engineering unit.

COORDINATING STAFF OFFICERS. The responsibilities and duties of the coordinating staff, as prescribed in *Field Manual 101-5*, are presented below. The G1 (personnel) is responsible for the personal readiness of soldiers. Thus all aspects of personnel administration and management fall under the purview of the G1. Key responsibilities include: unit strength maintenance; personnel service support; discipline, law, and order; civilian personnel; administrative support for other personnel; safety and accident prevention; and headquarters management.

The G2 (intelligence) collects, analyzes, and presents information about the enemy in order to provide the commander with a "view" of the entire battlefield. The G2 also identifies valuable targets and directs the intelligence and counterintelligence efforts of the division. Principal responsibilities include the production of intelligence, counterintelligence, and intelligence training.

The G3 (operations) has functional responsibilities that require extensive coordination with other staff. Chief responsibilities include operations, organization, and training. The G3 staff maintain the current "estimate of the situation"; prepare and publish the commands, operation plans, and orders for the division; and allocate critical resources, including personnel, supplies, and equipment.

The operations officer coordinates the activities of different units, for example, keeping air defense units away from the areas of the battlefield where nuclear or chemical weapons will be used. The G3 recommends the location of command posts and is responsible for their security from attack and electronic surveillance. This officer must coordinate closely with intelligence.

The G4 (logistics), which must coordinate closely with the G3 (operations), has the following responsibilities: supply, maintenance, transportation, and services. The logistics officer coordinates the implementation of automated logistics systems, which are similar to inventory control and shipping systems. The G4 also monitors equipment readiness and maintenance priorities as well as the distribution and reallocation of ammunition, weapons, equipment, and supplies, including fuel, food, and clothing. The connections with the personnel function, and thus the collocation of the G1 and G4, are obvious.

Finally, the G5 (civil-military operations) has primary responsibility for civil affairs and civil/military relationships. Civil affairs includes the effects of military activities on the civilian population, government, economy, infrastructure, and cultural resources. The G5 is also concerned with refugees, evacuees, and displaced persons and coordinates with other U.S., foreign, and nongovernmental agencies to carry out its responsibilities. Civil/military relationships include those areas of the social order that affect military operations, such as the maintenance of public support, the activities of civil defense forces, and the effects of nuclear and chemical weapons on the civilian population.

Command and Control at the Division Level

ROLES AND RELATIONSHIPS. According to U.S. Army doctrine in the mid-1980s: "Command and control is the process through which the activities of military forces are directed, coordinated, and controlled to accomplish the mission. This process encompasses the personnel, equipment, communications, facilities, and procedures necessary to gather and analyze information, to plan for what is to be done, to issue instructions, and to supervise the execution of operations."[6] Moreover, the commander is responsible not only for accomplishing the mission of the organization but also for ensuring the morale, health, welfare, and training of assigned and attached personnel.

The command-and-control system at the divisional level comprises three interrelated parts: (1) organization of the headquarters for operations, (2) the command-and-control decisionmaking process, and (3) the facilities that support command and control. The commander has limited flexibility in the organization of staff roles, relationships, responsibilities, and functional groupings. The decisionmaking process includes the procedures used to receive, analyze, and communicate information. The facilities for information processing include both command posts and the information systems that support them.

The command-and-control system has evolved as new technologies become available and as doctrine develops to take account of technological changes in weapons systems, communications, and data processing capabilities. A major difference between the command-and-control function in most civilian organizations and in military operations lies in the extraordinary stress under which a military organization must function during battle; time-critical decisions must be made and communicated under conditions of rapid change, high uncertainty, ambiguity, and severe physical and emotional stress. It is critical to keep the decisionmaking cycle more rapid than that of the enemy in order to maintain advantage.

COMMAND AND STAFF RELATIONSHIPS. The commander communicates with staff through the chief of staff. Similarly, the chief of staff directs and supervises the staff in support of the commander. (At lower levels of command, the executive officer performs parallel functions.) The military staff has responsibility for "[assisting the] commander in decisionmaking by acquiring, analyzing, . . . coordinating . . . , [and] presenting essential information to the commander with a recommendation [for action]. The staff, organized functionally, also monitor the progress of decisions, . . . estimate future requirements, and prepare plans and orders."[7]

At the level of the division, staff are responsible for combat, combat support, and combat service support with an emphasis on planning and supervising tactical operations. Special staff function both as staff officers and subordinate unit commanders. This structure is replicated roughly in smaller unit staffs. At lower levels, functions parallel those described above for division staff.

The Implementation of MCS2

As the high-technology testbed for the army, the Ninth Infantry Division was a center for the development, testing, and use of automation for battlefield planning and management. An important but criticized component of the management of the division was the development of systems using nondevelopmental items—that is, computers and equipment purchased "off-the-shelf" and adapted where necessary rather than developed for the army using military specifications, a much more expensive process.[8] In addition, the army has found that it could use what it calls "ruggedized" equipment—nondevelopmental items adapted for use in adverse environmental conditions—rather than militarized hardware designed and built specifically for military use.

The Maneuver Control System, Version 2.0

The Maneuver Control System, version 2.0, was designed both to support one of the five battlefield functions, maneuver control, and to serve as a force-level control system for all five battlefield functions by providing an interface that allows access to "common collateral-level" databases and an infrastructure for data transfer throughout the division.[9] Thus it formed not only one of the five points of the army command-and-control system star but also the hub, or center, connecting the points of the star. These concepts marked the beginning of networked command-and-control doctrines.

The MCS2 was defined broadly by the army to include "computer equipment, software, communications interface devices, equipment shelters, training programs, personnel and procedures combined to support the tactical command and control requirements of the 9th Infantry Division."[10] Development of the overall battlefield automation system for the Ninth Infantry Division began in 1983 and was known at that time as the Distributed Command and Control System.[11]

MCS2 was meant to enhance a commander's control of combat forces. Visual displays were intended to provide quick and accurate snapshots of the current situation and the availability of resources. Command staff used the system to analyze battlefield information and to generate and transmit battle plans, orders, and situation reports on friendly and enemy locations; to monitor progress toward the completion of plans and orders; and to modify plans rapidly as situations and resource levels changed. Fundamentally, the strategic importance of the use of automation lies in the ability to "get inside the decision cycle of the enemy"—that is, to process information, make decisions, and communicate orders more quickly than an enemy can react to them.

The system was also intended to allow commanders access to reliable data at dispersed locations, thus freeing them to move about the battlefield as the situation dictates, rather than being tied to a central command post. Data updates were to be immediately replicated throughout the network. Moreover, the dispersal of current information throughout subordinate units allowed for more decentralization of control by providing subordinate commanders with equal access to information about the entire system and creating a broader context within which to interpret and implement plans and orders.

As the high-technology testbed for the army during the 1980s, the Ninth Division took the lead in the use of cutting-edge networked computing to experiment with command, control, communications, and intelligence in tactical electronic warfare. As a quintessential traditional bureaucracy, an army division exhibits the distinguishing characteristics of all large, routinized organizations, including long chains of command, specific spans of control, clear hierarchy, strict authority relations, prescribed communication channels, and highly formalized routines or performance programs. Moreover, the army possesses deeply institutionalized norms and values. The organization is therefore an almost ideal place to systematically examine the effects of networked computing on a formalized structure with a "strong" culture and deep commitment. The use of an intranet, similar in structure and function to the Internet but restricted to the division, provides an early example of the challenges of working across the logics of information technology, networked organization, and institutions. This examination focuses in detail on the interaction of technology, structure, and institutions within one government organization.

The Virtual Military Organization

Even before the availability of the personal computer and its "revolution," military theorists and reformers envisioned a high-tech army. In 1970 testimony to Congress, General William Westmoreland outlined "the battlefield of the future" in which "enemy forces will be located, tracked, and targeted almost instantaneously through the use of data links, computer-assisted intelligence evaluation, and automated fire control. . . . I am confident [that] the American people expect this country to take full advantage of its technology—to welcome and applaud the developments that will replace wherever possible the man with the machine."[12]

The needless loss of life caused by doctrinal and organizational failures during the war in Vietnam, as well as the necessity of building conventional deterrence in Europe during the 1970s, forced the United States to modernize its basic doctrine for warfare. Since the Civil War, army doctrine had been premised on attrition warfare. The 1976 version of *Field Manual (FM) 100-5, Operations*, the basic training document used by the army, although touted as a revision, merely rearticulated the fundamentals of a war of attrition. A second revision, developed by military reformers and issued in 1982, represented what most experts felt was "the most extensive change in the fundamentals of U.S. military doctrine since the Civil War."[13]

Modernization Efforts in the U.S. Army

New technologies and changes in the politico-economic structure of the world have led to decreased emphasis on the threat of nuclear war and on a large-scale land war pitting the United States against the Soviet Union in Europe, and, concomitantly, to a partial reappraisal of tactical strategies and concentration on the development of high-technology, nonnuclear weapons.[14] Highly accurate, dizzyingly fast weapons systems have in turn outstripped the organizational capacity of decisionmakers to manage and plan their use and to react to similar systems of potential foes. Increasing rationalization of command post functions follows logically and of necessity from the introduction of more sophisticated and mobile enemy forces.

In 1985, *Field Circular 101-55* introduced the organizational concept of mobile, survivable, standardized command posts to support division-level command staff as a response to the evolution of command-and-control doctrine and procedures. MCS2 was designed as an essential infrastructural element for force management in such command posts.

The concept of command staff organization, although eminently logical, is relatively new.[15] Of course commanders have always relied on staff and aides; however it was not until the Civil War that the organizational form of a command staff organization was refined because of the need to plan for and manage an expanded force structure consisting of divisions, corps, and armies. During World War I new military technologies pushed the organizational form toward further standardization and elaboration as the trend toward larger functionally differentiated and specialized staffs continued.

By the end of World War II, operations had become even more specialized. The staff organization manual in use at that time separated the functional organization of staff into personnel (G1), intelligence (G2), operations (G3), and logistics (G4), with several units combining the intelligence and operations (G2/G3) and the personnel and logistics (G1/G4) functions.[16] More hierarchical differentiation occurred within functions as staff were layered into forward and rear echelons in order to further task specification.

After World War II ended and fear of nuclear war developed, further echelonment of command posts occurred to enhance the survivability of command. The increased technological complexity of weapons and communication during the 1950s led to the establishment of an additional subunit, the technical operations center, within the main command post.

Elaboration of the organizational form notwithstanding, as late as the Vietnam War these centers of battlefield planning and management were generally fixed (or at least semipermanent), large, and elaborate units. During the 1970s, when the importance of command posts as primary targets in battle began to be appreciated, the emphasis on survivability increased. The development of applications and systems to detect the electronic signatures given off by the equipment in command posts and to attack command posts with great speed and pinpoint accuracy has driven the further refinement of the staff organization and its physical environment in order to ensure continuity of battlefield planning and management.[17]

The U.S. Army has sought to rapidly implement information technology as a means of realizing mobile, survivable, and complex command post structures. Beginning in 1976 the army initiated several programs to automate battlefield functions and improve communications under the umbrella term the Army Command and Control System (ACCS). The Maneuver Control System both supports the functional area of maneuver control and integrates the five battlefield functional areas.

The five battlefield functions identified for development were control and direction of artillery (fire support), control of short-range air defense weapons (air defense), intelligence and electronic warfare, combat service support (including the management of personnel, medical needs, transportation, maintenance, and supply), and the monitoring and management of battlefield conditions and the movement of troops (maneuver control). A network of automated systems designed to work within and among the five functional areas is being developed to assist commanders in battlefield management. ACCS allows individual battlefield systems to exchange data using standard army tactical communication systems.

The 1982 version of *Field Manual 100-5* combined the German tradition of mission-oriented command and control, *Auftragstaktik*—in which relatively independent, highly trained, mobile units went into battle with an overarching grasp of the mission—with cutting-edge distributed computing like that used in business. AirLand Battle called for achieving victory not through a war of attrition, with its unacceptable loss of life, but through tight integration of "land, sea, and air combat systems" such that the U.S. military would be able to conduct "simultaneous offensive operations over the length and breadth of the battlefield." Tight integration, achieved through networked computing, would allow commanders to quickly move and focus "decisive combat power, both fire and maneuver, at the proper time and place on the battlefield."[18] The organizational and information processing implications of such a doctrine are enormous. The challenge to military organizations is exacerbated by the presence of enemy forces with potentially disruptive digital technologies who could destroy or obstruct the flow of information electronically.[19]

During the 1980s the Defense Advanced Research Projects Agency (DARPA) launched a strategic computing initiative for the military. In addition to developing autonomous vehicles and a "smart" robotic pilot's assistant, the Initiative focused on battle management in an integrated digital environment. In 1983, Richard Cooper, director of DARPA, reported to Congress that "with increasingly massive amounts of valuable data collected, no commander can possibly keep up and make full use of the information, making an accurate picture even less likely . . . [R]evolutionary improvements in computer technology are required."[20] The long-standing support of DARPA for research in computing has been directly oriented toward battlefield management requirements to align military organization and decisionmaking with the logics of high-tech weaponry.

Enacting Technology in the High-Tech Testbed

Members of the Ninth Infantry Division tested automated battlefield management systems at division headquarters at Fort Lewis and in war games conducted in the desert in Yakima, Washington. They enacted battlefield management technologies in at least three ways. First, they defined and described the information systems through the ways they used them rather than through some set of objective characteristics of the technologies. Second, the officers used the MCS to replicate, or reproduce, institutionalized practices and processes—in other words, they used new technology in ways that would preserve already institutionalized arrangements. Third, officers reinterpreted and redefined central concepts of command, including the critical roles played by the intuition and experience of commanders, in light of the increasing dominance of formalized and rigid logics embedded in information systems that threatened the traditional role of the commander.

Enacting Technology and Performance Programs

Most behavior, both within and outside organizations, is organized into performance programs. Staff officers in the Ninth Division were easily able to automate several lower-level performance programs. A second set of lower-level performance programs, those that combined both routine tasks and a great amount of operator discretion, were also quickly automated, with significant unanticipated consequences. Finally, performance programs that crossed organizational boundaries linking the organization to, for example, its supply of resources, produced unexpected and important effects on enactment.

ENACTING TECHNOLOGY AND LOWER-LEVEL PERFORMANCE PROGRAMS. Rarely does an organization comprehensively reassess the hundreds of performance programs that structure much of its human information processing capacity. In contrast, routines and operating procedures typically are amended in ad hoc fashion. As staff officers in the Ninth Division tried to implement the maneuver control system, they did not expect to have to modify performance programs. Instead, they used the technology to enact existing programs. They automated the status quo.

Indirect evidence for this claim is provided by noting the pattern of use of MCS2 applications by members of the Ninth Division.[21] Table 10-1 reports the relative use of nine applications in MCS2 by three categories of organizational actors. Members of the division, regardless of hierarchical position, most frequently used the applications that only slightly perturbed their existing routines. Applications with potentially important benefits to the division but whose implementation would cause officers to modify existing routines were relatively neglected.

Table 10-1. Descriptive Statistics for Software Use by Functional Group

	Commanders and principal staff (N = 17–20)		MCS2 staff users (N = 21–23)		Operators and system specialists (N = 19–21)	
Electronic mail	4.00	(1.17)	4.35	(1.18)	4.00	(1.22)
Communications	3.81	(1.47)	3.94	(1.39)	3.55	(1.67)
Database	3.78	(1.38)	3.74	(1.41)	2.76	(1.87)
Word processing	3.35	(1.70)	3.42	(1.64)	3.33	(1.42)
Situation reports	3.30	(1.64)	3.24	(1.75)	2.65	(1.81)
User-defined reports	2.32	(1.70)	1.56	(1.25)	1.75	(1.55)
Map graphics	2.18	(1.62)	1.80	(1.36)	1.50	(1.43)
Spreadsheet	1.56	(1.59)	1.89	(1.28)	1.35	(1.18)
Graphics	1.18	(1.14)	1.22	(1.11)	.68	(1.11)

Source: Data presented in Table 10-1 were collected by means of a questionnaire designed and administered in 1987 to MCS2 users by the Experimentation Division of the Army Development and Employment Agency. I conducted the data analysis.

Notes: The category "Commanders and principal staff" includes chiefs of staff and executive officers; "MCS2 staff users" represents staff ranked higher than system specialists; and "Operators and system specialists" indicates enlisted personnel trained to use technical systems. Participants reported their use of applications by using a "5" for an application used every hour, "4" for an application used every six hours, "3" for daily use, "2" for occasional use of a "vital" application, "1" for occasional use of a nonvital application, and "0" if an application was not used.

The initial implementation strategy for MCS2 involved placing personal computers with simple applications such as word processing, electronic mail, and database management systems at the disposal of the users. Managers and consultants assumed that if users were allowed to become comfortable with the system any resistance to the technology would be overcome and they would gravitate naturally toward those functions best suited to automation. The approach, a novel one for the army, was known as "evolutionary design and development," or "build a little, test a little." One of the objectives was to get users involved in the development and implementation of the technology, known as the "user as developer" approach. By closely involving users in the design of automation, the army hoped to save money, produce better systems suited to human needs, and shorten the cycle time of development.

A lieutenant colonel explained the process of socialization and the evolutionary development of system use from his perspective:

You're the old colonel or the old sergeant major who has been very successful in his trade. . . . And you've been very successful at using pencils and papers and textbooks to do your trade and managing your people and your materiel, resources, and other things. And now somebody brings this strange electronic device into your working area and says, "Now this is what you're going to use now because we have determined that this will help you do your job better." Your first and most immediate reaction is, "It will make me look dumb. I'm good at what I do. I'm smart at what I do. I'm efficient at what I do by doing it my way and now somebody wants me to do it another way."

And so to use a rather crass comparison, they feel as though they're going to get electronic AIDS by touching this thing. And they will be less effective and spend more time learning how to use the computer than utilizing the skills and experience they've acquired in the trade over a number of years. . . . So the step, if you will, in, as we call it, socialization to automation is to start displaying some of the benefits and use *terribly* simple descriptions. . . . The first to use the system are your lower-ranking soldiers, your clerk typists . . . not your sergeants and colonels and majors . . . because Sarge says, "You've got to use this now instead of your typewriter because that's what they gave us now.". . . Then all of a sudden Sarge and the young officers think, "If they can do it, I can do it." Or "He's not here, and someone's got to do it." So they start doing it.

But I found the real test, the absolute test, is when the commander says, "Put one in my office.". . . If the boss is sending messages on the computer and knows how to use it, sure and be damned his support types and staffs and support commanders will learn more rapidly. We found that everywhere we went. . . . And after they start to use it, the more they use it the more they convince themselves that "I can do it faster with this machine.". . . The final step to winning their hearts and minds is when they say, "God, this thing does this thing really good and this thing really good. . . . But it really needs to do this other thing." That's when the hook is set. And now your automation is on the success curve because you're meeting [the commander's] needs, his real needs, his current needs.

Not surprisingly, word processing and other general-purpose applications, such as electronic mail and communications, were among the most frequently used applications at all levels of the staff hierarchy. Applications that require more substantial modifications of performance programs, such as transmitting information by computer rather than by radio, were less frequently employed, although their potential benefit to battlefield management was far greater. In general, those routines that could be enacted with little modification were the first to be automated.

ENACTING TECHNOLOGY AND OSTENSIBLY LOW-LEVEL ROUTINES. In contrast to highly routinized low-level performance programs, some lower-level performance programs require a large measure of discretion, judgment, and contextual knowledge. The enlisted personnel, or operators, responsible for enacting those programs tend to be high school graduates with little computer experience. Responding to a skill deficit in the enlisted ranks and the reality of a volunteer army, the military has tried to substitute technology for human intelligence and skills. One strategy for information technology use, known as "black-boxing," involves embedding in software the algorithms, or decision rules, that historically formed part of the skill base operators obtained through training and experience. Thus applications may be designed and used to deskill low-level operator positions.[22]

The maneuver control system was enacted in conformance with an institutionalized view of operators as "button pushers"—people who did not need much intelligence or judgment to carry out their tasks. Operators were trained to use the system mechanically with little conceptual understanding of the data reduction tasks being performed. But implementing the system to encompass only the rote aspects of tasks that also required some discretion and judgment had the unintended and perverse consequence that operators and system specialists became unable to recognize erroneous output. For example, by removing skill from operators it became impossible for them to discern whether output from the computer system made sense. If an operator recognized that something generated from the information system was nonsensical, he or she would not be able to identify what had caused the error. For example, output from the MCS might not make sense because of a typographical error in the input of information in any one of several subunits. Or an operator might produce erroneous output by using the wrong version of a software package. And errors or nonsensical results could be produced if a data tape were worn out.

The deskilling or black-boxing strategy also had serious implications for mid-level users of MCS2, who received data organized and entered by lower-ranking operators and system specialists. One of the jobs of mid-level staff was to "recontextualize" the data using their professional knowledge and expertise. They would then transmit their enriched information to the command level, where life-and-death decisions would be made based in part on the information provided by staff. But the "knowledge deficit" created at the operator level by deskilling modified the performance programs, or routines, of the mid-level staff. They were forced to make sense of the output their subordinates produced without the benefit of clarification and details that operators and system specialists had traditionally supplied verbally. Thus middle managers were forced to take on some of the highly discretionary tasks that experienced operators and system specialists were once able to perform. The information system had not completely replaced the knowledge that operators used to have; but it caused a shift in its locus. It shifted data reduction tasks that required some specialized knowledge up a level and made them more centralized. In time, some operators and system specialists will become mid-level staff users, but it is not clear at what point they will acquire the conceptual skills needed to perform higher-level tasks.

A mid-level staff user explained the shift in the locus of knowledge:

The average soldier does not walk into a headquarters or a TOC [tactical operations center] and know what's going on, the dynamics of controlling the battle using the information. . . . He's dealing in data, not in information, and generally does not readily get the feeling of the whole system. It takes the operational guy, who is the senior NCO [non-commissioned officer] or the officer now, who has maybe a better concept of what's happening with all that data and transforming it into information. He essentially becomes the operator of the system. . . . The nature of the beast kind of moves the burden of the administrative stuff up a couple of levels. . . . It all shifts up! And the management of it shifts up. . . . As we high-tech the system, it moves up and becomes very centralized to one or two people at the battalion level.

Thus the automation of routines and procedures gives operators few opportunities to develop their understanding of subtle differences in situations or an appreciation of the combinations of constraints. The manual collection and organization of data allowed operators to see the steps involved in processing data. MCS2 was used, or enacted, in a way that shifted task characteristics, role relationships, and the location of specialized knowledge in the organization.

Another mid-level staff user discussed the additional managerial tasks the specific implementation of the maneuver control system had created:

> Before, I could say to [the operators], "OK, we're going to go and set up this system. Go program your switchboard." And they would punch it in manually. Now it's centralized, where I do the planning in my shop on my computer, and they come with their computers, and I just dump in their respective programs, and they go and do the stuff. So for them it's time saving and again the management of it has come back to me. . . . Basically what we've done is change the whole work force.

The shift in routines and "the management burden" has serious implications for organizational learning, staff development, error recognition and correction, and system refinement. Officers of the Signal Battalion, by virtue of their technological proficiency, had absorbed much of the additional workload introduced by MCS2. They were particularly concerned about the unintended loss of expertise among operators:

> [Officer A:] Normally . . . we would . . . [describe technical specifications] with a stubby pencil on a form that we have which is recognizable. Now we tend to automate that, so the form is now in this computer. But you still cannot get away from the basics of how you compile the data to put it into this form. And the best way that we used to do it before was just by making the lieutenant or that young buck sergeant sit there and take his pencil. And he didn't go home until he mastered that. And it was a way of training him by repetition. . . . But now we tend to get away from that basic ground step. . . . Things get past them.

> [Officer B:] He [the operator or system specialist] has no idea what's happening. . . . And if . . . all of a sudden [there's a glitch], it becomes difficult to understand what's happening and work a fix.

> [Officer A:] And what happens if this computer breaks down and we had to revert back to the old way? Can they do it? No, they can't because they don't know the mechanics of how this computer suddenly spat these three forms out there.

Enacting Technology and Control Systems

The Maneuver Control System was designed as both a centralized and a decentralized system to allow commanders access to reliable data at different locations, thus freeing them to move about the battlefield rather than tying them to a central command post. The internal network, the heart of MCS2, was designed so that modifications to data were immediately transmitted, or replicated, throughout the network. For example, just as spreadsheet software automatically updates all relevant cells when one cell is modified, the replicated database automatically adjusted information at the division and brigade levels every time new data from subordinate units, battalions, were entered.

The intranet dispersed the same information widely throughout the battlefield and thus enhanced the survivability of the command-and-control system through redundancy and the reconstitutability of system nodes. In addition, by distributing current battlefield information throughout subordinate units, control of the division could be decentralized. Subordinate commanders, those at the brigade and battalion levels, would have equal access to information about the entire system. With a view of the entire battlefield, commanders throughout the division would have a broader context within which to interpret and implement plans and orders.

Before the introduction of computers, staff reports, which contained information about location and resources of units, were produced manually. Updates required copying data from one document to another, recalculating figures, and regenerating the entire report, a process that introduced errors and consumed time. A decentralized electronic database streamlined the tasks required of a logistics staff member (see box). MCS2 automatically sent data to several report-writing programs and automatically sent required reports to higher headquarters units at prescribed times and in prescribed formats.

A central report, the Division Commander's Situation Report, contains information about "pacer" items, equipment selected by commanders as key criteria for decisionmaking. Threshold percentages ranging from indications of critical needs to high operating levels could be selected by the user and color-coded for quick visual recognition of levels. Figure 10-1 presents the format for a situation report.

To illustrate how the control system shaped the enactment of MCS2, this section addresses three issues. First, organizational actors overloaded

Selected Tasks of Logistics Staff

Assistant chief of staff, G4 (coordinate logistics)

Provide input to the planning and decision-making process

1. Develop plans
2. Make recommendations
3. Prepare plans and orders
4. Provide staff supervision of decision policy
5. Provide continuity for completed staff actions
6. Coordinate and monitor supply and operations
7. Maintain information on the status of supplies
8. Supervise collection and distribution of excess, salvage, and captured materials
9. Coordinate reception of augmentations
10. Monitor type of tactical operations
11. Coordinate and monitor field services
12. Monitor status of field service support units
13. Coordinate reception of CSS augmentation
14. Monitor type of tactical operations
15. Coordinate and monitor maintenance operations
16. Maintain records of the status of maintenance
17. Coordinate reception of augmentations
18. Monitor type of tactical operations

Source: U.S. Army *Field Circular 101-55*, 1985.

the database to such an extent that its use by the entire division remained degraded for years. Second, although division officers appreciated the implications of data overload and its negative effects on the networked system, no viable solution could be found, in spite of repeated discussion. Third, officers were unable to specify which data belonged in the MCS2 database. Commanders and staff officers were unable to clearly specify what data and information were needed to support commanders and their objectives. The system was meant to be a commander's decision support system, but it became a repository for staff data.

A battalion commander from a maneuver division commented on the propensity of MCS2 to become a staff tool rather than a command tool, and a continuing source of tension within the division. He observed that

Figure 10-1. Format for Operational Situation Report

Copy no. ____ of ____ copies

Issuing headquarters

Place of issue
Date-time group of signature
Message reference number

OPERATIONAL SITUATION REPORT NO. _____

Period covered: (date and time to date and time).
References: Maps (series number, sheet(s), edition, scale).

1. ENEMY
    a. Units in contact.
    b. Enemy reserves that can affect local situation.
    c. Brief description of enemy activity during period covered by report.
    d. Brief description and results of operations during period of report.
    e. Conclusions covering courses of action open to enemy.

2. OWN SITUATION
    a. Location of forward elements.
    b. Location of units, headquarters, and boundaries.
    c. Location of adjacent units and supporting troops.
    d. Brief description and results of operations during period of report.
    e. Noneffective units.

3. COMBAT SERVICE SUPPORT General statement of the CSS situation, if other than normal, as it directly affects the tactical situation.

4. GENERAL Information not covered elsewhere.

5. COMMANDER'S EVALUATION To be completed when directed by higher authority.
Acknowledgement instructions.

_____
Commander

Authentication
Annexes:
Distribution:

_____
(Classification)

Source: U.S. Army, "Staff Organization and Operations," *Field Manual 101-5*, p. B-6.

when logisticians and personnel officers started using the system for their own purposes it ceased to become a commander's system.

But logisticians and personnel officers who used MCS2 to build staff support capability did not recognize their behavior as a problem. Their design and use of MCS2 was logical from their perspective. The responsibility for apportioning parts of the database as a resource resided at the command level because only at that level could critical decisions about the data needs for command be made. The need for command-level participation was fully recognized by mid-level staff, who enacted MCS2 by automating their performance programs, such as those for inventory management and personnel functions. But the pursuit of their subunit goals came at the expense of enacting the technology in ways that would enhance command and control from the perspective of the headquarters command staff.

Although most officers observed that over a period of two or three years the primary focus of MCS2 had shifted from staff needs to command decisionmaking, major problems continued to plague the information system. One key problem was a glut of information viewed by command staff as nonessential. It clogged lines of communication and slowed the processing time of the system so severely that manual methods of calculation often outpaced the computer. One colonel in a headquarters unit complained that so many data elements had been added to the system that they actually detracted from decision support. A subordinate officer echoed that sentiment and explained the organizational logic that led to continued data overload: "To the guy that was responsible for that part of the database, that stuff's important to him. He was that commodity manager and responsible for that part of the database. . . . He had to get it in there."

Thus, in spite of broad consensus on the existence of data overload, the database remained glutted because each group felt strongly, according to the institutionalized requirements of its professional role, that its inputs were vital to command decisionmaking. Absent clear direction from commanders, staff had little choice but to carry out their prescribed roles. As a colonel from the command staff observed:

> One commander or chief of staff or G3 doesn't have enough exposure to the system to get comfortable with what his critical elements of information are. We're constantly fluctuating back and forth as to what needs to be in that machine—and [that] causes that clog of

information. What we tend to do with the computer because it's a quick processor is glut it with information. Our demands on it are totally unrealistic. Totally unrealistic. We think it's a savior for everything.

An unresolved and important conflict exists between the routinizing imperatives of information systems and the idiosyncrasies of decision-makers. An underlying assumption in the automation of decisionmaking is that the key elements of decision can be isolated, formalized, and programmed. But knowledgeable actors disagree about the key data elements for decisionmaking, and it is not clear that training them to conform to one set of decision rules would improve command decisionmaking. In fact, decision rules used by one person may vary with the context of the decision. As one officer noted:

One of the things that seems to be central is the impact of the automation system on the decision process. . . . You really have got to understand that decision process and what information is there. . . . In a changing situation—when you get into battle it changes hour by hour. . . . The person making the decision based on information has to be really flexible in understanding the limitations of what the machine is giving him to make his decision. If he gets tied into it too much, then he probably doesn't need to be there. His decisions could be automated. . . . And the hardest question was going to a commander . . . and getting him to tell you what he needs. . . . He can't define it.

Several officers stressed the difficulty of enacting rigid applications so that they are comfortable with them and can tailor them to their own uses. A battalion commander added his observations concerning the propensity of staff, in addition to commanders, to use the system according to their professional roles and interests:

The staff guy wants it to become a product to satisfy his needs. The guy at battalion level, the operations officer, wants to use it to satisfy his needs. The commander at battalion level wants it to satisfy different needs than the commander at brigade level. . . . During this testing that we did, it became an opportunity for a lot of players to develop and design something that . . . they needed—as opposed to what the real intent of the process was. And I think we lost control there for awhile. Just in terms of the overall project, we began to lose control and then we were able to bring it back into perspective again.

Uncertainty about how the commander's tool should be designed, specifically uncertainty about the data elements required for decision (if, indeed, they can be isolated) and which commander's decisionmaking styles should be codified (if, indeed, the system is flexible enough to incorporate such diversity) generated conflict. The result was an intractable data overload problem with significant implications for the quality of automated battlefield management. Decisionmaking was retarded, system performance was degraded, and burdens on the system caused it to "crash" at exactly the times when the need for it became most intense.

Enactment of Deep Institutions

Why did commanders fail to take the lead in building the database, the heart of the decision support system, which was ostensibly designed to support their work? One explanation may be that some of the deep institutions of the army had a profound effect on the organization's perceptions and use of the technology. One institution, the role of the commander, is embodied in the often-used phrase "Commanders command." A related institution, the role of lower-level staff and other soldiers, is aptly summarized as "Soldiers do," that is, they follow orders.

The institutionalized role of the commander is changing because of networked computing. For example, in order to remain unfettered by the enormous volume of information flowing through command centers, commanders—like most executives—have developed an institutionalized "distance" from routine information processing. Commanders tend to avoid direct analysis of information, a staff function. But for this reason, commanders tended to have little direct training in IT, also perceived to be a staff function. Not surprisingly, therefore, commanders also tended not to use computers directly or to understand their strengths and limitations. These institutionalized behaviors and attitudes prevented MCS2 from developing beyond a staff tool.

The irony here is that the institutionalized distance of the commander from the flood of information received by a division command post is critical during battle. Data overload would prove overwhelming, distracting, and disabling for commanders. The historic role of the commander has serious, and as yet unaddressed, implications for the use of networked computing to support command and control.

Commanders and their subordinates concur completely with U.S. Army doctrine that the chief contribution of the commander in the decisionmaking process is his or her experience, intuition, wisdom, and judgment. These qualities are extremely difficult to define in a formalized technological logic. External actors—typically contractors who, ironically, tend to be former army officers—clearly see the constraints posed by institutionalized thinking. One contractor explained:

> The command-and-control environment is very much like an office. But automation threatens the senior guy. The senior may have to do something himself. The top guys delegate to staff. [So a hands-on, computerized environment is very] threatening. The technology's there. [What's needed is] cultural change. Whether it's command-and-control or office applications, it's all the same thing. Paper allows you to hide behind the various stations of the cross. There's no excuse with technology for not getting the right information into the right hands.

Proponents of new technology interpret commanders' avoidance of it as obstinacy or defensiveness. One retired colonel-turned-consultant criticized army commanders for missing important opportunities to field advanced information systems by failing to "move through the window of socialization: What are the data elements that are needed for command? The army can't even figure this out. If they did, we could build an expert system. The army is just not there yet. . . . The tools are there." The gap between contractor optimism about networked computing and commanders' appropriately cautious stance is striking. The implications of this gap for technology enactment are serious given the heavy reliance on contractors and external experts by the military. The gap points to the critical differences between technological and organizational logics and the propensity of technical contractors to ignore deep institutions, social relations, and cognitive complexity.

Conclusion

Technology enactment illuminates the struggle of organizational decisionmakers and actors to integrate the capabilities of a new information technology with their existing organizational and institutional arrangements. Members of the organization enacted their routinized performance programs with little awareness or understanding of the transformative potential of the computer networks at their disposal. As institutional theory would predict, organizational structure and practices shaped not only the actions of organizational members but also their perceptions and interests. The intractability of the database overload problem could have been interpreted as an example of political players engaged in a stalemate. However, this interpretation would fail to account for the actors' cognitive dilemmas as they attempted to formalize the data requirements of highly complex, contextual, and dynamic command decisions.

The use of IT in command implicitly calls into question the value and role of commander experience, intuition, and judgment in decisionmaking. Deep suspicion of technology's potential effects on executive decisionmaking combined with equally deep ignorance of the significant changes induced by automating operator tasks resulted in a transformation of the division into one in which staff officers with technical competence and facility became the de facto decisionmakers. No simple model of technology adoption or use explains these transformations. As the action-reaction chains of enactment unfold, a new structure is negotiated.

The cognitive, cultural, and sociostructural embeddedness of organizational practices and relationships helps to explain their surprising resilience in the face of new information and communications technologies. The stability of organizational forms demonstrates the importance of an institutional perspective in a terrain that has been dominated by the assumption that technology drives structure. Society has almost certainly entered the information age, with major structural changes attending technological change. However, it would be wrong to attribute structural change primarily to technology when organizational and institutional arrangements play such a key role.

Networked computing in the Ninth Division was enacted by the organization's members to maintain performance programs, role definitions, and role relationships—in fact, to maintain the status quo. Army officers would like to have mapped MCS2 on their existing organization, retaining its essential elements but making them work more accurately and quickly. This was not possible. The introduction of networked communications changed the role of some soldiers and lower-level officers from skilled to less skilled as computer programs internalized the rules they would have learned through drill and practice. The deeply institutionalized role of the commander also began to change from intuitive warrior to high-level data analyst. Consequently, role relationships were altered. This case examines some of the micro-level social and structural details of the technology enactment framework.

Epilogue

In August 1990, less than two years after I followed army officers and operators through a war game in the desert of Yakima, Washington, Iraqi forces invaded Kuwait on the assumption that the United States would not engage Iraqi forces in the desert. The stunning success of American forces in February 1991 removed any doubt about U.S. military capability in the Middle East. This success was all the more gratifying because the war had provided the first test of the new high-tech military. As Rochlin writes: "The war demonstrated dramatically the possibilities of the still-ongoing technological revolution in weapons and warfare. Many of the platforms, weapons, and systems were used in combat for the first time, and most performed superbly. . . . But this technological euphoria over-looked the special conditions under which the war was fought. . . . The war also exposed serious vulnerabilities in the network of intelligence, logistics, communications, and other infrastructure required to support the sophisticated and complex military technologies."[23]

Not surprisingly, the victory in the Gulf War was used to strengthen arguments for further expenditures for high-tech weapons and the high-tech military organization required to manage and integrate them. But nearly every system used in the Gulf War provided surprises. The F-16 fighter planes had onboard computers so heavily loaded with information that they lacked enough memory for updates that would allow their electronic countermea-sure pods to respond to new weapons systems.[24] More important, perhaps, personal computers and laptops, the equipment upon which a distributed command-and-control organization had been built, failed under the climatic conditions of the Arabian desert. This is ironic given that war games in the United States are typically played in American deserts. Since then, ruggedized computers, specially equipped computers in boxes that protect them from adverse temperatures and sand, have replaced the off-the-shelf items.[25] The degree of "friendly fire" by U.S. troops was surprising and unacceptably high, a consequence of deskilled operators using blindingly fast information processing. Moreover, because the Iraqis had no capacity for electronic warfare, the electronic command-and-control systems of the U.S. forces were never subjected to electronic countermeasures.

As a small group of military and socio-technical system experts have argued, behind high-tech weaponry must lie an increasingly sophisticated organization to provide support and management. Most discussions of military modernization focus on weaponry and neglect the critical role of organization. The gap between the increasing complexity of weapons and the commensurate complexity of military organization is a recipe for disaster.

CHAPTER ELEVEN

Conclusions

A S A MEANS OF bringing together dominant themes in the previous chapters and drawing out a few of the implications of this book, I address three critical topics here: (1) the contributions of this study to institutional theory; (2) the practical implications for public management of integrating new information technologies into the machinery of the state; and (3) technology enactment as state-building.

Accounting for Technology in Institutional Theory

Institutional theory has not accounted for information technology (IT) and its multifaceted role in changing the contours of the landscape within which rules and structure influence perception and action. The Internet is a revolutionary lever for institutional change. Yet inside the machinery of the state, amid a web of institutional structures that offer perverse incentives for innovation and efficiency gains, the action of this lever is complex, indirect, and mediated significantly by institutional and organizational arrangements.

The central purpose of this book is the extension of institutional theory to account for information technology. The Internet and its effects, although indirect, invite institutional theorists to rethink the interpenetration of organizational settings and their networked environments. Rationalization of formal organizational systems and of society is being catalyzed by technological logics and the efficiencies of connectivity, standards, and interoperability. The empirical evidence in this study documents deep changes in industry structure, international flows of goods and information, national security, roles, authority relationships, and ultimately, modifications of the bureaucratic state, the role of the public servant, and citizenship. As these developments unfold, the continued absence of the Internet and related information technologies from institutional theory is puzzling. The puzzle is even more interesting because institutional theorists seek to explain the very phenomena and processes deeply affected by the Internet, including the diffusion of new organizational forms, the role and transformation of symbolic orders, and the structuration of organizational fields. The next logical step for institutional theory is to conceptualize the roles of IT in these social processes.

Two parallel streams of research have been increasing in importance but have not yet intersected. Their partial intersection would further institutional perspectives. Researchers, including institutionalists, have become greatly interested in a phenomenon variously referred to as collaboration, cooperation, social capital, interorganizational networks, and strategic alliances. Their interest stems from what appears to be a small but growing change in organizational and managerial behavior that allows a greater possibility for cross-boundary networks of many kinds. Social capital—a powerful concept that combines network dynamics, trust, and the role of norms—provides an underlying substrate upon which cooperative interjurisdictional arrangements might flourish. The network form has been contrasted with both hierarchy and market to distinguish its features and dynamics from both forms of organization. Interorganizational cooperation and the role of managerial craftsmanship has been explored. The importance of public-private partnerships as means of improving production processes and gaining market efficiencies is now well known. These and other developments in networked arrangements were taken up in detail in Chapter 5.

A parallel stream of research focuses on networked computing and its role in organizational structure and process. It is less well known in public management, organization theory, and economic sociology. Researchers have traced the effect of new information technologies on roles, role relationships, and consequently, organizational arrangements. Other researchers have contrasted information flows and social relationships in high-technology industry clusters. Still others have unpacked the relationships among information technologies, structure, and control in firms and industries. Knowledge management is, in part, concerned with externalizing and leveraging the collective, intrinsic knowledge in the social networks of professionals by using IT as a key organizational tool.

The parallelism of these two streams is curious given the intrinsic and well-known interrelatedness of technology, structure, people, and process. In organization theory, the term "technology" continues to evoke the industrial production technologies of machine-age bureaucracies, contingency theory, and the socio-technical school. Although these older perspectives have something to say to managers grappling with IT, their referent technology is focused on production rather than information. Public management has not typically included leveraging IT in the necessary toolkit of managers. Research on public organizations has not yet recognized it as a strategic tool, focusing instead on the difficult procurement processes for new computer systems and traditional information resource management issues.

The technology enactment framework brings the two streams together within a theoretical perspective. Rather than separating social organization and relationships from technological infrastructure, technology enactment theory recognizes the interplay between these two modes. In contrast to the buffering of technology management from core strategic concerns of public organizations, the enactment framework invites close analysis of the strategic and transformative role of information technology. It extends institutional and public management research by conceptualizing IT in at least three critical roles.

First, information technology functions in enactment theory as a tool that public managers, or bureaucratic policymakers, can use or misuse. Enacted technology is a product of design, negotiation, politics, understanding, social construction, entrepreneurship, and leadership. Information technologies are not simply purchased and plugged in, even when off-the-shelf products and services are procured for government organizations. They are always subject to extensive design of their use within an organization and must be integrated with work processes, communication channels, means of coordination, culture, authority structures—every central element of an organization.

The second role of IT is as a vital infrastructure in governments. Once built, this infrastructure becomes part of the institutional structure of constraint and opportunity. This is due to the high sunk costs of constructing large information systems, their tendency to persist even when technology changes rapidly, their influence on future actions, and their role as part of the brain or nervous system of organizations. Information systems quickly become intertwined in hundreds of ways with performance programs, routines, communication modes, and power. Thus they are difficult to change when their enactment is deeper than the "plug and play" level.

Third, information technology, particularly the Internet, serves not only as an enabler of change, but also as a strong catalyst for organizational change. Dramatic potential efficiency gains and opportunities to improve productivity and control align seamlessly with the prevalent logics of the bureaucratic state. Thus it is increasingly difficult for public managers to resist using technologies to produce efficiencies even if they avoid transformation. As a catalyst, the Internet increases the probability that a reaction—or some form of institutional change—will take place, given the appropriate elements.

Catalysts also increase the rate at which a reaction takes place. The Internet, not merely through its internal technical logic but also through the rhetoric and myth that surround it in American culture, forces a pace of change too rapid for many institutions. The pace and logic of social network construction are at odds with those of networked computing. Public managers who have already developed social capital are able to use the Internet to quickly leverage their collective capacity. But where mistrust characterizes a policy network, the Internet may exacerbate conflict by removing the buffers and slack that allowed agencies and policies in conflict to coexist peacefully.

The institutional design of the bureaucratic state overwhelmingly structures behavior within agencies rather than between agencies. Incentives in government flow from this institutional structure, which includes oversight and the budget processes that assume and reinforce agency autonomy and competition. It is difficult to develop cross-program initiatives because of these processes. Congressional committees are structured and staffed to align with agencies and agency programs. Congress has yet to adequately recognize or oversee cross-agency initiatives, although networks are proliferating and significant efficiencies and capacity from integration are possible.

Similarly, the Office of Management and Budget (OMB)—still much more oriented toward budget than management—is organized and staffed by agency, program, and line item. Budget examiners tend to find "messy" network arrangements at odds with their routines. Cross-agency initiatives cut against OMB procedures, practices, and organization. When such initiatives are relatively new and do not yet have strong support from constituents, they are easily squashed by the oversight process.

When federal agencies first developed plans to use IT more vigorously in government, at the beginning of the Clinton administration, cross-agency initiatives such as virtual agencies lay in the future. Budgets, plans, designs, and personnel were all developed with agency-based information systems as the dominant mental model. During the 1990s a number of cross-agency bodies were formed to rectify this problem and to enlarge the focus of technological change. The National Performance Review (NPR) explicitly encouraged the development of governmentwide systems. The Government Information Technology Services Board, now part of the Chief Information Officers (CIO) Council, was initiated to implement information systems recommended by NPR. Following the executive order that mandated a chief information officer for each federal agency, the Chief Information Officers Council was created to encourage knowledge transfer throughout the federal government. However, often the chief information officers have risen through the ranks of information resource management rather than strategic information technology. Their individual career focus on efficiency rather than on the larger institutional impact of technology biases their perceptions and limits their experience with networked initiatives. To date, interagency bodies have lacked the leadership, resources, and authority to conceptualize and build cross-agency or governmentwide information systems. The Clinger-Cohen Act of 1996, legislation that guides agency IT planning, procurement, and implementation, was written on the assumption that single agencies build information systems.[1] Agencies that conform to the letter of Clinger-Cohen cannot easily initiate horizontal, interagency networks. And the General Accounting Office and other oversight bodies use Clinger-Cohen to evaluate technology efforts. These formal and legal institutions cast technology enactment in the mold of the bureaucratic state.

The interagency board established to guide the International Trade Data System (ITDS) also lacked precedent, legitimacy, and power. Drawn from the agencies chiefly involved with the system, board members were ultimately forced to choose whether to weaken their alliances with the U.S. Customs Service in order to further an interagency network qualitatively different from its predecessor. But because weaker ties to Customs would mean poorer access to information, inspections, cargo, and technology in the medium term, most board members calculated the risk not worth taking.

The institutional setting within which government managers make and implement policy poses a puzzle. On the one hand, the claim that our institutions must be modernized so that agency heads can take advantage of new technologies and opportunities to develop networked capacity in government is both appealing and plausible. On the other hand, the stability and certainty provided by this institutional setting reduces the pace of change in government and allows for more considered and careful approaches to the reconstruction of the state.

Implications for Public Management

Theory and practice are, of course, separable only in the abstract. Without extending institutional theories to account for and explain the role of information technology in social systems and institutions, a solid body of practical advice to public managers will not follow. As the social psychologist Kurt Lewin said: There is nothing so practical as a good theory.

The role of public managers is critical to understanding how IT is being used to develop a virtual state. It is public managers who puzzle over structural and process arrangements, new technologies, and the implementation of policy within institutions. Hugh Heclo observed:

> Governments not only "power". . . they also puzzle. Policy-making is a form of collective puzzlement on society's behalf; it entails both deciding and knowing. The process of making . . . policies has extended beyond deciding what "wants" to accommodate, to include problems of knowing who might want something, what is wanted, what should be wanted, and how to turn even the most sweet-tempered general agreement into concrete collective action. This process is political, not because all policy is a by-product of power and conflict but because some men have undertaken to act in the name of others.[2]

Heclo continues that civil servants "have consistently made more important contributions to . . . policy development than political parties or interest groups." Socioeconomic change stimulates only intermittent attention from parties and interest groups. Civil servants, drawing on "administrative resources of information, analysis, and expertise" often envisage new policymaking to be "corrective[s] less to social conditions as such and more to the perceived failings of previous policy" in terms of "the government bureaucracy's own conception of what it has been doing."[3]

Public managers in a networked environment are the central enactors of technology in the state. They can no longer afford the luxury of relegating technology matters to technical staff. The questions and dilemmas raised by this book should convince public managers and senior executives in government of the strategic and political centrality of enacting technology. In some instances enactment furthers agency or program mission. In others technology plays a transformative role that leads to the expansion, contraction, or rethinking of mission. In each case transformation of mission follows from fundamental change in coordination, control, and communication. Often these modifications comprise unanticipated consequences of technology enactment. For example, even an interagency web portal will require managers to rethink, modify, and integrate organizational processes behind the web in what are called "back channels."

Several decades of institutional history, culture, and professionalization do not bode well for public managers taking a strategic perspective on IT in government. Current staffing systems and government occupations in information technology reflect a preoccupation with information resources management. The strategic technology executives needed in government are unlikely to come from the ranks of professionals who have climbed information resource management career ladders. Even more problematic is the "brain drain" of IT specialists from government to the private sector, ironically to firms that specialize in selling digital government solutions to public agencies. The likelihood of such exits increases as the use of the Internet in government gains force during a period of shrinking government by decreasing headcount in the civil service.[4]

The rules of the game in public management have long rewarded agency-specific endeavors. Agency autonomy would protect the integrity of policy areas, programs, and clients. Success meant increasing or maintaining budget, staff, and resources. Internal agency conflicts could be reconciled or at least buffered through bureaucratic governance structures and processes. If all attempts at resolution failed, miscreants could be banished to remote field offices.

The rules of the game for managers in a networked environment are qualitatively different. In the most highly calculative models of strategic alliances, individual organizations seek partnerships in which they can extract maximum value from others while losing as little of their own value as possible. This calculative game might work in economic fields in which multiple partners are available and in which alliances form to work on discrete projects and then disband. But networks of the type that are often formed in the public and nonprofit sectors are more firmly embedded in ongoing professional relationships in which reciprocity is extended rather than immediate (I may not pay you back immediately, but I will pay you back in the future) and in which capacity for joint policy and problem solving is often the chief value added. In this sense, ongoing interorganizational networks for leveraging knowledge or other cooperative partnerships provide more realistic models than temporary strategic alliances.

Flexible public managers will adapt to the new rules of the game. The technology enactment framework depicts how multiple rules and multiple games are currently in play, each of which possesses a different internal logic. Public managers must learn to be astute players of the bureaucratic game. They must also master the network game if they are to establish productive and useful partnerships in a time of scarce and diminishing government resources and rapidly changing environments. Finally, they must master the networked computing game if they are to use the Internet strategically rather than simply following fashion, contractors, or the behavior of "best practice" agencies in their field. Thus the art and science of public management have become more differentiated and complex. The balancing of mission, support from the authorizing environment, and administrative capacity is more challenging in a networked government. Not only is administrative capacity now an open systems game, but different actors in the authorizing environment also may hold different perceptions of the rules that are appropriate or in force. And the Internet, in its role as catalyst, infrastructure, and tool, adds another layer of complexity.

Multiple rules and games provide scope for strategic action and institutional change. Bureaucratic policymakers and other strategic actors transform institutions by consciously framing, managing, interpreting, and leveraging these contradictions. The use of new technologies and new organizational arrangements holds operational and strategic value but carries high rhetorical and symbolic value as well. Although networks are difficult to develop, their value and use are increasingly legitimized as appropriate for government because of opportunities to reduce overlap and redundancy, to pool resources and expertise, to attack policy problems that would otherwise fall between the bureaucratic stools, and to better serve the public by integrating fragmented programs and services.

Getting information and services over the web, a first-stage use, is highly appealing to that part of the public that has access to the Internet.

Much public management and network research takes for granted the overarching institutions in which individuals and organizations operate. In traditional public management scholarship, astute public managers are those who can work effectively within a given institutional system whose structure and practices are unlikely to change. Less often are they portrayed as agents of institutional change at an interagency level. But if the Internet is as revolutionary as its attributes indicate, if it is a new infrastructure for communication, coordination, and control, deeper structural change in institutions is likely and will be carried out primarily by civil servants and their policy networks. Public management and research on interorganizational networks might be extended to account for the fluidity, as well as the stability, of some institutions. For it is likely that the budget process, oversight processes, and committee structures will be modified to better align with the growth of interagency and intersectoral networked arrangements for policymaking, implementation, service delivery, and enforcement.

The technology enactment framework provides the basis for research to move beyond truisms such as "the Internet changes everything," which implies that the Internet is creating a network society, a networked government, and webbed structures. Finer-grained examination of current organizations and institutions reveals that in spite of access to the Internet many potential connections remain unforged, and numerous opportunities to gain stunning efficiencies, cost savings, integrated services and joint problem solving in complex policy areas lie fallow. The Internet is used often to reinforce old institutional structures rather than to open communications. Channel development occurs selectively and is controlled by public managers.

The dot-coming of government is just beginning. The average number of services provided over the web by state governments is only four.[5] Agencies are still in the process of putting basic information on the web and institutionalizing secure methods and authentication so that web-based payments become possible and personal documents, such as social security benefit information and tax files, can be transmitted safely over the Internet. England under Prime Minister Tony Blair promised to put a significant percentage of government transactions on the web by 2005. Former mayor Stephen Goldsmith of Indianapolis wondered publicly why anyone should have to come to city hall to transact business with the government.

The many examples and cases throughout the preceding chapters provide a sense of the cutting edge in digital government.

The beauty of virtuality obscures the difficulty of making institutional changes, and for the time being has delayed them. But web-based efforts at integration also reveal the "cracks" in the machinery of the bureaucratic state: the extent of fragmentation and lack of fit among programs, data measures, information, rules, and services in government. The promise of a seamless interface with the public at the level of a computer screen is the promise of the first wave of G2C digital government. The second wave, G2G, is integration and connection across jurisdictions and programs behind the interface, in the bricks and mortar of government. The second wave is about politics and the structure of the state.

Experienced political actors are fond of dismissing the significance of technological change by arguing that politics will not change. They are both right and wrong. They are wrong because, in the long run, technological change as significant as the Internet will lead to deep structural changes in government, although the contours are indeterminate. But they are correct to remind us that too few studies of digital government treat politics seriously, as if the Internet alone would usher in a transformation of the state and as if politics and institutions ceased to exist or to have force. This inquiry challenges that assumption.

Public managers need to better understand the politics of networked computing. Regardless of far-reaching and dramatic changes in IT, political actors will continue to pursue their own interests as they understand them. Absent changes in incentives and norms, agency heads and their staffs will continue to marshal resources in the form of budget, staff, and jurisdiction. The executive, legislative, and judicial branches will continue to jostle for position and primacy. These realities are not in question. But the transformation of information processing engenders political challenges that are at once familiar and qualitatively different. The Internet does not diminish politics or power as some cyberutopians have claimed. But it does change the contours of the playing field and some of the rules of the game.

Dramatic cost savings are anticipated from the development of cross-agency, G2G relationships. These networks will take longer to implement, and the resultant costs and benefits are more difficult to measure than other uses of networked computing in government because they derive from organizational and structural changes. The International Trade Data System demonstrates the type of dramatic gains possible to government and business from greater integration of the federal agencies with jurisdiction over trade administration. A more integrated, streamlined trade system has become a necessary adjunct to just-in-time, global business processes. But this case also demonstrates the political and institutional struggles on the horizon in several policy domains as some government actors attempt to maintain existing relationships of power while others seek to develop new coalitions and institutional arrangements in order to change the distribution of benefits from electronic government.

A critical set of governance questions bears on the nature of public-private policy networks and their appropriate role in the design, development, management, control, and in some respects, ownership of the virtual state. Private sector vendors of digital government and professional service firms have aggressively targeted the construction and operation of the virtual state as an enormous and lucrative market to be tapped. Economic incentives in the private sector generate rapid, innovative solutions and applications that should not be ignored by government actors. Yet information architecture, both hardware and software, is more than a technical instrument; it is a powerful form of governance. As a consequence, outsourcing architecture is effectively the outsourcing of policymaking. Governments must be careful, in their zeal to modernize, not to unwittingly betray the public interest. It will remain the province of public servants and elected officials to forge long-term policies that guard the interests of citizens, even when those policies seem inefficient, lacking in strategic power, or unsophisticated relative to "best practice" in the economy.

Technology Enactment as State-Building

When bureaucrats manage public programs, government operations, service delivery, and policy implementation, their activities may properly be called "public management." But when their activities move beyond the management of agency and program change to institutional change, their activities constitute state-building, the construction or reconstruction of the nation-state. The structure of the state will change largely to the extent that changes in information infrastructure catalyze modifications in communication, coordination, and control. I use the language of the state to indicate that the Internet signals not simply more efficient, effective government structured largely according to present arrangements, but deeper institutional change. Building a virtual state is about the process and politics of institutional change rather than a set of predictions about the end result. And this process is partially about rethinking the role of the state in relation to the economy and society.

Max Weber, echoing other nineteenth-century German social theorists, focused on the state as an institution whose structure has a significant effect on civil society. The state as a compulsory association is unique in its powers of coercion and control over territories and populations. The "administrative, legal, extractive, and coercive organizations" that constitute the state are at its center.[6] As fundamental modifications in these organizations accumulate, so proceeds change in the structure and role of the state. Alfred Stepan argued persuasively that the state is more than simply "government." Its structures and systems influence not only relationships between governing bodies and civil society but also central relationships within the economy and society.[7] Intellectual activities and decisions of civil servants working for long periods on policy questions are arguably more powerful and influential than the sporadic attention of legislators to particular policies. The activities of the civil servants and military officers who will construct trade administration processes for a global trading environment such as those analyzed in the development of the International Trade Data System, interagency advisor portals such as the U.S. Business Advisor, and the military of the future through battlefield management systems shape political forces and the path of future policy decisions. Their deep tacit knowledge of their agencies and policy domains, strong relationships with powerful economic actors, and experience in federal politics means that their policymaking behavior far exceeds administrative functions and public management.[8]

Policy networks link government with private and nonprofit organizations. These institutionalized policymaking structures pattern state and society relations. Research on the state suggests that variation among policy networks and the power, skill, interests, and resources of actors within them is likely to translate to variation in technology enactment across policy domains. In any analysis of state structure and capacity and its interrelationship with networked computing, one should expect variation across policy domains conditioned on financial resources, available policy instruments, the level of expertise and experience of bureaucratic policymakers, interest group structure, history and culture, and external events that might precipitate action.[9]

As students of government institutions have argued for more than a century, the structure and capacity of the state is of central importance because the state shapes politics and social relationships. It is not an arena in which interest groups compete, a black box in which inputs are transformed into outputs, or an instrument of class or business rule. Structural change in the state of the kind likely to occur as a result of networked computing disrupts complex ecologies of institutionalized power relationships among public and private organizations in the state and society.

Several topics of importance beyond the scope of this study bear mention. As of July 1999, the gap between information haves and have-nots was growing. Urban households with incomes of $75,000 or more are at least twenty times more likely to be connected to the Internet and nine times as likely to have a personal computer in the home as those households at the lowest income levels. African American and Latino households in the United States are two-fifths as likely to have access to the Internet as white households.[10] These inequalities must be considered in any political analysis of the use of the Internet in American government. The cases in this inquiry indicate that preferred "customers" receive preferred treatment in government enactment of the Internet. If this happens throughout government, then enacting technology with a "customer focus" and without conscious efforts to reduce inequality may exacerbate the digital divide in ways that extend beyond simple inequality of access.

An increasingly digital government favors those with access to computers, modems, and search tools and the education to use them. Text-based service delivery over the Internet means no service at all for those without literacy or English language proficiency. Further, the complexity and sheer amount of government information available electronically requires search and query skills not possessed by large segments of the population.

Yet even those without access to the Internet and the web are likely to be monitored by them: databases used in law enforcement, welfare, and other entitlement programs collect and integrate information about citizens. The protection of privacy looms as a set of central and pressing legislative and regulatory problems. The virtual state raises a new set of questions regarding the ownership, control, use, and manipulation of what have traditionally been government data. A recent Supreme Court decision enjoined government from selling some types of government data to private firms. The current legal structure is inadequate as a protector of property rights in a government whose networked computers extend from state to economy and blur the distinctions between them.

The potential benefits of networked institutions must also be balanced against other risks and externalities. Rationalization and standardization of the administrative state may allow bureaucrats less opportunity to use their accumulated experience and judgment, or tacit knowledge, to consider exceptional cases that do not conform to standardized rule-based systems. Security will be an increasingly pressing policy problem as the government makes it possible for citizens to transfer funds and private information such as that found in tax returns, financial aid applications, medical histories, and social security filings. Information systems are vulnerable to white-collar criminals, hackers, and "bugs" or errors in computer programs caused by decades of incremental and at times poorly documented software programs. Networked connections also increase the vulnerability of systems to a variety of threats.

A century ago the American state was dramatically different in structure, scope, and capacity from its counterpart today. The modern American bureaucratic state was constructed during the twentieth century through political and institutional processes. Some theorists predicted that the Internet would lead to the demise of the nation-state. More recently, it has become clear that the state is not likely to wither away, although researchers have shifted their attention to supra- and subnational governance structures. Few studies have focused on the changing structure of the American state. This book seeks to fill that gap. The state is being reconstructed as organizational actors enact new technologies to reshape relationships in the state and the economy.

Notes

Chapter One

1. For more detailed estimates regarding the economic implications of networked computing in government, see Jane E. Fountain with Carlos A. Osorio-Urzua, "Public Sector: Early Stage of a Deep Transformation," in Brookings Task Force on the Internet, *The Economic Payoff from the Internet Revolution* (Brookings, 2001).

2. Secretariat on Electronic Commerce, *The Emerging Digital Economy* (U.S. Department of Commerce, 1998), table 6, pp. A4–36 (www.ecommerce.gov/EmergingDig.pdf [August 14, 2000]).

3. See Fountain with Osorio-Urzua, "Public Sector: Early Stage of a Deep Transformation." These data are from a telephone interview with David Temoshok, General Services Administration, June 23, 2000. See also David Longenecker, "Student Loans—Applying for Federal Financial Aid Electronically," in *Reinventing Government to Get Results Americans Care About* (National Partnership for Reinventing Government, March 3, 1998) (www.npr.gov/library/announc/customer.html [April 1, 2001]).

4. See Fountain with Osorio-Urzua, "Public Sector: Early Stage of a Deep Transformation." The authors estimated the volume of a subset of routine government-to-citizen (G2C) transactions from the following data sources: the U.S. Census Bureau at: (www.census.gov/population/projections/nation/detail/componen.a);

(www.census.gov/population/socdemo/voting/history/htab01.txt); (www.census.gov/population/socdemo/school/taba-1.txt); and New Privately Owned Housing Units Authorized Unadjusted Data for United States (www.census.gov/const/C40/Table1/table1a.txt); 1999 U.S. Statistical Abstract, table 1439, Transportation Indicators for Motor Vehicles and Airlines: 1900 to 1998, 20th Century Statistics; table 893, Patents and Trademarks: 1980 to 1997; Section 17, Business Enterprise. The projections of transactions in 1999 and 2000 were made by Osorio-Urzua using Excel's system of linear best-fit trend. They are not provided in the government data.

5. Jeremy Sharrard with John C. McCarthy, Michael J. Tavilla, and Jay Stanley, "Sizing US eGovernment" (Cambridge, Mass.: Forrester Research Report, August 2000).

6. For the results of a survey of the information and services provided by the fifty state government websites see Jane E. Fountain, "Digital Government: A View from the States," working paper, Harvard University, Kennedy School of Government, 2001.

7. Bureau of Economic Analysis, "Government Consumption Expenditures and Gross Investment by Type (1959–1999)," U.S. Department of Commerce, table 307 (www.bea.doc.gov/bea/dn/seltabs.exe [July 10, 2000]).

8. "Government and the Internet: The Next Revolution," *Economist*, June 24, 2000, p. 4.

9. Fountain with Osorio-Urzua, "Public Sector: Early Stage of a Deep Transformation."

10. Robert A. Dahl, *Democracy and Its Critics* (Yale University Press, 1989), p. 91.

11. John Stuart Mill, *Considerations on Representative Government* (Indianapolis: Bobbs-Merrill, [1861] 1958). See Dahl, *Democracy and Its Critics*, pp. 93–95, for a persuasive argument that one can separate the protection of individual rights and interests in Mill from narrower arguments in favor of utilitarianism.

12. The following streams of new institutionalism, closely aligned with rational choice theory, are of less importance to this study but are of central significance to the institutional perspective as a whole. The new institutional economics adds realism to standard neoclassical economic accounts of behavior while retaining many standard economic assumptions of self-interest, rational choice, and the primacy of exchange and transaction costs. See, for example, Oliver E. Williamson, *Markets and Hierarchies* (Free Press, 1975); Douglass C. North, *Structure and Change in Economic History* (W. W. Norton, 1981); Richard Nelson and Sidney Winter, *An Evolutionary Theory of Economic Change* (Harvard University Press, 1982); Douglass C. North, "Government and the Cost of Exchange in History," *Journal of Economic History*, vol. 44, no. 2 (1984): 255–64; Oliver E. Williamson, *The Economic Institutions of Capitalism* (Free Press, 1985); Douglass C. North, "Economic Performance through Time," lecture delivered

after receiving the Alfred Nobel Memorial Prize in Economic Sciences, Stockholm, Sweden, December 9, 1993, printed in Mary C. Brinton and Victor Nee, eds., *The New Institutionalism in Sociology* (Russell Sage Foundation, 1998).

The positive theory of institutions in political science has focused on the effects of political structure on political outcomes. Institutions in this perspective typically are viewed as rational responses to collective action problems that economize on transaction costs, structure cooperation, and dampen opportunism. This view has been criticized for its functionalist assumptions that the institutions that are developed are the functional outcome of bargaining. See, for example, Kenneth A. Shepsle and Barry Weingast, "Structure-Induced Equilibria and Legislative Choice," *Public Choice*, vol. 37, no. 3 (1981): 503–19; Terry Moe, "The New Economics of Organization," *American Journal of Political Science*, vol. 78, no. 4 (1984): 739–77; Elinor Ostrom, "An Agenda for the Study of Institutions," *Public Choice*, vol. 48, no. 1 (1986): 3–25; Kenneth A. Shepsle, "Institutional Equilibrium and Equilibrium Institutions," in Herbert F. Weisberg, ed., *Political Science: The Science of Politics* (New York: Agathon, 1986); Kenneth A. Shepsle and Barry Weingast, "The Institutional Foundations of Committee Power," *American Political Science Review*, vol. 81, no. 1 (1987): 85–104; Kenneth A. Shepsle, "Studying Institutions: Some Lessons from the Rational Choice Approach," *Journal of Theoretical Politics*, vol. 1, no. 2 (1989): 131–37; Terry Moe, "Political Institutions: The Neglected Side of the Story," *Journal of Law, Economics, and Organization*, vol. 6 (1990): 213–53.

13. Robert D. Putnam with Robert Leonardi and Raffaella Y. Nanetti, *Making Democracy Work: Civic Traditions in Modern Italy* (Princeton University Press, 1993). Robert D. Putnam, *Bowling Alone: The Collapse and Revival of American Community* (Simon and Schuster, 2000).

14. James G. March and Johan P. Olsen, *Rediscovering Institutions: The Organizational Basis of Politics* (Free Press, 1989).

15. Robert O. Keohane and Joseph S. Nye, *Power and Interdependence: World Politics in Transition* (Little, Brown, 1977); R. O. Keohane, "International Institutions: Two Research Programs," *International Studies Quarterly*, vol. 32, no. 4 (1988): 379–96; Robert O. Keohane and Joseph S. Nye Jr., "Power and Interdependence in the Information Age," in Elaine Ciulla Kamarck and Joseph S. Nye Jr., eds., *democracy.com? Governance in a Networked World* (Hollis, N.H.: Hollis, 1999).

16. See, for example, Stephen D. Krasner, *International Regimes* (Cornell University Press, 1983); Robert O. Keohane, *After Hegemony* (Princeton University Press, 1984); Keohane, "International Institutions"; Frederick Kratochwil and J. G. Ruggie, "International Organization: A State of the Art on the State of the Art," *International Organization*, vol. 40, no. 4 (1986): 753–76; Stephen D. Krasner, "Sovereignty: An Institutional Perspective," *Comparative Political Studies*, vol. 21, no. 1 (1988): 660–94.

17. See H. T. Wright, "Recent Research on the Origin of the State," *Annual Review of Anthropology*, vol. 6: 379–97; Jack Hayward and R. N. Berki, eds., *State and Society in Contemporary Europe* (St. Martin's, 1979); Stephen Skowronek, *Building a New American State: The Expansion of National Administrative Capacity 1877–1920* (Cambridge University Press, 1982); Peter B. Evans, Dietrich Rueschemeyer, and Theda Skocpol, eds., *Bringing the State Back In* (Cambridge University Press, 1985); Peter Hall, *Governing the Economy: The Politics of State Intervention in Britain and France* (Oxford University Press, 1986).

18. See, for example, Hugh Heclo, *Modern Social Politics in Britain and Sweden: From Relief to Income Maintenance* (Yale University Press, 1974); Hugh Heclo, *A Government of Strangers: Executive Politics in Washington* (Brookings, 1977); Theda Skocpol, "Political Response to Capitalist Crises: Neo-Marxist Theories of the State and the Case of the New Deal," *Politics and Society*, vol. 10, no. 2 (1980): 155–201; Theda Skocpol and Kenneth Finegold, "State Capacity and Economic Intervention in the Early New Deal," *Political Science Quarterly*, vol. 97, no. 2 (1982): 255–78; Edward O. Laumann and David Knoke, *The Organizational State: Social Choice in National Policy Domains* (University of Wisconsin Press, 1987); Aaron Wildavsky, "Choosing Preferences by Constructing Institutions: A Cultural Theory of Preference Formation," *American Political Science Review*, vol. 81, no. 1 (1987): 3–22.

19. I use "policy" to mean a course of action rather than a formal program, following Heclo, *Modern Social Politics*, p. 4.

20. Ibid.

21. March and Olsen, *Rediscovering Institutions*; Walter W. Powell and Paul J. DiMaggio, *The New Institutionalism in Organizational Analysis* (University of Chicago Press, 1991); Brinton and Nee, *The New Institutionalism in Sociology*.

22. Émile Durkheim, *The Rules of Sociological Method*, 2d ed. (Free Press, [1895] 1958).

23. See John W. Meyer and Brian Rowan, "Institutionalized Organizations: Formal Structure as Myth and Ceremony," *American Journal of Sociology*, vol. 83, no. 2 (1977): 340–63; John W. Meyer and W. Richard Scott with Brian Rowan and Terrence Deal, eds., *Organizational Environments: Ritual and Rationality* (Beverly Hills, Calif.: Sage, 1983); Charles Perrow, "Overboard with Myth and Symbols," *American Journal of Sociology*, vol. 91, no. 1 (1985): 151–55.

24. Paul J. DiMaggio and Walter W. Powell, "The Iron Cage Revisited: Institutional Isomorphism and Collective Rationality in Organizational Fields," *American Journal of Sociology*, vol. 48, no. 2 (1983): 147–60.

25. Brinton and Nee, *The New Institutionalism in Sociology*.

26. Mark Granovetter, "Economic Action and Social Structure: The Problem of Embeddedness," *American Journal of Sociology*, vol. 91, no. 3 (1985): 481–510.

27. Ibid., p. 483.

28. Walter W. Powell, "Neither Market nor Hierarchy: Network Forms of Organization," in Barry Staw and L. L. Cummings, eds., *Research in Organiza-*

tional Behavior, vol. 12 (Greenwich, Conn.: JAI Press, 1990); Sharon Zukin and Paul DiMaggio, "Introduction," in Sharon Zukin and Paul DiMaggio, *Structures of Capital: The Social Organization of the Economy* (Cambridge University Press, 1990); Ronald Burt, *Structural Holes: The Social Structure of Competition* (Harvard University Press, 1992); Michael Gerlach, *Alliance Capitalism: The Social Organization of Japanese Business* (University of California Press, 1992); Alejandro Portes and Julia Sensenbrenner, "Embeddedness and Immigration: Notes on the Social Determinants of Economic Action," *American Journal of Sociology*, vol. 98, no. 6 (1993): 1320–50; Joel Podolny, "Market Uncertainty and the Social Character of Economic Exchange," *Administrative Science Quarterly*, vol. 39, no. 3 (1994): 458–83; Neil J. Smelser and Richard Swedberg, eds., *The Handbook of Economic Sociology* (Princeton University Press, 1994); Sumantra Ghosal and Peter Moran, "Bad for Practice: A Critique of the Trasaction Cost Theory," *Academy of Management Review*, vol. 21, nol. 1 (1996): 13–47; Brian Uzzi, "The Sources and Consequences of Embeddedness for the Economic Performance of Organizations," *American Sociological Review*, vol. 61, no. 4 (1996): 674–98; Brian Uzzi, "Social Structure and Competition in Interfirm Networks: The Paradox of Embeddedness," *Administrative Science Quarterly*, vol. 42, no. 1 (1997): 35–67; Victor Nee and Paul Ingram, "Embeddedness and Beyond: Institutions, Exchange, and Social Structure," in Brinton and Nee, *The New Institutionalism in Sociology*.

29. Max Weber, *Economy and Society: An Outline of Interpretive Sociology*, Guenther Roth and Claus Wittich, trans. and eds. (New York: Bedminster Press, [1922] 1968).

30. Alfred D. Chandler Jr., *The Visible Hand: The Managerial Revolution in American Business* (Belknap Press of Harvard University Press, 1977).

31. James R. Beniger, *The Control Revolution: Technological and Economic Origins of the Information Society* (Harvard University Press, 1986).

32. JoAnne Yates, *Control through Communication: The Rise of System in American Management* (Johns Hopkins Press, 1989).

33. Stephen R. Barley, "Technology as an Occasion for Structuring: Evidence from Observations of CT Scanners and the Social Order of Radiology Departments," *Administrative Science Quarterly*, vol. 21, no. 1 (1986): 81; Stephen R. Barley, "Technology, Power, and the Social Organization of Work: Toward a Pragmatic Theory of Skilling and Deskilling," in Nancy DiTomaso and S. B. Bacharach, eds., *Research in the Sociology of Organizations*, vol. 6 (Greenwich, Conn.: JAI Press, 1988); Stephen R. Barley, "The Alignment of Technology and Structure through Roles and Networks," *Administrative Science Quarterly*, vol. 35: 61–103; Siobhan O'Mahony and Stephen R. Barley, "Do Digital Telecommunications Affect Work and Organization? The State of Our Knowledge," *Research in Organizational Behavior*, vol. 21 (Greenwich, Conn.: JAI Press, 1999): 125–61.

34. Shoshana Zuboff, *In the Age of the Smart Machine: The Future of Work and Power* (Basic Books, 1984); Michael S. Scott Morton, ed., *The Corporation*

of the 1990s: Information Technology and Organizational Transformation (Oxford University Press, 1991); Lee Sproull and Sarah Kiesler, *Connections: New Ways of Working in the Networked Organization* (MIT Press, 1991); Michael Hammer and James Champy, *Reengineering the Corporation: A Manifesto for Business Revolution* (HarperCollins, 1993); Thomas H. Davenport, *Process Innovation: Reengineering Work through Information Technology* (Harvard Business School Press, 1993); Maryellen R. Kelley, "Productivity and Information Technology: The Elusive Connection," *Management Science*, vol. 40, no. 11: 1406–25; Janet Fulk and G. DeSanctis, "Electronic Communication and Changing Organizational Forms," *Organization Science*, vol. 6, no. 6 (1995): 337–49; J. M. Pickering and John L. King, "Hardwiring Weak Ties: Interorganizational Computer-Mediated Communication, Occupational Communities, and Organizational Change," *Organization Science*, vol. 6, no. 4 (1995): 479–86; Manuel Castells, *The Information Age: Economy, Society and Culture*, 3 vols. (Oxford: Blackwell, 1996); Manju K. Ahuja and Kathleen Carley, "Network Structure in Virtual Organizations," *Journal of Computer-Mediated Communication*, vol. 3, no. 4 (1998); JoAnne Yates, Wanda J. Orlikowski, and K. Okamura, "Explicit and Implicit Structuring of Genres in Electronic Communication: Reinforcement and Change in Social Interaction," *Organization Science*, vol. 10, no. 1 (1999): 83–112; Eric Brynjolfsson and Lorin M. Hitt, "Beyond Computation: Information Technology, Organization Transformation and Business Performance," *Journal of Economic Perspectives*, vol. 10, no. 4 (2000).

35. Laurence J. O'Toole Jr., "Treating Networks Seriously: Practical and Research-Based Agendas in Public Administration," *Public Administration Review*, vol. 57, no. 1 (1997): 45.

36. John J. DiIulio Jr. and Donald F. Kettl, "Fine Print: The Contract with America, Devolution, and the Administrative Realities of American Federalism," Report 95-1 (Brookings, Center for Public Management, March 1995), p. 17.

37. Brinton H. Milward, ed., Symposium on "The Hollow State: Capacity, Control and Performance in Interorganizational Settings," *Journal of Public Administration Research and Theory*, vol. 6, no. 2 (1996): 193–313; Brinton H. Milward and Keith G. Provan, "The Hollow State: Private Provision of Public Services," in Helen Ingram and Steven R. Smith, eds., *Public Policy for Democracy* (Brookings, 1993).

38. Heclo, *Modern Social Politics*, p. 1.

39. W. Richard Scott, "Unpacking Institutional Arguments," in Walter W. Powell and Paul J. DiMaggio, eds., *The New Institutionalism in Organizational Analysis* (University of Chicago Press, 1991), p. 167.

40. See, for example, Peter Drucker, *Post-Capitalist Society* (Boston: Butterworth-Heinemann, 1993); Scott Morton, *The Corporation of the 1990s*.

41. O'Mahony and Barley, "Do Digital Telecommunications Affect Work and Organization?"

42. Harold J. Leavitt and Thomas L. Whisler, "Management in the 1980's," *Harvard Business Review*, vol. 36, no. 6 (1958): 41–48.

43. Fernand Braudel, *The Structures of Everyday Life: The Limits of the Possible*, vol. 1 of *Civilization and Capitalism: 15th–18th Century* (Harper and Row, 1981).

44. See, for example, Scharrard, "Sizing eGovernment."

Chapter Two

1. National Performance Review, "From Red Tape to Results: Creating a Government That Works Better and Costs Less" (Government Printing Office, 1993). For a brief history of the National Performance Review, see John Kamensky, "A Brief History," National Partnership for Reinventing Government, Washington, D.C. (www.npr.gov/cgi-bin/print_hit_bold.pl/whoweare/history2.htm?Kamensky [March 13, 2001]); Kamensky, "A Brief History of NPR," (www.npr.gov/library/papers/bkgrd/brief.html [March 13, 2001]); and Kamensky, "The U.S. Reform Experience: The National Performance Review," (www.npr.gov/library/papers/bkgrd/Kamensky.html [March 13, 2001]). Among the important critiques of the NPR see John J. DiIulio Jr., Gerald Garvey, and Donald F. Kettl, *Improving Government Performance: An Owner's Manual* (Brookings, 1993); Donald F. Kettl and John J. DiIulio Jr., eds., *Inside the Reinvention Machine: Appraising Governmental Reform* (Brookings, 1995); and Ronald C. Moe, "The 'Reinventing Government' Exercise: Misinterpreting the Problem, Misjudging the Consequences," *Public Administration Review*, vol. 54, no. 2 (1994): 125–36.

2. See Michael Barzelay, *The New Public Management: Improving Research and Policy Dialogue* (University of California Press, 2001); Alan Doig and John Wilson, "What Price New Public Management?" *Political Quarterly*, vol. 69, no. 3 (1998): 26–76; Fred Thompson and L. R. Jones, *Reinventing the Pentagon: How the New Public Management Can Bring Institutional Renewal* (San Francisco. Jossey-Bass, 1994), Joel D. Aberbach and Bert A. Rockman, "Policy and the New Public Management in the United States," *Journal of Managerial Issues*, vol. 2 (Winter 1990): 371–81.

3. John Kamensky, "The U.S. Reform Experience, 1997" (www.npr.gov/library/papers/bkgrd/kamensky.html [February 2000]).

4. Executive Order 12862, "Setting Customer Service Standards," September 11, 1993.

5. National Performance Review, "Reengineering through Information Technology," Accompanying Report of the National Performance Review, September 1993 (www.npr.gov/library).

6. Janet Abbate, *Inventing the Internet* (MIT Press, 1999).

7. The Internet browser Mosaic was developed in 1993 by Marc Andreesen, then a student at the University of Illinois. Netscape, the commercial product

based on Mosaic and cofounded by Andreesen, formed a major starting point to the opening of the Internet to the general population of computer users. As the first successful graphical browser, Mosaic allowed computer users to "surf" the Internet by clicking a mouse on hypertext links to reach computer files located on computers around the globe.

8. T. A. Kalil, "Leveraging Cyberspace," *IEEE Communications Magazine* (July 1996): 82.

9. Steven D. Whitehead, "Auto-FAQ: An Experiment in Cyberspace Leveraging," Electronic Proceedings of the Second International World Wide Web Conference, 1994 (www/ncsa/uiuc.edu/SDG/IT94/Proceedings [March 13, 2001]).

10. Joshua Dean, "The IT Pioneers," *Government Executive* (www.govexec.com/features/1299/1299s6.htm [March 23, 2001]).

11. Ibid.

12. Ibid.

13. I am indebted for this explanation to James Martin, *Cybercorp* (New York: Amacom, 1996), p. 115. See also, Nitin Nohria and James D. Berkeley, "The Virtual Organization," in Anne Donnellon and Charles Heckscher, eds., *The Post-Bureaucratic Organization* (Thousand Oaks, Calif.: Sage). Packet switching, or the sending of messages in uniformly sized "packets," is central to distributed communcations systems. For an account of its development and integration into the Internet, see Abbate, *Inventing the Internet*, chap. 1.

14. The success of Asian economies in the 1980s spurred political, economic, and scholarly interest in network structures, specifically dense interorganizational networks and management practices. See, for example, Mark Granovetter, "Economic Action and Social Structure: The Problem of Embeddedness," *American Journal of Sociology*, vol. 91, no. 3 (1985): 481–510; F. P. Contractor and P. Lorange, *Cooperative Strategies in International Business* (Lexington, Mass.: Lexington Books, 1988); Robert G. Eccles and Dwight B. Crane, "Managing through Networks in Investment Banking," *California Management Review*, vol. 30, no. 1 (1987): 176–96; Walter Powell, "Neither Market nor Hierarchy: Network Forms of Organization," in B. Staw and L. L. Cummings, eds., *Research in Organizational Behavior* (Greenwich, Conn.: JAI Press, 1990); Michael Gerlach, *Alliance Capitalism: The Social Organization of Japanese Business* (University of California Press, 1992).

15. Lucian W. Pye, ed., *Communications and Political Development* (Princeton University Press, 1963).

16. For recent examples of client-based, cross-agency portal efforts in the U.S. federal government see the National Partnership for Reinventing Government website (www.npr.gov); FirstGov.gov, a portal providing access to the entire U.S. government holidngs on the web; Access America for Seniors (www.seniors.gov); Access America for Students (www.students.gov); and the Business Advisor (www.business.gov), discussed in Chapter 9 in this volume.

17. Information Network for Public Health Officials (INPHO), Public Health Practice Program Office, Centers for Disease Control, Department of Health and Human Services, semifinalist application 288, Innovations in American Government, 1995 Awards Program, Kennedy School of Government, Harvard University.

18. Nuclear Suppliers Group—Information Sharing, Office of Arms Control and Nonproliferation, Export Control Division, Department of Energy, semifinalist application 247, Innovations in American Government, 1996 Awards Program, Kennedy School of Government, Harvard University.

19. See www.dtic.mil/staff/cthomps/webmaster96/800.html (January 2000); "Migrating into the Digital World" (slide from presentation on the virtual social work agency) (www.socialworkmanager.org/virtualsocialwork/V-SWK/sld007.htm).

20. www.hud.gov (November 2000).

21. "Status of the Original NPR Information Technology Reengineering Initiatives," Appendix C, *Access America Initiatives*, accompanying report, no date (www.accessamerica.gov/docs/appndxc.html [April 2, 2001].

22. Ibid.

23. See, for example, Murray Edelman, *The Symbolic Uses of Politics* (University of Illinois Press, 1964).

Chapter Three

1. See Ithiel de Sola Pool, *Technologies of Freedom* (Harvard University Press, 1983); Fernand Braudel, *The Perspective of the World*, vol. 3: *Civilization and Capitalism: 15th–18th Century* (Harper and Row, 1984), pp. 566ff.; Manuel Castells, *The Rise of the Network Society*, vol. 1: *The Information Age: Economy, Society and Culture* (Cambridge, Mass.: Blackwell, 1996), esp. chap. 3, pp. 151ff.; Merritt Roe Smith and Leo Marx, eds., *Does Technology Drive History? The Dilemma of Technological Determinism* (MIT Press, 1994), JoAnne Yates, *Control through Communication: The Rise of System in American Management* (Johns Hopkins University Press, 1989); James Beniger, *The Control Revolution*. Using detailed evidence, Yates argues that technological innovations in communications in the nineteenth century were not used in the economy, in some cases, for fifty years. Braudel argues also, with respect to the industrial revolution in Great Britain, that technological innovations must wait for the economy to use them. James Beniger argues that control technologies developed in industry in the nineteenth and twentieth centuries were adopted and implemented before consumer demand for them developed.

2. For elaboration on these and other effects, see, for example, George P. Huber, "The Nature and Design of Post-Industrial Organizations," *Management Science* (August 1984): 928–51; Michael Scott Morton, ed., *The Corporation of*

the 1990s: Information Technology and Organizational Transformation (Oxford University Press, 1991); Philip Evans and Thomas Wurster, "Strategy and the New Economics of Information, *Harvard Business Review* (September–October 1997): 70–83.

3. Shared databases are digital files of organized data and information that can be accessed and used simultaneously by large numbers of people anywhere on the globe provided a person has a computer, connection to the database, and permission to access the information.

4. Joshua Dean, "The IT Pioneers," *Government Executive*, December 1, 1999 (www.govexec.com/features/1299/1299s6.htm [March 28, 2001]).

5. Goals 2000 Teacher Forum, U.S. Department of Education, semifinalist application 1209, 1996 Awards Program, Innovations in American Government Program, Kennedy School of Government, Harvard University.

6. As a government official reported: "The single most important achievement to date regarding the development of the ACE System is the increased speed at which FEMA processes home inspections. The Northridge earthquake generated nearly 700,000 requests for assistance, with approximately 600,000 requiring an inspection. At Disaster plus sixty days, 291,000 ACE inspections had been completed. At Disaster plus sixty days after Hurricane Andrew, 90,000 inspections had been accomplished. This latter figure represents the maximum that could be achieved using the paper system. This increased ability to respond to the needs of the disaster victims has expedited the award process and increased the ability of the disaster victims to make repairs of their damaged homes." Automated Construction Estimating, 1995 Awards Program, semifinalist application 558, 1995 Awards Program, Innovations in American Government, Kennedy School of Government, Harvard University.

7. William J. Bruns and F. Warren McFarlan, "Information Technology Puts Power in Control Systems," *Harvard Business Review* (September–October 1987): 89–96.

8. Harry Braverman, *Labor and Monopoly Capital: The Degradation of Work in the Twentieth Century* (New York: Monthly Review Press, 1998).

9. Even the efficiencies created by the division of labor have been overstated in many cases. See Richard Hackman and Greg Oldham, *Work Redesign* (Reading, Mass.: Addison-Wesley, 1980) on the relationship between individual motivation and the design of work. The socio-technical perspective in organization theory has always stressed the importance of "meaningful" tasks or segments of work large enough to have intrinsic interest to workers.

10. See, for example, Todd R. LaPorte, ed., *Organized Social Complexity: Challenge to Politics and Policy* (Princeton University Press, 1984); Huber, "The Nature and Design of Post-Industrial Organizations"; and Jay R. Galbraith, *Designing Complex Organizations* (Reading, Mass.: Addison-Wesley, 1973).

11. United States General Accounting Office, "Federal Downsizing: Better Workforce and Strategic Planning Could Have Made Buyouts More Effective," GAO/GGD-96-62, August 1996.

12. Harold J. Leavitt and Thomas L. Whisler, "Management in the 1980s," *Harvard Business Review* (November–December 1958): 41–48. Their forecast was based on the obsolescence of middle management in light of office automation. That their prediction took more than thirty years to come to fruition merely illuminates the uncertainties of making deep structural modifications in complex organizations.

13. Interview conducted by the author with an INS branch chief, New York City, July 1993.

14. Al Gore, "Businesslike Government: Lessons Learned from America's Best Companies," National Performance Review, October 1997, pp. 20–22; Linda Kaboolian, "Ruthless with Time, Gracious with People," Kennedy School of Government Teaching Case, Harvard University, 1994.

15. For negative accounts of increases in employee discretion and autonomy see, for example, *Administrative Science Quarterly*, Special Issue: "Critical Perspectives on Organizational Control" (June 1998); Gene Rochlin, *Trapped in the Net: The Unanticipated Consequences of Computerization* (Princeton University Press, 1997). Positive views pervade the popular management literature as well as recent government reports and publications in public management and reform efforts. See, for example, National Performance Review, *From Red Tape to Results: Creating a Government That Works Better and Costs Less* (Government Printing Office, 1993).

16. Dean, "The IT Pioneers."

17. Ibid.

18. Ibid. The system was developed at the cost of $4.6 million dollars and was tested in pilot studies at LaGuardia Airport in New York, Chicago's O'Hare International Airport, and Denver International Airport.

19. Ibid.

20. Bruns and McFarlan, "Information Technology."

21. Savings Institution Risk Management Program, Office of Thrift Supervision, Department of the Treasury, semifinalist application 270, 1995 Awards Program, Innovations in American Government, Kennedy School of Government, Harvard University, p. 7.

22. Interview with Michael Gomez, program manager of IHPES, reported in Dean, "The IT Pioneers." IHPES supports thirty-one of the forty-nine IHS hospitals as well as tribally operated facilities.

23. Consolidated Planning/Community Connections, Department of Housing and Urban Development, winner, 1996 Awards Program, Innovations in American Government, Kennedy School of Government, Harvard University.

24. James G. March and Herbert Simon, *Organizations* (John Wiley, 1958); Richard Cyert and James G. March, *A Behavioral Theory of the Firm* (Prentice-Hall, 1963); Beniger, *The Control Revolution*; Paul S. Adler and Bryan Borys, "Two Types of Bureaucracy: Enabling and Coercive," *Administrative Science Quarterly* (March 1996): 61–89.

25. Braverman, *Labor and Monopoly Capital*; Shoshana Zuboff, *In the Age of the Smart Machine: The Future of Work and Power* (Basic Books, 1984); Adler and Borys, "Two Types of Bureaucracy."

26. Zuboff, *In the Age of the Smart Machine*; Paul S. Adler, *Technology and the Future of Work* (Oxford University Press, 1992); Adler and Borys, "Two Types of Bureaucracy."

27. Adler and Borys, "Two Types of Bureaucracy," p. 68.

Chapter Four

1. For an earlier perspective on the need for a complex administrative state in which bureaucrats indeed play a decisionmaking role, see Fritz Morstein Marx, *The Administrative State: An Introduction to Bureaucracy* (University of Chicago Press, 1957).

2. Max Weber, *An Outline of Interpretive Sociology: Economy and Society,* 2 vols., ed. Guenther Roth and Claus Wittich (University of California Press, [1922] 1978).

3. James R. Beniger, *The Control Revolution: Technological and Economic Origins of the Information Society* (Harvard University Press, 1986).

4. Charles Perrow, *Complex Organizations: A Critical Essay*, 3d ed. (Random House, 1986).

5. Weber, *Economy and Society*, vol. 2, chap. 11.

6. Or "levels of graded authority" in a different translation; see Hans Gerth and C. Wright Mills, eds., *From Max Weber: Essays in Sociology* (Oxford University Press, 1946).

7. Weber, *Economy and Society*, vol. 2, chap. 11, p. 956.

8. James March and Herbert Simon, *Organizations* (John Wiley, 1958).

9. Luther Gulick and Lyndall Urwick eds., *Papers on the Science of Administration* (Columbia University Institute of Public Administration, 1937).

10. Richard M. Cyert and James G. March, *A Behavioral Theory of the Firm* (Prentice Hall, 1963).

11. Graham Allison, *Essence of Decision: Explaining the Cuban Missile Crisis* (Little, Brown, 1971).

12. James Q. Wilson, *Bureaucracy: What Government Agencies Do and Why They Do It* (Basic Books, 1989).

13. Beniger, *The Control Revolution: Technological and Economic Origins of the Information Society* (Harvard University Press, 1986), pp. 6ff.

14. JoAnne Yates, *Control through Communication: The Rise of System in American Management* (Johns Hopkins University Press, 1989).

15. Herbert A. Simon, "The Architecture of Complexity," *Proceedings of the American Philosophical Society* 106 (December 1962): 467–82.

16. Several theorists at least partially reject the idea of bureaucratic neutrality; see, for example, Chester Barnard, *The Functions of the Executive* (Harvard University Press, 1948); March and Simon, *Organizations*; Anthony Downs, *Inside Bureaucracy* (Little, Brown, 1967); and Oliver E. Williamson, *The Economic Institutions of Capitalism* (Free Press, 1985).

17. See the analysis of Weber's theory of bureaucracy in W. Richard Scott, *Organizations: Rational, Natural and Open Systems*, 2d ed. (Prentice Hall), pp. 40–45.

18. Frederick Winslow Taylor, *The Principles of Scientific Management* (W. W. Norton, [1911] 1967).

19. Gerald Garvey, "False Promises: The NPR in Historical Perspective," in Donald F. Kettl and John J. DiIulio Jr., eds. *Inside the Reinvention Machine: Appraising Governmental Reform* (Brookings, 1995), p. 90.

20. Stephen Skowronek, *Building a New American State: The Expansion of National Administrative Capacity 1877–1920* (Cambridge University Press, 1982).

21. Garvey, "False Promises," n. 7.

22. See Dennis Dresang, "Whither Civil Service? Wither Civil Service?" working paper (LaFollette Institute, University of Wisconsin, Madison, 1993).

23. Garvey, "False Promises," pp. 90–91.

24. In this section of the chapter I draw upon and extend a framework developed by Henry Mintzberg in *The Structuring of Organizations: A Synthesis of the Research* (Prentice Hall, 1979). Mintzberg, summarizing several streams of research and theory in organizational analysis (including Herbert Simon, *Administrative Behavior: A Study of Decision-Making Processes in Administrative Organization* [Macmillan, 1947]; March and Simon, *Organizations*; and Jay Galbraith, *Designing Complex Organizations* [Reading, Mass.: Addison-Wesley, 1973]) suggested that organizations structure themselves through coordination (using mutual adjustment, supervision, and standardization), functions (executive, technical, and operational), and systems of regulated flows.

25. I use the term "coordination" to convey the image as well as the importance of the links within flows of information. Some, including Beniger and students of cybernetic theory and its successors, subsume coordination under control. Although I agree with their argument, I use "coordination" to mean the flows or movements of information within and across organizations. I use "control" to mean the measures used to ascertain the degree to which objectives are met.

26. Charles E. Lindblom, *The Intelligence of Democracy: Decision Making through Mutual Adjustment* (Free Press, 1965), pp. 9–10; emphasis in original.

27. Ibid., p. 91.

28. Ibid., p. 89.

29. See Douglas Yates, *Democratic Bureaucracy: The Search for Democracy and Efficiency in American Government* (Harvard University Press, 1982).

30. Beniger, *The Control Revolution*, p. 15.

31. March and Simon, *Organizations*, p. 162.

32. Charles Lindblom, *Inquiry and Change: The Troubled Attempt to Understand and Shape Society* (Yale University Press, 1990), esp. chap. 12.

33. See also Simon, *Administrative Behavior*; March and Simon, *Organizations*; and Mintzberg, *The Structure of Organizations*.

34. See Michael Hammer and James Champy, *Reengineering the Corporation: A Manifesto for Business Revolution* (HarperCollins, 1993); and Thomas H. Davenport, *Process Innovation: Reengineering Work through Information Technology* (Harvard Business School Press, 1993).

35. March and Simon, *Organizations*, pp. 164–65.

36. See the special issue of *Administrative Science Quarterly*, "Critical Perspectives on Organizational Control," vol. 43 (June 1998), especially John M. Jermier, "Introduction: Critical Perspectives on Organizational Control," pp. 235–56; and Graham Sewell, "The Discipline of Teams: The Control of Team-Based Industrial Work through Electronic and Peer Surveillance," pp. 397–428. See also Frederick M. Gordon, "Bureaucracy: Can We Do Better? We Can Do Worse," in Charles Heckscher and Anne Donnellon, eds., *The Post-Bureaucratic Organization: New Perspectives on Organizational Change* (Thousand Oaks, Calif.: Sage, 1994).

37. See, for example, James Burnham, *The Managerial Revolution: What Is Happening in the World* (John Day, 1941); William H. Whyte Jr., *The Organization Man* (Simon and Schuster, 1956).

38. United States Department of Commerce, Office of Technology Policy, Technology Administration, "America's New Deficit: The Shortage of Information Technology Workers" (Fall 1997).

Chapter Five

1. Lawrence Lessig, *Code and Other Laws of Cyberspace* (Basic Books, 1999).

2. For exceptions see Nitin Nohria and Robert G. Eccles, "Face-to-Face: Making Network Organizations Work," in Nohria and Eccles, eds., *Networks and Organizations: Structure, Form, and Action* (Harvard Business School Press, 1992); Siobahn O'Mahony and Stephen R. Barley, "Do Digital Telecommunications Affect Work and Organizations? The State of Our Knowledge," *Research in Organizational Behavior*, vol. 21 (1999): 125–61; Manju K. Ahuja and Kathleen M. Carley, "Network Structure in Virtual Organizations," *Journal of Computer-Mediated Communication*, vol. 3, no. 4 (1998).

3. Joel M. Podolny and Karen L. Page, "Network Forms of Organization," *Annual Review of Sociology*, vol. 24 (1998): 59.

4. Christine Oliver, "Determinants of Interorganizational Relationships: Integration and Future Directions," *Academy of Management Review*, vol. 15, no. 2 (1990): 241.

5. See Podolny and Page, "Network Forms of Organization," p. 59.

6. See Mark Granovetter, "Economic Action and Social Structure: The Problem of Embeddedness," *American Journal of Sociology*, vol. 91, no. 3 (1985): 481–510; Brian Uzzi, "Social Structure and Competition in Interfirm Networks: The Paradox of Embeddedness," *Administrative Science Quarterly*, vol. 42, no. 1 (1997): 35–67; Brian Uzzi, "The Sources and Consequences of Embeddedness for the Economic Performance of Organizations," *American Sociological Review*, vol. 61, no. 4 (1996): 674–98; Alejandro Portes and Julia Sensenbrenner, "Embeddedness and Immigration: Notes on the Social Determinants of Economic Action," *American Journal of Sociology*, vol. 98, no. 6 (1993): 1320–50; Joel A. C. Baum and Christine Oliver, "Institutional Embeddedness and the Dynamics of Organizational Populations," *American Sociological Review*, vol. 57, no. 4 (1992): 540–59.

7. Manuel Castells, *The Rise of the Network Society*, vol. 1 of *The Information Age: Economy, Society, and Culture* (Oxford: Blackwell, 1996); Mark Granovetter, "Coase Revisited: Business Groups in the Modern Economy," *Industrial and Corporate Change*, vol. 4, no. 1 (1995): 93–131; Rosabeth Moss Kanter, "The Future of Bureaucracy and Hierarchy in Organizational Theory: A Report from the Field," in Pierre Bourdieu and James S. Coleman, eds., *Social Theory for a Changing Society* (Boulder, Colo.: Westview, 1991); Edward Laumann, "Comment on 'The Future of Bureaucracy and Hierarchy in Organizational Theory: A Report from the Field,'" in Bourdieu and Coleman, *Social Theory for a Changing Society*.

8. Podolny and Page, "Network Forms of Organization"; James R. Lincoln, Michael L. Gerlach, and Christina Ahmadjian, "Keiretsu Networks and Corporate Performance," *American Sociological Review*, vol. 61, no. 1 (1996): 67–88; Michael L. Gerlach, *Alliance Capitalism: The Social Organization of Japanese Business* (University of California Press, 1992).

9. Oliver E. Williamson, "Comparative Economic Organization: The Analysis of Discrete Structural Alternatives," *Administrative Science Quarterly*, vol. 36, no. 2 (1991): 269–96; Oliver E. Williamson, *The Economic Institutions of Capitalism: Firms, Markets, and Relational Contracting* (Free Press, 1985).

10. John R. Harbison and Peter Pekar Jr., *Smart Alliances: A Practical Guide to Repeatable Success* (San Francisco: Jossey-Bass, 1998).

11. Peter Pekar Jr. and Robert Allio, "Making Alliances Work—Guidelines for Success," *Long Range Planning* vol. 27, no. 4 (1994): 54–65; Jane E. Fountain

and Robert D. Atkinson, "Innovation, Social Capital, and the New Economy: New Federal Policies to Support Collaborative Research," Washington, D.C., Progressive Policy Institute, July 1998.

12. Podolny and Page, "Network Forms of Organization," p. 58.

13. Walter W. Powell, "Neither Market nor Hierarchy: Network Forms of Organization," in Barry Staw and L. L. Cummings, eds., *Research in Organizational Behavior*, vol. 12 (Greenwich, Conn.: JAI Press, 1990); Jeffrey L. Bradach and Robert G. Eccles, "Price, Authority, and Trust: From Ideal Types to Plural Forms," *Annual Review of Sociology*, vol. 15 (Palo Alto, Calif.: Annual Reviews, 1989); Walter W. Powell, Kenneth W. Koput, and Laurel Smith-Doerr, "Interorganizational Collaboration and the Locus of Innovation," *Administrative Science Quarterly*, vol. 41, no. 1 (1996): 116–45.

14. Edward O. Laumann and David Knoke, *The Organizational State: Social Choice in National Policy Domains*, (University of Wisconsin Press, 1987); David Knoke, Franz Urban Pappi, Jeffrey Broadbent, and Yutaka Tsujinaka, *Comparing Policy Networks: Labor Politics in the U.S., Germany, and Japan* (Cambridge University Press, 1996).

15. Hugh Heclo, *A Government of Strangers: Executive Politics in Washington* (Brookings, 1977), p. 132.

16. Ronald Burt, *Structural Holes: The Social Structure of Competition* (Harvard University Press, 1992).

17. Granovetter, "Economic Action and Social Structure"; Brian Uzzi, "Embeddedness in the Making of Financial Capital: How Social Relations and Networks Benefit Firms Seeking Capital," *American Sociological Review*, vol. 64, no. 4 (1999): 481–505; Brian Uzzi, "The Sources and Consequences of Embeddedness for the Economic Performance of Organizations: The Network Effect," *American Sociological Review*, vol. 61, no. 4 (1996): 674–98.

18. Nohria and Eccles, "Face-to-Face"; Ahuja and Carley, "Network Structure in Virtual Organizations."

19. Laurence J. O'Toole Jr., "Treating Networks Seriously: Practical and Research-Based Agendas in Public Administration," *Public Administration Review*, vol. 57, no. 1 (1997): 45; O'Mahony and Barley, "Do Digital Telecommunications Affect Work?"

20. Robert G. Eccles and Dwight B. Crane, *Doing Deals: Investment Banks at Work* (Harvard Business School Press, 1988), pp. 119ff.

21. Jeffrey L. Pressman and Aaron Wildavsky, *Implementation: How Great Expectations in Washington Are Dashed in Oakland*, 3d ed. (University of California Press, 1984); Ernest R. Alexander, *How Organizations Act Together: Interorganizational Coordination in Theory and Practice* (Amsterdam: Gordon and Breach, 1995); Eugene Bardach, *Getting Agencies to Work Together: The Practice and Theory of Managerial Craftsmanship* (Brookings, 1998).

22. Uzzi, "Social Structure and Competition"; Podolny and Paige, "Network

Forms"; Jane E. Fountain, "Social Capital: A Key Enabler of Innovation," in Lewis M. Branscomb and James H. Keller, eds., *Investing in Innovation: Creating a Research and Innovation Policy That Works* (MIT Press, 1998).

23. For research on interorganizational networks or partnerships in the public sector, see, for example, Bardach, *Getting Agencies to Work Together*; Alexander, *How Organizations Act Together*; Keith Provan and H. Brinton Milward, "A Preliminary Theory of Interorganizational Network Effectiveness: A Comparative Study of Four Mental Health Systems," *Administrative Science Quarterly*, vol. 40, no. 1 (1995): 1–33; Provan and Milward, "Integration of Community-Based Services for the Severely Mentally Ill and the Structure of Public Funding: A Comparison of Four Systems," *Journal of Health Politics, Policy and Law*, vol. 19, no. 4 (Winter 1994): 865–94; H. Brinton Milward and Keith R. Provan, "The Hollow State: Private Provision of Public Services," in Helen Ingram and Steven Rathgeb Smith, eds., *Public Policy for Democracy* (Brookings, 1993).

24. In developing a partial theory of why organizations set up such relationships, Oliver classified six broad determinants—necessity, asymmetry, reciprocity, efficiency, stability, and legitimacy—and linked those determinants to six types of networks. See Oliver, "Determinants of Interorganizational Relationships," pp. 241–65.

25. On the prevalence of mandated intergovernmental networks see, O'Toole, "Treating Networks Seriously"; John J. DiIulio Jr. and Donald F. Kettl, *Fine Print: The Contract with America, Devolution, and the Administrative Realities of American Federalism* (Brookings, 1995).

26. Oliver, "Determinants of Interorganizational Relationships."

27. T. K. Das and Bing-Sheng Teng, "Managing Risks in Strategic Alliances," vol. 13, no. 4 (1999): 50.

28. Castells, *The Rise of the Network Society*; Podolny and Paige, "Network Forms of Organization."

29. Robert M. Axelrod, *The Evolution of Cooperation* (Basic Books, 1984); Drew Fudenberg and Eric Maskin, "Folk-Theorem for Repeated Games with Discounting or with Incomplete Information," *Econometrica*, vol. 54, no. 3 (1986): 533–54.

30. Elinor Ostrom, *Governing the Commons: The Evolution of Institutions for Collective Action* (Cambridge University Press, 1990).

31. For a process perspective see Peter Smith Ring and Andrew Van de Ven, "Developmental Processes of Cooperative Interorganizational Relationships," *Academy of Management Review*, vol. 19, no. 1 (1994): 90–118.

32. This discussion of social capital is excerpted, with revision, from Fountain, "Social Capital."

33. James S. Coleman, *Foundations of Social Theory* (Harvard University Press, 1990), pp. 300–21; Robert Putnam, *Making Democracy Work: Civic Traditions in Modern Italy* (Princeton University Press, 1993), chap. 6.; Robert Putnam,

"The Prosperous Community: Social Capital and Public Life," *American Prospect* (March 21, 1993): 35–42. Glenn Loury first introduced the term "social capital" and noted its importance to economic development. See Glenn Loury, "A Dynamic Theory of Racial Income Differences," in Phyllis A. Wallace and Annette M. LeMond, eds., *Women, Minorities, and Employment Discrimination* (Lexington, Mass.: Lexington Books, 1977); and Glenn Loury, "Why Should We Care about Social Inequality?" *Social Philosophy and Policy*, vol. 5, no. 1 (1987): 249–71.

34. See Putnam, *Making Democracy Work;* Lewis M. Branscomb, "Social Capital: The Key Element in Science-Based Development," *Science-Based Economic Development: Case Studies around the World*, Annals of the New York Academy of Sciences, Vol. 798; Lewis M. Branscomb and Young-Hwan Choi, "A Framework for Discussing Korea's Techno-Economic Future," in Branscomb and Choi, eds., *Korea at the Turning Point: Innovation-Based Strategies for Development* (Westport, Conn.: Praeger, 1996).

35. Burt, *Structural Holes*, p. 12.

36. Putnam, "The Prosperous Community," p. 41.

37. For micro-level explanations of the development of interorganizational arrangements, see Ring and Van de Ven, "Developmental Processes."

38. See, for example, Christopher Matthews, *Hardball: How Politics Is Played, Told by One Who Knows the Game* (Simon and Schuster, 1988), chap. 3.

39. See Coleman, *Foundations of Social Theory*.

40. See Ostrom, *Governing the Commons*.

41. See, for example, Pressman and Wildavsky, *Implementation*; Eugene Bardach, *The Implementation Game: What Happens after a Bill Becomes Law* (MIT Press, 1977).

42. In an important study of mental health networks, Milward and Provan provide evidence to suggest that networks structured along clear authority lines— that is, a hierarchical network of organizations—will provide higher-quality, more cost-effective services. Provan and Milward, "A Preliminary Theory."

43. A rotating credit association consists of a network of carefully selected participants, each of whom makes monthly contributions and each of whom receives the "pot" in sequence. Failure to pay, even after receiving the combined contributions, is exceedingly rare. Members typically use the funds to begin or develop small businesses or to make home improvements. See Robert Putnam, *Making Democracy Work,* pp. 167–69; T. Besley, S. Coate, and G. Loury, "The Economics of Rotating Savings and Credit Associations," *American Economic Review* (September 1993): 792–811; Carlos G. Velez-Ibanez, *Bonds of Mutual Trust: The Cultural Systems of Rotating Credit Associations among Urban Mexicans and Chicanos* (New Brunswick, N.J.: Rutgers University Press, 1983); Clifford Geertz, "The Rotating Credit Association: A 'Middle Rung' in Development," *Economic Development and Cultural Change* (April 1962): 241–63.

44. Elinor Ostrom has systematically compared the management of common-pool resources in order to determine why some collective action arrangements succeed and others fail. See Ostrom, *Governing the Commons.*

45. Loury, "A Dynamic Theory of Racial Income Differences"; Loury, "Why Should We Care about Group Inequality?"; Xavier de Souza Briggs, "Brown Kids in White Suburbs: Housing Mobility and the Many Faces of Social Capital," *Housing Policy Debate,* vol. 9, no. 1 (1998): 177–221; Xavier de Souza Briggs, "Social Capital and the Cities: Advice to Change Agents," *National Civic Review,* vol. 86, no. 2 (1987): 111–17; Frances Moore Lappé and Paul Martin Du Bois, "Building Social Capital without Looking Backward," *National Civic Review,* vol. 86, no. 2 (1997): 129–30.

46. Robert O. Keohane and Joseph S. Nye, *Power and Interdependence: World Politics in Transition* (Little, Brown, 1977); Robert O. Keohane and Joseph S. Nye Jr., "Power and Interdependence in the Information Age," in Elaine Ciulla Kamarck and Joseph S. Nye Jr., eds., *democracy.com? Governance in a Networked World* (Hollis, N.H.: Hollis, 1999); Stephen D. Krasner, *International Regimes* (Cornell University Press, 1983); Robert O. Keohane, *After Hegemony* (Princeton University Press, 1984); Robert O. Keohane, "International Institutions; Two Approaches," *International Studies Quarterly* (December 1988): 379–96; Joseph M. Grieco, *Cooperation among Nations: Europe, America, and Non-Tariff Barriers to Trade* (Cornell University Press, 1990); Michael D. McGinnis, "Issue Linkage and the Evolution of International Cooperation," *Journal of Conflict Resolution,* vol. 30, no. 1 (1986): 141–70; Oran R. Young, *International Cooperation: Building Regimes for Natural Resources and the Environment* (Cornell University Press, 1989).

47. Bardach, *Getting Agencies to Work Together.*

48. For a detailed study of industry transformation in retail see Frederick H. Abernathy, John T. Dunlop, Janice H. Hammond, and David Weil, *A Stitch in Time: Lean Retailing and the Transformation of Manufacturing—Lessons from the Apparel and Textile Industries* (Oxford University Press, 1999).

49. See Daniel Roos, Frank Field, and James Neely, "Industry Consortia," in Branscomb and Keller, *Investing in Innovation,* chap. 15.

50. Bruce Kogut, "The Stability of Joint Ventures," *Journal of Industrial Economics,* vol. 38, no. 1 (1989): 1–16; Kathleen Eisenhardt and Claudia Bird Schoonhoven, "A Resource-Based View of Strategic Alliance Formation: Strategic and Social Effects in Entrepreneurial Firms," *Organization Science,* vol. 7, no. 2 (1996): 136–50; John Hagedoorn, "Understanding the Rationale of Strategic Technology Partnering: Interoganizational Modes of Cooperation and Sectoral Differences," *Stragegic Management Journal,* vol. 14, no. 5 (1993): 371–85.

51. Walter W. Powell, Kenneth W. Koput, and Laurel Smith-Doerr, "Interorganizational Collaboration and the Locus of Innovation: Networks of Learning in Biotechnology," *Administrative Science Quarterly,* vol. 41, no. 1 (1996): 116–45.

52. Burt, *Structural Holes*, pp. 13ff.

53. John F. Rockart and James E. Short, "The Networked Organization and the Management of Interdependence," in Michael S. Scott Morton, ed., *The Corporation of the 1990s* (Oxford University Press, 1991), p. 192.

54. See Heclo, *A Government of Strangers*; Burt, *Structural Holes*; Uzzi, "Social Structure and Competition."

55. Morton, *The Corporation of the 1990s*, "Introduction"; O'Mahony and Barley, "Do Digital Comunications Affect Work?"

56. Brian Kahin, "Beyond the National Information Infrastructure Initiative," in Branscomb and Keller, *Investing in Innovation*.

57. Granovetter, "The Embeddedness of Economic Relations."

58. Irving Janis, *Groupthink: Psychological Studies of Policy Decisions and Fiascoes*, rev. 2d ed. (Houghton Mifflin, 1983); Portes and Sensenbrenner, "Embeddedness and Immigration."

59. See Alejandro Portes and Patricia Landolt, "The Downside of Social Capital," *American Prospect* (May–June 1996): 18–21; and Portes and Sensenbrenner, "Embeddedness and Immigration."

60. Portes and Sensenbrenner, "Embeddedness and Immigration"; see also Uzzi, "Social Structure and Competition."

61. Oliver, "Determinants of Interorganizational Relationships."

62. The term *hyperarchy* is used to mean something different by Philip Evans and Thomas Wurster in "Strategy and the New Economics of Information," *Harvard Business Review* (September–October 1997): 71–82.

63. Jessica Lipnack and Jeffrey Stamps, *The Age of the Network: Organizing Principles for the 21st Century* (Wiley, 1994).

64. Ibid.

65. Herbert Simon, "The Architecture of Complexity," *Proceedings of the American Philosophical Society* (Philadelphia, 1962).

Chapter Six

1. This maxim is often referred to as "Miles's Law" after Rufus Miles, a seasoned senior federal executive, who is reputed to have coined it.

2. Douglass C. North, "Economic Performance through Time," lecture delivered in Stockholm, Sweden, upon receiving the Alfred Nobel Memorial Prize in Economic Science, December 9, 1993; reprinted in Mary C. Brinton and Victor Nee, eds., *The New Institutionalism in Sociology* (Russell Sage Foundation, 1998); see also James G. March and Johan P. Olsen, *Rediscovering Institutions: The Organizational Basis of Politics* (Free Press, 1989).

3. North, "Economic Performance through Time," p. 250.

4. Charles E. Lindblom, "The 'Science' of Muddling Through," *Public*

Administration Review, vol. 19, no. 2 (Spring 1959): 79–88; Aaron Wildavsky, *The Politics of the Budgetary Process*, 3d ed. (Little, Brown, 1979).

5. Barry Staw and Jerry Ross, "Commitment to a Policy Decision: A Multitheoretical Perspective," *Administrative Science Quarterly*, vol. 23, no. 2 (1978): 40–64; Barry Staw, S. Barsade, and Kenneth Koput, "Escalation and the Credit Window: A Longitudinal Study of Bank Executives' Recognition and Write-off of Problem Loans," *Journal of Applied Psychology*, vol. 82, no. 1 (1997): 130–42; Barry Staw and Jerry Ross, "Organizational Escalation and Exit: The Case of the Shoreham Nuclear Power Plant," *Academy of Management Journal*, vol. 36, no. 4 (1993): 701–32.

6. See, for example, Gene I. Rochlin, *Trapped in the Net: The Unanticipated Consequences of Computerization* (Princeton University Press, 1997).

7. For a current example of the systems approach applied to information technology and organizations, see James I. Cash Jr., Robert G. Eccles, Nitin Nohria, and Richard L. Nolan, *Building the Information-Age Organization: Structure, Control, and Information Technologies* (Boston: Irwin, 1994). For the traditional systems perspective applied to organizations, see H. J. Leavitt, "Applied Organizational Change in Industry: Structural, Technological, and Humanistic Approaches," in James G. March, ed., *Handbook of Organizations* (Rand McNally, 1965).

8. Michael T. Hannan and John Freeman, "Structural Inertia and Organizational Change," *American Sociological Review*, vol. 49, no. 2 (1984): 149–64.

9. See Michael Hammer and James Champy, *Reengineering the Corporation: A Manifesto for Business Revolution* (HarperBusiness, 1994); Michael Hammer and Steven A. Stanton, *The Reengineering Revolution: A Handbook* (HarperBusiness, 1995), for the details of business process reengineering. See Don Tapscott, *The Digital Economy: Promise and Peril in the Age of Networked Intelligence* (McGraw-Hill, 1996), pp. 3–4, on the failure rate of reengineering. In many cases, Tapscott notes, executive-level conflict, not operator-level resistance, slowed organizational restructuring.

10. For examples of this early stream of research see Henri Barki and Jon Hartwick, "Rethinking the Concept of User Involvement," *MIS Quarterly* (March 1989): 53–63; Shoshana Zuboff, *In the Age of the Smart Machine* (Basic Books, 1988); J. J. Baroudi, M. H. Olsen, and B. Ives, "An Empirical Study of the Impact of User Involvement on System Usage and User Satisfaction," *Communications of the ACM*, vol. 29, no. 3 (1986): 232–38; C. R. Franz and D. Robey, "Organizational Context, User Involvement, and the Usefulness of Information Systems," *Decision Sciences*, vol. 17, no. 3 (1986): 329–56; Tora K. Bikson and Barbara A. Gutek, "Advanced Office Systems: An Empirical Look at Utilization and Satisfaction," Rand Note (Santa Monica, Calif.: Rand Corp., February 1983); Tora K. Bikson and D. Mankin, "Factors in Successful Implementation of Computer-Based Office Information Systems: A Review of the Literature," mimeo, Rand

Corporation, 1983; M. L. Markus, "Power, Politics, and MIS Implementation," *Communications of the ACM*, vol. 26, no. 6 (1983): 430–44.

11. Zuboff, *In the Age of the Smart Machine*; A. M. Mohrman and E. E. Lawler, III, "A Review of Theory and Research," in F. Warren McFarlan, ed., *The Information Systems Research Challenge* (Harvard Business School Press, 1984).

12. Important critiques include: Siobahn O'Mahony and Stephen R. Barley, "Do Digital Telecommunications Affect Work and Organizations? The State of Our Knowledge," *Research in Organizational Behavior*, vol. 21 (JAI Press, 1999), pp. 125–61; Wanda J. Orlikowski and Jack J. Baroudi, "Studying Information Technology in Organizations: Research Approaches and Assumptions," *Information Systems Research*, vol. 2, no. 1 (1991): 1–28; Maryam Alavi and E. A. Joachimsthaler, "Revisiting DSS Implementation Research: A Meta-Analysis of the Literature and Suggestions for Researchers," *MIS Quarterly*, vol. 16, no. 1 (1992): 95–116.

13. Janet Fulk and Gerardine DeSanctis, "Electronic Communication and Changing Organizational Forms," *Organization Science*, vol. 6, no. 4 (1995): 337–49; J. M. Pickering and John L. King, "Hardwiring Weak Ties: Interorganizational Computer-Mediated Communication, Occupational Communities, and Organizational Change," *Organization Science*, vol. 6, no. 4 (1995): 479–86; Michael S. Scott Morton, *The Corporation of the 1990s: Information Technology and Organizational Transformation* (Oxford University Press, 1991); James I. Cash Jr., Robert G. Eccles, Nitin Nohria, and Richard L. Nolan, *Building the Information-Age Organization: Structure, Control, and Information Technologies* (Burr Ridge, Ill.: Irwin, 1994); Gerardine DeSanctis and Janet Fulk, eds., *Shaping Organization Form: Communication, Connection, and Community* (Thousand Oaks, Calif.: Sage, 1999).

14. Stephen R. Barley, "Technology as an Occasion for Structuring: Evidence from Observations of CT Scanners and the Social Order of Radiology Departments," *Administrative Science Quarterly*, vol. 21, no. 1 (1986): 81.

15. Stephen R. Barley, "The Alignment of Technology and Structure through Roles and Networks," *Administrative Science Quarterly*, vol. 35, no. 1 (1990): 61–103.

16. Brookings Task Force on the Internet, *The Economic Payoff from the Internet Revolution* (Brookings, 2001); Carl Shapiro and Hal R. Varian, *Information Rules: A Strategic Guide to the Network Economy* (Harvard Business School Press, 1999); Philip B. Evans and Thomas S. Wurster, "Strategy and the New Economics of Information," *Harvard Business Review* (September–October 1977): 71–82.

17. The concepts "enactment" and "the definition of the situation," first developed in the 1920s, were at the center of sociologist W. I. Thomas's research program. See William I. Thomas, "Situational Analysis: The Behavior Pattern and the Situation," in *Publications of the American Sociological Society*, vol. 22

(1927): 1–13; and William Isaac Thomas, *Social Behavior and Personality: Contributions of W. I. Thomas to Theory and Social Research*, Edmund H. Volkart, ed. (Westport, Conn.: Greenwood Press, 1981). March and Simon reinvigorated the concept and its relationship to bounded rationality in *Organizations* (Wiley, 1958). More recently, North has reiterated the need to integrate bounded rationality into rational choice, in part by recognizing the importance of framing, or the processes by which individuals form a "subjective representation" of a problem. See North, "Economic Performance through Time," p. 251.

18. March and Olsen, *Rediscovering Institutions*; Linda Smircich and Charles Stubbart, "Strategic Management in an Enacted World," *Academy of Management Review*, vol. 10, no. 4 (1985): 724–36; Karl E. Weick, *The Social Psychology of Organizing*, 2d ed. (Addison-Wesley, 1979).

19. Elizabeth Goodrick and Gerald Salancik found that actor discretion tended to be high when institutional uncertainty was present. In other words, when routines were not clear, actor discretion took precedence over institutions. See Elizabeth Goodrick and Gerald Salancik, "Organizational Discretion in Responding to Institutional Practices: Hospitals and Cesarean Births," *Administrative Science Quarterly*, vol. 41, no. 1 (1996): 1–28.

20. Barry Staw and Lisa D. Epstein, "What Bandwagons Bring: Effects of Popular Management Techniques on Corporate Performance, Reputation, and CEO Pay," *Administrative Science Quarterly*, vol. 45, no. 3 (2000): 523–56; Pamela R. Haunschild, "Interorganizational Imitation: The Impact of Interlocks on Corporate Acquisition Activity," *Administrative Science Quarterly*, vol. 38, no. 4 (1993): 564–92; Pamela R. Haunschild and Anne S. Miner, "Modes of Interorganizational Imitation: The Effects of Outcome Salience and Uncertainty," *Administrative Science Quarterly*, vol. 42, no. 3 (1997): 472–500; James G. March and Barbara Levitt, "Organizational Learning," *Annual Review of Sociology*, vol. 14 (Palo Alto, Calif.: Annual Reviews, 1988).

21. Philip Selznick, *TVA and the Grass Roots* (University of California Press, 1949). The quotation is from Philip Selznick, "Institutionalism 'Old' and 'New,'" *Administrative Science Quarterly*, vol. 41, no. 2 (1996): 270.

22. Selznick, "Institutionalism," p. 271.

23. Philip Selznick, *The Moral Commonwealth: Social Theory and the Promise of Community* (University of California Press, 1992), p. 232.

24. Sharon Zukin and Paul DiMaggio, "Introduction," in Zukin and DiMaggio, *Structures of Capital: The Social Organization of the Economy* (Cambridge University Press, 1990).

25. Ann Swidler, "Culture in Action: Symbols and Strategies," *American Sociological Review*, vol. 51, no. 2 (1986): 273.

26. W. Richard Scott, "Unpacking Institutional Arguments," in Walter W. Powell and Paul J. DiMaggio, eds., *The New Institutionalism in Organizational Analysis* (University of Chicago Press, 1991), p. 169.

27. This classification scheme is drawn, with slight revision, from Sharon Zukin and Paul DiMaggio, "Introduction," in Zukin and DiMaggio, eds., *Structures of Capital: The Social Organization of the Economy* (Cambridge University Press, 1990).

28. Anthony Giddens, *New Rules of Sociological Method: A Positive Critique of Interpretive Sociologies*, 2d ed. (Stanford University Press, 1993).

29. Ibid. This duality is present in Granovetter, "Economic Action and Social Structure," but missing from North, "Economic Performance through Time." In North's framework, individuals learn and through collective learning may modify institutions.

30. Ibid., pp. 4, 5, 6.

31. Thomas J. Fararo and John Skvoretz, "Action, Institution, Network and Function: The Cybernetic Concept of Social Structure," *Sociological Forum*, vol. 1, no. 2 (1986): 219–50; see also Jepperson's use of this framework, Ronald L. Jepperson, "Institutions, Institutional Effects, and Institutionalism," in Powell and DiMaggio, *The New Institutionalism*.

32. Jepperson, "Institutions," p. 145.

33. Anthony Giddens, *The Constitution of Society: Outline of the Theory of Structuration* (University of California Press, 1984); March and Olsen, *Rediscovering Institutions*; Granovetter, "Economic Action and Social Structure"; Goodrick and Salancik, "Organizational Discretion in Responding to Institutional Practices," *Administrative Science Quarterly*, vol. 41, no. 1 (1996): 1–28; Brian Uzzi, "Social Structure and Competition in Interfirm Networks," *Administrative Science Quarterly*, vol. 42, no. 1 (1997): 35–67; Jerry D. Goodstein, "Institutional Pressures and Strategic Responsiveness: Employer Involvement in Work-Family Issues," *Academy of Management Journal*, vol. 37, no. 2 (1994): 350–82; Steven Brint and Jerome Karabel, "Institutional Origins and Transformations: The Case of American Community Colleges," in Powell and DiMaggio, *The New Institutionalism*; Christine Oliver, "Strategic Responses to Institutional Processes," *Academy of Management Review*, vol. 16, no. 1 (1991): 145–79; Paul J. DiMaggio, "Interest and Agency in Institutional Theory," in Lynne G. Zucker, ed., *Institutional Patterns and Organizations: Culture and Environment* (Cambridge, Mass.: Ballinger, 1988).

34. March and Simon, *Organizations*; March and Olsen, *Rediscovering Institutions*; Roger C. Schank and Robert P. Abelson, *Scripts, Plans, Goals, and Understanding: An Inquiry into Human Knowledge Structures* (Hillsdale, N.J.: L. Erlbaum Associates, 1977).

35. Brian T. Pentland and Henry H. Rueter, "Organizational Routines as Grammars of Action," *Administrative Science Quarterly*, vol. 39, no. 3 (1994): 484–510.

36. Wanda J. Orlikowski and JoAnne Yates, "Genre Repertoire: The Structuring of Communicative Practices in Organizations," *Administrative Science Quarterly*, vol. 39, no. 4 (1994): 541–74.

37. Victor Nee and Paul Ingram, "Embeddedness and Beyond: Institutions, Exchange, and Social Structure," in Brinton and Nee, *The New Institutionalism in Sociology*, p. 19.

38. For a review of the few studies that relate social and computer networks, see O'Mahony and Barley, "Do Digital Telecommunications Affect Work?" See also Pickering and King, "Hardwiring Weak Ties."

39. These three reasons have been given for increased networking activity among high-tech as well as more traditional firms. The logic for using networks to pool resources and expertise applies equally well to policy domains and government. See Daniel Roos, Frank Field, and James Neely, "Industry Consortia," in Lewis M. Branscomb and James H. Keller, eds., *Investing in Innovation: Creating a Research and Innovation Policy That Works* (MIT Press, 1998); Jane E. Fountain, "Social Capital: A Key Enabler of Innovation," in Branscomb and Keller, *Investing in Innovation*.

40. Mark S. Ackerman, "Expertise Networks as an Enabling Technology for Cyberspace Use," invited paper, PARC White House Leveraging Cyberspace Conference, October 1996 (www.ics.uci.edu/~ackerman/pub/96f03/leveraging.fmt.html [March 22, 2001]).

41. Ibid.

42. Walter W. Powell, "Neither Market nor Hierarchy: Network Forms in Organizations," *Research in Organizational Behavior*, vol. 12 (JAI Press, 1990); Walter W. Powell, Kenneth W. Koput, and Laurel Smith-Doerr, "Interorganizational Collaboration and the Locus of Innovation: Networks of Learning in Biotechnology," *Administrative Science Quarterly* (March 1996): 116–45; Joel M. Podolny and Karen L. Paige, "Network Forms of Organization," *American Review of Sociology*, vol. 24 (1998): 57–76.

43. See Access America for Seniors (www.seniors.gov).

44. See the Wilderness Information Network (www.wilderness.net).

45. See Jane Fountain, "The Paradoxes of Public Sector Customer Service," *Governance*, vol. 14, no. 1 (2001): 55–73.

Chapter Seven

1. This study of the International Trade Data System began in June 1996. Unless otherwise indicated, the quotations of government executives and technical specialists in Chapters 7 and 8 are taken from interviews I conducted between 1996 and 2000. Zachary Tumin, a research associate during part of the data collection effort, also conducted some of the interviews quoted from in these chapters. We conducted more than fifty face-to-face interviews with civil servants from the Customs Service, including ITDS project staff; ITDS board members (from the Department of the Treasury, the Department of Transportation, the Census Bu-

reau, the Immigration and Naturalization Service); industry representatives; GAO staff; congressional staff; and other government and nongovernment analysts and trade specialists. The transcriptions of those taped interviews total more than 600 pages. Data sources also include a comprehensive review of government documents (including congressional hearings; GAO reports; and unpublished white papers produced by the ITDS project office) and periodicals, especially those that specialize in trade processing issues.

A site visit in 1996 to the Otay Mesa, California, port of entry included field observation of border crossing operations and technologies, observation of North American Trade Automation Prototype (NATAP) training for operators and supervisors; a meeting with participants in NATAP from the trade community; and interviews with Customs Service operators, supervisors, managers, private contractors, trade community participants, ITDS project staff, and other federal employees working at the port. On April 24–25, 1997, I was a participant-observer at a meeting of the NATAP Tri-lateral Evaluation Subcommittee held in Mexico City, Mexico. The field visit included interviews with Canadian, Mexican, and U.S. project managers and staff.

I was ably assisted in the data collection effort by Zachary Tumin, who conducted interviews, reviewed the periodical literature on the Customs Service under Commissioner William von Raab, and drafted a teaching case on automation in the Customs Service for the Strategic Computing Program at the Kennedy School of Government that provides critical information on automation efforts during the 1980s before the National Performance Review. Laurel Blatchford assisted with the identification of relevant government documents.

2. The estimate was calculated by the United Nations Council on Trade and Development and verified as an accurate overhead figure for U.S. international trade by the House Government Reform and Oversight Subcommittee on Government Management and Information Technology. Government Reform and Oversight Subcommittee on Government Management and Information Technology, Hearing on Oversight and Implementation of the Clinger-Cohen Act, October 27, 1997.

3. IT06 Task Force, "Concepts and Recommendations for an International Trade Data System," Report for the Government Information Technology Working Group of the National Information Infrastructure Task Force, May 16, 1995.

4. Ibid., p. 23.

5. Council of Economic Advisers, *Annual Report of the Council of Economic Advisers, 1998* (Government Printing Office, 1998), p. 216.

6. World Bank, *Workers in an Integrating World: World Development Report, 1995* (Oxford University Press, 1995), p. 51.

7. A significant increase in unilateral, bilateral, and multilateral trade agreements has added complexity to the international trade policy domain. Each new trade agreement, especially those between two nations or among small groups of

nations, creates new provisions relating to specific goods or business matters for only those signatories, forcing businesses to adhere not only to requirements for the General Agreement on Tariffs and Trade/World Customs Organization (GATT/ WCO) agreements, but also to follow all the smaller agreements and regulatory rules that apply within each trading country.

8. An internationalization of trade in services is also occurring, but that development is not relevant to this discussion of international trade.

9. On structural changes in business resulting from technological change, see, for example, Frederick H. Abernathy, John T. Dunlop, Janice H. Hammond, and David Weil, *A Stitch in Time: Lean Retailing and the Transformation of Manufacturing—Lessons from the Apparel and Textile Industries* (Oxford University Press, 1999); Jane E. Fountain, "Social Capital: A Key Enabler of Innovation," in L. Branscomb and J. Keller, eds., *Investing in Innovation: Creating a Research and Innovation Policy That Works* (MIT Press, 1998); U.S. Department of Commerce, "Meeting the Challenge: U.S. Industry Faces the Twenty-First Century" (August 1995); Michael Baum and Henry Perritt Jr., *Electronic Contracting, Publishing and EDI Law* (Wiley, 1991); and Michael Piore and Charles Sabel, *The Second Industrial Divide: Possibilities for Prosperity* (Basic Books, 1984).

10. This overview of the Customs Service before the Clinton administration is excerpted, with revisions, from "Automate or Perish," draft teaching case written by Zachary Tumin under the direction of Jane Fountain, Strategic Computing Program, Kennedy School of Government, Harvard University, March 2000.

11. Catherine Collins, "Letting the Public in on Which Firm Ships What Technology to Whom," *Los Angeles Times*, June 16, 1991, Sunday home edition, p. 11.

12. Nancy M. Davis, "Changing Customs: A Whistleblower and a New Commissioner Take Aim at the Customs Service's Long-Standing History of Financial Mismanagement," *Government Executive*, December 1990.

13. Haynes Johnson, "Customs Service Tries to Do More with Less; Mission Grows but Staff Shrinks," *Washington Post*, August 24, 1986, Sunday final edition.

14. Davis, "Changing Customs."

15. Vanessa Jo Grimm, "Customs Says System Can Replace Staff," *Government Computer News*, March 13, 1987, p. 1.

16. H. G. Reza, "Border Inspections Eased and Drug Seizures Plunge," *Los Angeles Times*, February 13, 1995.

17. Bureau of National Affairs, "Ways-Means Approves 1985 Authorizations for ITC, USTR, Customs," *Daily Report for Executives*, April 4, 1984.

18. James T. McKenna, "Agency Will Mothball Cargo Computer System Unless New Operator Is Found," *Aviation Week and Space Technology*, December 12, 1988, p. 129.

19. Joseph Bonney, "Forwarders Seek to Work with ISA, Information Systems Agreement," *American Shipper*, October 1994, p. 74.

20. Lawrence Stevens, "Users Say EDI Cuts Inventory Costs, Speeds Product Delivery," *Computerworld*, May 2, 1988.

21. Judith A. Fuerst, "Shipper's or Smuggler's Blues; U.S. Customs Service," *Handling & Shipping Management*, February 1986.

22. Vanessa Jo Grimm, "Customs Requests More Funds for Automated Systems," *Government Computer News*, April 29, 1988.

23. Michael Hammer and James Champy, *Reengineering the Corporation* (HarperCollins, 1993).

24. Don Steinberg, "Customs Service's Data Link Raises Stakes for U.S. Firms," *PC Week*, January 12, 1988.

25. During this period, Singapore already had developed and implemented TradeNet, the world's first automated, fully integrated trade processing system; it linked all government agencies and trade businesses throughout the small country. Its initiative, widely reported in the press and business journals, turned the port of Singapore into one of the fastest, and most profitable, deep-water ports in the world. An automated trade data system was an idea whose time had come. John L. King, "Singapore TradeNet," Harvard Business School Teaching Case series.

26. Joseph F. Dunphy, "Streamlining the Paperwork of Trade," *Chemical Week*, July 9, 1986.

27. Davis, "Changing Customs."

28. Bureau of National Affairs, "Customs Refused to Enforce Laws Unless Agencies Picked Up Costs, House Panel told," *Daily Report for Executives*, August 9, 1984.

29. Johnson, "Customs Service Tries to Do More."

30. 105 Cong. 1 sess., House Committee on Ways and Means, Subcommittee on Trade, testimony of Linda D. Koontz, associate director, Information Resources Management and General Government Issues Accounting and Information Management Division, General Accounting Office, May 15, 1997.

31. Davis, "Changing Customs."

32. Bill Pietrucha, "Customs to Format Data to International Standard," *Government Computer News*, April 29, 1988.

33. For an analysis of the contradictions between Customs modernization using accounts management and the requirements of NAFTA see Carol Metzger, U.S. Customs Service, "U.S. Customs Modernization and NAFTA Administration: Conflicting Agendas," paper presented at the Symposium on Innovations in Trade: Customs in the 21st Century, International Tax Program and Harvard Institute for International Development, Harvard University, November 14–15, 1996.

34. U.S. Department of the Treasury, Customs Service, "Automated Commercial System Fact Sheet," February 1993, p. 1.

35. National Performance Review, *Reengineering through Information Technology: Recommendations and Actions*, "IT06: Establish an International Trade Data System," 1993, p. 1.

36. "Automated Commercial System Fact Sheet," p. 3.

37. Vice President Al Gore, "From Red Tape to Results: Creating a Government That Works Better and Costs Less: Reengineering through Information Technology," Accompanying Report of the National Performance Review, September 1993. The other policy areas included: integrated electronic benefit transfer for the distribution of food stamps, Social Security benefits, and veterans' benefits; "integrated electronic access to government information and services" (electronic access resulted in the U.S. Business Advisor, among other similar efforts); the development of a national law enforcement and public safety network, a wireless network to coordinate federal, state, and local entities; intergovernmental tax filing, reporting, and payments processing; a national environmental data index; and governmentwide electronic mail.

38. IT06: Establish an International Trade Data System, 1993.

39. Ibid.

40. IT06 Task Force, "Concepts and Recommendations for an International Trade Data System," Report for the Government Information Technology Working Group of the National Information Infrastructure Task Force, May 16, 1995, p. 7.

41. 106 Cong. 1 sess., Senate Committee on Ways and Means, Subcommittee on Trade, testimony of John P. Simpson, deputy assistant secretary of the Treasury, April 13, 1999.

Chapter Eight

1. See 106 Cong. 1 sess., House Committee on Ways and Means, Trade Customs Service, Trade Representative Authorizations, testimony of John P. Simpson, deputy assistant secretary of the Treasury, April 16, 1999.

2. See 105 Cong. 1 sess., House Committee on Government Reform and Oversight, Subcommittee on Government Management, Information and Technology, Hearing on Oversight and Implementation of the Clinger-Cohen Act, October 27, 1997 (see especially the testimony of John P. Simpson, deputy assistant secretary of the Treasury; Alan Proctor, chief information officer, Federal Trade Commission; Robert W. Ehinger, ITDS project office, Department of the Treasury; and Michael D. Cronin, assistant commissioner of inspection, Immigration and Naturalization Service).

3. Unless otherwise indicated, the quotations of government executives and technical specialists in Chapters 7 and 8 are taken from interviews I conducted between 1996 and 2000. Zachary Tumin, a research associate during part of the data collection effort, also conducted some of the interviews quoted from in these chapters.

4. Gene Linn, "Backers Claim Support for Single Electronic Gateway," *Journal of Commerce*," January 6, 1999, p. 1A.

5. Quoted in Bill Mongelluzzo, "Trade Sectors Unite on ITDS," *Journal of Commerce*, June 8, 1999, p. 1.

6. Ibid.

7. This estimate was arrived at by summing the cost of filing all international trade forms with federal agencies holding jurisdiction over trade administration and enforcement.

8. Gene Linn, "Backers Claim Support for Single Electronic Gateway," *Journal of Commerce*, January 6, 1999, p. 1A.

9. See, for example, "An Independent and Objective Perspective on the U.S. Customs Approach to and Delivery of Information Technology," testimony (prepared statement) by J. Kurt Zimmer, vice president, Gartner Group, before the House Committee on Ways and Means, Subcommittee on Trade, April 13, 1999.

10. GAO/AIMD-99-41, February 1999, cited in 106 Cong. 1 sess., House Committee on Ways and Means, Subcommittee on Trade, testimony of Randolph C. Hite, associate director, Governmentwide and Defense Information Systems, General Accounting Office, "Customs Service Modernization: Actions Needed to Correct Serious ACE Management and Technical Weaknesses," April 13, 1999. See also Randolph C. Hite's testimony, Senate Finance Committee, Customs Service Enforcement and Management Oversight Hearing, May 17, 1999.

11. Testimony of Randolph C. Hite, May 17, 1999.

12. Ibid. See also testimony of the commissioner of Customs, April 13, 1999.

13. Ibid.

14. Jack Lucentini, "Trade Sector Fears More Delay If Data System Is Implemented," *Journal of Commerce*, March 12, 1999, p. 12A.

15. 106 Cong. 1 sess., Senate Finance Committee, Customs Service Enforcement and Management Oversight Hearing, testimony of Raymond W. Kelly, commissioner of the U.S. Customs Service, May 17, 1999.

16. 106 Cong. 1 sess., House Committee on Ways and Means, Subcommittee on Trade, testimony of Ronald Schoof on behalf of the Joint Industry Group, April 13, 1999.

17. 106 Cong. 1 sess., House Committee on Ways and Means, Subcommittee on Trade, testimony (prepared statement) of James A. Rogers, Air Courier Conference of America, International, April 13, 1999.

18. Ibid.

19. Ibid.

20. See, for example, 106 Cong. 1 sess., House Ways and Means, Trade Customs Service, Trade Representative Authorizations, testimony of Richard J. Salamone, customs manager and employee of BASF Corporation, April 16, 1999; and Senate Finance Committee, Customs Service Enforcement and Management Oversight Hearing, testimony of Raymond W. Kelly, customs commissioner, May 17, 1999.

21. Testimony of Ronald Schoof.

22. Linn, "Backers Claim Support."

23. Ibid.

24. Ibid.

25. Bill Mongelluzzo, "Customs Secures Oversight of Import Filing Program," *Journal of Commerce*, September 17, 1999.

Chapter Nine

1. The narrative portions of this chapter draw from several sources, noted in the text, and in particular from "www.business.gov: Building an Interagency Web Site," written by David Eddy Spicer under the supervision of Associate Professor Jane Fountain. Copyright © 1999 by the President and Fellows of Harvard College. Excised with revisions with the permission of the Kennedy School of Government, Case Program, Harvard University, case no. C16-99-1497.0. The online version of this case includes hyperlinks to relevant websites, video clips, and an archived early version of the Business Advisor website (www.ksg.harvard.edu/ case/advisor). See this case for additional details regarding the early development of the Business Advisor. All quotations, unless otherwise indicated, are from interviews with public managers and political appointees conducted by Spicer or Fountain between 1996 and 2000. Interviews were tape recorded and transcribed for thematic analysis.

2. The author gratefully acknowledges several public servants who granted interviews and supplied documents about the Business Advisor. In particular, I am grateful to James Van Wert. Sections of this chapter draw from the web-based teaching case "The Virtual Department of Business: Building an Interagency Web Site," written by David Eddy Spicer for Jane Fountain. The case is available from the Kennedy School of Government Case Program.

3. The statistics about SBA in this section are from U.S. Small Business Administration, *Opportunities for Success*, SBA Fiscal Year 1999 Annual Performance Report (www.sba.gov/aboutsba/1999performancereport.pdf [April 2, 2001]); and James Van Wert, prepared remarks, conference on Stimulating Small Business Formation through "Cutting Red Tape," Brussels, Belgium, March 8, 1999.

4. Sarah S. McCue, "The Federal Role in Export Assistance to Small Businesses: Helpful, Harmful, Necessary?" Ph.D. dissertation, University of Michigan Political Science Department, 1998; Trade Promotion Coordinating Committee, "The National Export Strategy," Sixth Annual Report to the United States Congress, October 1998.

5. Spicer, www.business.gov, p. 6.

6. Ibid., p. 5.

7. Ibid., p. 8.

8. Michael Selz, "From Uncle Sam Direct to Entrepreneur: Vice President Unveils Internet Service," *Wall Street Journal*, February 14, 1996, p. B2.

9. Eddy Spicer, "www.business.gov," p. 1.

10. Ethan Wallison, "Web Site Provides Regulatory Information," *Milwaukee Journal Sentinel*, February 26, 1996, p. 7.

11. Eddy Spicer, "www.business.gov," p. 12.

12. David Osborne and Peter Plastrik, "What Works WWW.GOV," *Washington Post*, August 10, 1997, p. W05, final edition.

13. Barbara J. Saffir, "Government Expands Its Claim on the Web," *Washington Post*, March 18, 1997, p. A15, final edition.

14. "Help Is Available for Small Businesses with Tax-Related Issues," Business Wire, June 22, 1999.

15. "Network Solutions and inc.com link with the Small Business Administration to Help Small Businesses Grow," Business Wire, November 16, 1999.

16. 106 Cong. 1 sess., House Committee on Small Business, testimony of SBA Assistant Administrator Daniel Hill, May 26, 1999.

17. "The President Announces Electronic Government Services to Better Serve Students," M2 Presswire, January 21, 1999.

18. Mary Beth Marklein, "Feds Launch On-line Student Aid Program," *USA Today*, January 19, 1999, p. 4D.

19. "NCS Launches Access America Student Account Manager for the U.S. Dept of Education," Presswire, August 27, 1999.

20. University of Northern Colorado President Hank Brown in "UNC Part of Pilot Program to Get Students Financial Aid," AP Newswire, January 14, 1999.

21. "NCS Launches Access America Student Account Manager for the U.S. Dept. of Education," Presswire, August 27, 1999.

22. Marklein, "Feds Launch On-line Student Aid Program."

23. Stephen Skowronek, *Building a New American State: The Expansion of National Administrative Capacities 1877–1920* (Cambridge University Press, 1982), p. 6.

Chapter Ten

1. Unless otherwise indicated, all of the observations by military personnel and other experts quoted in the text were made during fifty semistructured interviews with army and other allied officers, civilian military employees, defense contractors, and civilian defense experts conducted as part of in-depth field research at the headquarters of the Ninth Infantry Division (Motorized), Fort Lewis, and at the Yakima Firing Range, both in the state of Washington, between June and October 1988. Almost all of the interviews were tape recorded and transcribed for later thematic analysis.

2. Greg Jaffe, "Tug of War: In the New Military, Technology May Alter Chain of Command," *Wall Street Journal*, March 30, 2001, p. 1.

3. This question echoes similar concerns about democratic control of nuclear forces. See Robert Dahl, *Controlling Nuclear Weapons: Democracy versus Guardianship* (Syracuse University Press, 1985); and Gene I. Rochlin, *Trapped in the Net: The Unanticipated Consequences of Computerization* (Princeton University Press, 1997).

4. In contrast there are 17,000 men and women in a heavy (armored or mechanized) division, of which there were ten in the U.S. Army when this case study was researched. These figures changed rapidly in the late 1980s and 1990s as the Department of Defense reconfigured and markedly decreased the size of U.S. forces. Most analysts during this period called for 25 percent cuts in the number of divisions.

5. Brigade commanders, who hold the rank of colonel, generally command approximately three thousand soldiers.

6. U.S. Army Command and General Staff College, *Corps and Division Command and Control, Field Circular 101-55* (Fort Leavenworth, Ks.: February 28, 1985), p. 1-1.

7. Ibid., pp. 1-1–4-5.

8. The General Accounting Office has criticized the Army Command and Control System program for its assumption that off-the-shelf computer systems are available to meet its requirements and for its consolidated acquisition plan, which assumes that economies of scale due to buying in bulk outweigh the economies available from acquisition of tailored, specialized systems. U.S. General Accounting Office, *Tactical Computers: Army's Maneuver Control System Procurement and Distribution Plan*, GAO\IMTEC-86-21FS, May 1986; U.S. GAO, *Battlefield Automation: Status of the Army Command and Control System Program*, GAO\NSIAD-86-184FS, August 1986; U.S. GAO, *Battlefield Automation: Status of Army Command and Control Systems Acquisition Cost and Schedule Changes*, GAO\NSIAD-88-42FS, December 1987; U.S. GAO, *Battlefield Automation: Better Justification and Testing Needed for Common Computer Acquisition*, GAO\IMTEC-88-12, December 1987.

9. Francine Manna, *the MCS2 Introductory Guide* (Fairfax, Va.: BDM Management Services, September 1987).

10. U.S. Army, "Distributed Command and Control System (DCCS)," unpublished manuscript, 1985.

11. David Warren, "Lessons Learned from MCS2," Fort Lewis, Wash.: PEO-CCS Field Office, 1987, mimeo.

12. Quoted in Gary Chapman, "The Next Generation of High-Technology Weapons," in David Bellin and Gary Chapman, eds., *Computers in Battle: Will They Work?* (Harcourt Brace Jovanovich, 1987), p. 61.

13. Rochlin, *Trapped in the Net*, p. 199. Also see Bellin and Chapman, *Computers in Battle*, for a detailed account of the evolution of military doctrine and the transition to electronic warfare.

14. Commission on Integrated Long-Term Strategy, *Discriminate Deterrence:*

Report of the Commission on Integrated Long-Term Strategy (Government Printing Office, 1988).

15. Interestingly, the development of the command staff organization parallels that of the management structure and professionalization of managers of other types of bureaucracies and complex organizations from the late nineteenth century forward.

16. Civil-military operations (G5) and the fire-support coordinator functions were added to the staff after World War II.

17. Martin Van Creveld, *Technology and War: From 2000 B.C. to the Present* (Free Press, 1989); U.S. Army Command and General Staff College, *Corps and Division Command and Control*.

18. United States, Department of Defense, *Conduct of the Persian Gulf War: Final Report to Congress* (Government Printing Office, April 1992).

19. Strategic command and control has similar vulnerabilities. For early analyses of this problem see Bruce G. Blair, *Strategic Command and Control: Redefining the Nuclear Threat* (Brookings, 1985); Paul J. Bracken, *The Command and Control of Nuclear Forces* (Yale University Press, 1983); Ashton B. Carter, John D. Steinbruner, and Charles A. Zraket, eds., *Managing Nuclear Operations* (Brookings, 1987).

20. Jonathan Jacky, "The Strategic Computing Program," in Bellin and Chapman, *Computers in Battle*, pp. 181–82.

21. Data presented in table 10-1 were collected by means of a questionnaire designed and administered in 1987 to MCS2 users by the Experimentation Division of the Army Development and Employment Agency. I conducted the data analysis. Regression of measures of user attitude on several independent variables, including measures of location and time in the division, amount and perceived adequacy of training, and perceived expertise and amount of computer use are reported in Jane E. Fountain, "Bureaucratic Politics in the Information Age: Organizational Position, Training, Use and Attitudes toward Technology," Faculty Research Working Paper Series, John F. Kennedy School of Government, Harvard University, October 1995. Results of regression analyses indicate that a combination of organizational location, training, and use explain one third of the variance in the distribution of attitudes for the full sample of users of MCS2. Organizational location is a more powerful antecedent of user perceptions toward the information system than either training or system utilization. User type also has an effect on perceptions of system effectiveness. A user's function and unit membership were both found to be significant. These results did not support the hypothesis that user attitude varies by user experience even when several measures of experience were used.

22. For a detailed critique of "black-boxing" and its implications for military personnel and equipment readiness, see Chris C. Demchak, *Military Organizations, Complex Machines* (Cornell University Press, 1991).

23. Gene Rochlin, *Trapped in the Net*, p. 172. See also Gene I. Rochlin and Chris C. Demchak, "Lessons of the Gulf War: Ascendant Technology and Declining Capability," Policy Papers in International Affairs (University of California, Berkeley, Institute of International Studies, 1991).

24. Michael J. Mazarr, Don M. Snider, and James A. Blackwell Jr., *Desert Storm: The Gulf War and What We Learned* (Boulder, Colo.: Westview, 1993).

25. Rochlin, *Trapped in the Net*, p. 175.

Chapter Eleven

1. The Clinger-Cohen Act (PL 104-106) was originally called the Information Technology Management Reform Act (ITMRA).

2. Hugh Heclo, *Modern Social Politics in Britain and Sweden: From Relief to Income Maintenance* (Yale University Press), p. 305.

3. Ibid.

4. See Paul C. Light, *The True Size of Government* (Brookings, 1999); Donald F. Kettl, *Sharing Power: Public Governance and Private Markets* (Brookings, 1993).

5. Author's analysis based on a survey of all state government websites conducted in July 2000.

6. Peter B. Evans, Dietrich Rueschemeyer, and Theda Skocpol, eds., *Bringing the State Back In* (Cambridge University Press, 1985), p. 7.

7. Alfred Stepan, *The State and Society: Peru in Comparative Perspective* (Princeton University Press, 1978).

8. For a detailed analysis along these lines see Theda Skocpol and Kenneth Finegold, "State Capacity and Economic Intervention in the Early New Deal," *Political Science Quarterly*, vol. 97, no. 2 (1982): 255–78.

9. These ideas extend analysis of state structure and behavior to the problem of networked computing and its relationship to state-building. See Steven Kelman, *Regulating America, Regulating Sweden: A Comparative Study of Occupational Health and Safety Policy* (MIT Press, 1981); Hugh Heclo, *Modern Social Politics in Britain and Sweden*; Edward O. Laumann and David Knoke, *The Organizational State: Social Choice in National Policy Domains* (University of Wisconsin Press, 1987); Evans, Rueschemeyer, and Skocpol, *Bringing the State Back In*; Skocpol and Finegold, "State Capacity and Economic Intervention"; Stepan, *The State and Society*; Peter Katzenstein, ed., *Between Power and Plenty: Foreign Economic Policies of Advanced Industrial States* (University of Wisconsin Press, 1978).

10. U.S. Government, National Telecommunications and Information Administration, *Falling through the Net: Defining the Digital Divide*, July 1999.

Index

243